D1087632

Retirement Solutions

Retirement Solutions

Financial Strategies for Today's Retirees

First Edition

Michael Dallas, CFP®

Franklin & Grant
PUBLISHING

Franklin & Grant PUBLISHING

Published by:
Franklin & Grant Publishing
Michael Dallas, CFP®
817-763-8191
800-747-RETIRE (7384)

Hardback: 978-0-9776986-2-2
Paperback: 978-0-9776986-3-9
eBook: 978-0-9776986-4-6

Printed in the United States of America

Editing: Christine Keleny
Cover and Interior Design: Ghislain Viau

Table of Contents

Foreword

by Jeanette Alexander, CFP®

Although it's been over three decades since I started my career in the finance world, I remember it as if it happened yesterday. My hopes were high, yet I had no idea how rewarding my new professional life would be. The best unforeseen benefit was spending the better part of a decade working aside my son, Michael Dallas. The days we spent creating Retirement Solutions for our clients were some of the happiest times of my life.

Of course, every mother is proud of her children. In my case, however, I've got plenty of reasons to brag. Over the years, Michael has accomplished so much, and it's been an honor and a pleasure watching him exceed my expectations. Even when he was a little boy, I saw the same drive and ambition that I see in Michael today. Exceptionally bright and exceedingly hard working, Michael continually amazed me over the years with his long list of achievements. Our family didn't blink an eye when we found out he would close out his college years as a summa cum laude graduate with a 4.0 (straight A) average or that he aced his CFP exam on his first attempt.

Let me assure you, though, Michael's success is not just a by-product of his intelligence and diligence – it's also because he genuinely cares about people. Case in point: While in his early 20s, Michael befriended an elderly lady who resided in his neighborhood. Struggling to maintain her independence, she needed assistance but had no one to help. Of his own accord, Michael ran errands for her and did minor fix-it jobs at her home several times a week. While he's a bit older now, my son is still the same kind-hearted, helpful man he always has been. When I watch him speak to groups, consult with someone requesting his help, or devise a financial solution for a retiree, Michael's concern radiates. It really is no wonder that his clients trust and adore him.

Best of all, though, I am grateful for our wonderful friendship. I look back with such fondness at the years we spent co-hosting our call-in radio program here in the Fort Worth-Dallas area. I can't tell you how many listeners remarked with delight about our close bond, which to this day remains rooted in equal measures of love and respect.

Quality is intrinsic to Michael's business philosophy. This book is no exception. Of all the tenets and topics he explores on these pages, I think Michael's positive focus on financial solutions impresses me most of all. He sincerely wants to minimize worries and maximize results to help his readers achieve the best retirement possible. In his typical easy-to-grasp way, Michael presents the information simply and succinctly. By incorporating individual case studies based on real-life scenarios, he adds a personal touch absent from typical financial books. Readers truly will feel as if he's talking directly to them. As a retiree myself, I appreciate that. I know you will too.

So sit back, relax, and read this incredible book, written by one of the most talented financial experts out there, Michael Dallas, CFP®. After you finish, you will be armed with the tools you need to become a worry-free retiree.

Jeanette Alexander, CFP®

Acknowledgments

Writing a book is, for the most part, a solitary experience. Authors spend hours on end in front of a screen, recording their ideas, watching as words turn into sentences and sentences into chapters. As their volume starts to take shape, however, most writers look to others for opinions on how the project is shaping up. In my case, that small but savvy group of advisors included my mother, Jeanette Alexander, CFP®. I am eternally grateful for the time she spent painstakingly reading, proofing, and providing her industry expertise to help *Retirement Solutions* become the best it could possibly be.

In fact, the inspiration for this book – individualized solutions to optimize retirement years – came in large part from working with Mother for more than 10 years. One of the most generous, caring people I know, my mom sincerely wanted the best for each of our clients. I watched closely as she helped them map out the most rewarding retirements possible, gleaning priceless wisdom along the way. Teacher, mentor, and friend … my mother served all of those roles.

Her remarkable influence, however, doesn't end there. A three-time cancer survivor who resigned from hospice care alive and well, my mother is a beacon of hope and a testament to the power of positivity. Ever the optimist, she's taught me the value of hard work and the importance of following your dreams.

Thank you, Mother.

Michael Dallas, CFP®

In everything I do, I believe people are important.

Michael Dallas, CFP®

Chapter 1

Seeking Solutions?
This Book Is For You

I 've worked with retirees for many years, and while each person's situation is unique, a common thread unites them all: Each person wants the absolute best retirement possible. After raising kids, climbing career ladders, and managing the typical minutiae of life, they all are hoping their "golden years" will be a time when they can finally relax and reap the rewards of their many labors. After sitting down and putting pen to paper, though, what they quickly find is this: Realizing that vision is achievable only with the proper solutions in place.

Many decisions regarding myriad financial issues must be made. For example, retirees have to know how much cash to set aside for living expenses, as well as how much money to keep invested. They want to have enough finances to live comfortably – with some earmarked for fun activities like the vacations of which they've always dreamed – but they also need to ensure they have plenty set aside to pay their bills. It's a lot to think about. It's also a lot to worry about. The strategy I always prescribe? I study my client's situation and, based on their individual needs, supply specific tools to help them achieve their goals in the most stress-free way possible.

This book is your toolbox. Not every tool will apply to you, but many will. Pick and choose what you need. Then get ready to chart the retirement course you've always hoped for.

Looking Back

Remember 1975? A gallon of gas was 59 cents. Bread cost 75 cents. An average new home could be purchased for less than $40,000. Someone with a pension of $1000 per month felt secure about the future. It is a drastic understatement to say prices have risen since then. Inflation can easily strangle unwary, fixed-income retirees and prevent them from fully enjoying the best years of their life.

Inflation, of course, is only one of the many perpetual changes affecting retirees. Tax laws change. Medicare and health insurance benefits change. New investment opportunities become available every day. Information, and misinformation, abounds. Who do you listen to? How do you find the worry-free solutions that are best-suited for your retirement needs?

Why This Book Is Different

Over the years, I have conducted hundreds of workshops and spent tens of thousands of hours helping retirees create individualized Retirement Solutions. Without fail, the most frequent question my clients ask is, "What book should I buy to learn more?"

If you've shopped for books lately, you know there are hundreds of books classified under the subject of "financial planning and investing." Of those countless volumes, you will find a dearth of quality books written solely for retirees. That's why this book is different. What also sets this book apart is that I use the term *retirement solutions* instead of *financial planning*. A financial plan is just that: a plan. Implicit in the word *solution*, however, is the idea of answers and results. You now hold a volume that provides an entire toolbox of results-oriented solutions tailored to your particular needs.

Repeated Information Is Intentional. As you read through the chapters, you'll notice that some of the information and ideas are repeated. This redundancy is not an accident. I intentionally duplicated ideas so that each chapter could stand on its own. This technique should allow you to go right to the chapters you need and have the necessary background information to understand the concepts.

It Gets Complicated At Retirement

If you were able to keep your financial situation simple during your working career, you have found (or soon will find) that things get complicated at retirement. Decisions must be made regarding Social Security, Medicare, IRAs, estates, pensions, rollovers, tax management and, last but not least, your investment portfolio. While these issues are important for everyone, they are absolutely critical for retirees. One bad decision can be financially devastating – and can completely crumble your dreams for an ideal retirement.

To further complicate matters, each of these areas is interrelated. For example, portfolio decisions affect taxes. Estate decisions affect IRA beneficiary decisions. Deciding when to retire affects Social Security and Medicare benefits. If you have the right tools in your retirement arsenal, however, coordinating all of these critical decisions does not have to be a worrisome task.

If You Feel Like a Novice, You're Not Alone

In my years of conducting workshops, I've found that many people are reluctant to admit that they don't know much about the various pieces of retirement. If this is you, don't feel bad. It is not your fault. Learning how to devise successful Retirement Solutions is not something that's taught in school. You have to acquire that knowledge on your own. The important thing is that you're taking time now to gain that wisdom. The time invested in reading this book will pay huge dividends over your retirement years. Remember: My goal with this book is to help erase the worry of retirement and help you create the most rewarding and pleasurable retirement possible.

You Need To Be In Control

Even if you already have a competent financial advisor, you still need this book. Without a doubt, engaging a highly qualified financial professional can be one of your greatest assets in establishing and maintaining a worry-free retirement. Nevertheless, just as every person is different, so too is every retirement situation.

Of course, I cannot teach you everything there is to know in one short book about creating Retirement Solutions. The subject can fill many thick volumes. Instead, I want to use a broad brush to paint a picture of the fundamental issues that need to be addressed. *Retirement Solutions* is designed to raise your awareness and to provide an easy-to-understand outline, accompanied by clear-cut tactics you can begin using from day one.

Over the past few years, our society has been awash with information regarding retirement – both good and bad. The fact that our country – indeed, our entire world – has experienced financial and economic turmoil over the past few years has made separating the wheat from the chaff more challenging than ever before. This book is designed to cut through that clutter and equip you with tried-and-true solutions to help ensure your retirement years are the absolute best years of your life.

Specific Objectives

After reading *Retirement Solutions,* you will be able to say:
- I understand the various types of investments available.
- I know how decisions should be made regarding my pension and IRA.
- I understand how taxes and inflation affect my retirement and my investment decisions.

- I understand the steps needed to increase my returns.
- I know how to use all of these tools to turn my questions into solutions and ensure my retirement years are free of worry and full of life.

Furthermore, you will be transformed in the way you view – and experience – your retirement. You will become an exceptional retiree. What do I mean by that?

- The average retiree makes investment decisions by anxiety and greed; the exceptional retiree makes decisions through sensible, well-balanced solutions.
- The average retiree impatiently bets on his or her future; the exceptional retiree patiently invests in it.
- The average retiree focuses on short-term performance; the exceptional retiree focuses on achieving long-term goals.
- The average retiree tries to guess the future; the exceptional retiree relies on sound financial strategies that alleviate anxiety and doubt.
- The average retiree worries about his or her security; the exceptional retiree has peace of mind.
- The average retiree earns dismal returns and consistently underperforms the markets; the exceptional retiree steadily maximizes his or her returns.
- Finally, the average retiree loses sleep stressing about finances and how to make ends meet; the exceptional retiree employs specialized tools to maximize his or her outcome and design the best, most worry-free Retirement Solutions possible.

You too can become an exceptional retiree with a bright future ahead. This book will provide the tools you need to do just that.

Conclusion

You've worked hard. You've paid your dues. Now, as a retiree, it is finally *your* time. It is time to relish the rewards of your retirement years.

That, of course, is easier said than done.

I wrote *Retirement Solutions* to help ensure that your retirement is free from financial headache and hassle, replete with the best things life has to offer. Whatever the "best" means to you, I want you to experience it without worry or doubt.

Whether you read this book from cover to cover or study only the chapters that apply to your situation, the book you hold in your hands will be your personal roadmap to retirement rewards.

The best years of your life are yours for the taking. *Retirement Solutions* will be your trusted companion on that journey. ◆

Chapter 2

Four Steps To
Your Retirement Solutions

When speaking to groups about creating Retirement Solutions, I start by providing an overview of the process we need to follow. As I look around the room at my audience, I inevitably spot one or two people who are fidgeting and looking off into space. I can almost read their minds: "When are we going to get to the good stuff – the investing part?" What they need to understand is that to do the "investing part" correctly, we need to follow a process. Investing is simply one piece of your overall Retirement Solutions.

To make your best years worry-free, you must do the following and in this order:

1. Determine where you are financially.
2. Create clear goals.
3. Create solutions for the Five Important Retirement Issues.
4. Track your progress.

Step 1: Determine Where You Are Financially

While this sounds elementary, it is extremely important. Knowing where you are financially is a necessary prerequisite to creating sound

Retirement Solutions. Start by listing all your resources, assets, and sources of income. These will include Social Security benefits, pensions, investments, and any other sources of income. Amazingly, people often make all types of decisions before completing this first, fundamental step, and the results can be disastrous.

Before reading any further, gather together all of the following items that apply to you:

- Retirement plan distribution statements
- Employee benefit statements
- Deferred compensation and stock option agreements
- Latest statements from pension, Keogh, or IRA accounts
- Latest statements from brokerage accounts
- Latest statements for mutual fund accounts
- Latest bank account statements
- Copies of any stock certificates or bond certificates not held in a brokerage account (include a note telling where the original certificates are located)
- Latest wills and trust documents
- A list of safety deposit box assets (include the location of the box, the location of the key, and the contents of the box)
- A list of any other financial assets or sources of income

Next, compile the following documents in one easy-to-find location. They will help you with the development of your Retirement Solutions, and should something happen to you, the administrator of your will and your heirs will find it particularly helpful to have all these documents in one place:

- The names and phone numbers of your financial advisor, your attorney, your tax preparer, and so on.
- An outline of your family tree (include parents, siblings, children, and grandchildren)

- Any outstanding powers of attorney
- Other important documents: birth certificates, passports, adoption papers, military service records, marriage certificate, and divorce decree(s)

From these documents, create a list of your assets and liabilities. Identify sources of income that you will be receiving, such as Social Security benefits and pensions. Itemize your debts including interest rates, payments, and maturity dates. Once this task is completed, you will have a comprehensive view of your financial picture.

Please, read no further until this step is taken. Stop and do it now. Finding out where you are is absolutely critical to the success of your retirement.

Step 2: Create Clear Goals

The next step in creating sound Retirement Solutions is to develop a clear, specific goals list. Each goal must have a time frame and a cost attached. For example, a goal is not, "I want to have enough money to live on for the rest of my life." That may be your desire and dream, but it is not a goal. A goal is specific; a goal has a time frame and a particular dollar amount: "I would like to retire January 1 next year with $50,000 per year in income, which increases each year with inflation." Notice how this goal is specific; it has a time frame (January 1 next year) and a dollar amount ($50,000 per year) attached. The only other requirement for this objective to become a goal is for it be written down.

Get a pen and some paper out right now and make a list. Write down everything that you think you might like to do with the rest of your life. Don't be surprised if this requires a little soul-searching. What exactly do you want to accomplish? Where do you want to go? What do you want to do? Do you want to volunteer? Work part-time? Visit friends and family? Travel? Take up a new hobby? The answers to these questions are different for every person. Be imaginative. Don't limit yourself or have preconceived ideas about what is or is not possible. Brainstorm. Have fun with it!

Step 3: Create Solutions For Five Important Retirement Issues

This is the step where the rubber meets the road. Step 3 works to bring together steps 1 and 2. Once you know where you are (what resources are available) and where you want to go (what you want to do), you will need Retirement Solutions to get from here to there. Nothing is more fundamental to creating a successful retirement than having well-thought-out solutions.

Retirement Issue 1: Investment Portfolio

For most retirees, the management of their life savings is critical. This money will provide security against unforeseen expenses (e.g., emergencies) and often provides the necessary supplement to other sources of income such as Social Security and pensions. It is important that your *Portfolio Solution* provides the appropriate safety and growth you need for a successful and happy retirement.

Retirement Issue 2: Retirement Income

A doctor once told me, "My goal is to have my money last until I turn room temperature." While this doctor stated the idea in a euphemistic, amusing way, every retiree wants to know the answer to the same question: "Am I going to get checks every month for life?" This question addresses the second part of providing a lifetime income – creating a sound *Income Solution*.

To find out whether your money will last, you need to peer into your crystal ball. You need to create simulations of the future – often referred to as *projections*. These projections combine resources, goals, Portfolio Solution, and a few assumptions about the future. Retirement projections help you evaluate your Retirement Solutions: Will it work?

Does it have problems? When the projections show a problem, it is time to go back and reevaluate the goals. Later, I'll show you examples of what projections look like.

Retirement Issue 3: Risk Assessment

Your Retirement Solutions need to address provisions for unexpected catastrophes. These areas include estate planning, health care, and liability risks. If you do everything else right yet neglect your *Risk Solution*, all your Retirement Solutions could be destroyed.

Several years ago, I created Retirement Solutions for a client named Leonard, who was then in his early 50s. Among my recommendations, I suggested that Leonard purchase what is called an *umbrella insurance policy*. This policy increases and extends liability coverage beyond the standard automobile and home liability policies. In Leonard's case, I suggested that he buy at least one million dollars in coverage. While this policy sounds expensive, it is not. At the time I made the recommendation, a million-dollar umbrella policy cost less than $200 per year. (In my opinion, an umbrella policy is one of the best insurance values one can get, and no one should even think of going without this coverage.)

A year later, I got a call from Leonard, who sounded very distraught. Tragedy had struck. He needed me to liquidate his investment accounts. His teenage son was driving the family car and accidentally ran into another driver. The injured motorist was suing Leonard for damages. Unfortunately, his auto coverage had quickly run out. Leonard informed me that he had never gotten around to purchasing the umbrella policy. Now he deeply regretted his procrastination.

The only way Leonard could make ends meet was to liquidate his retirement accounts. The sad thing was that Leonard did not need the money to pay a judgment but rather to pay his attorney's fees. Had he purchased the umbrella policy, he would have been covered, and the insurance company's lawyers would have been there to defend him.

Leonard's story is not unique, I'm sorry to say. I could fill many pages with horror story after horror story of similar tragedies. The bottom line is that under no circumstances should you consider retiring without making provisions for sickness, disability, death, and legal entanglements.

Retirement Issue 4: Estate Planning

When people think of estate planning, they usually think of wills. However, estate planning is far more than "who gets what" at death. A good estate plan outlines who your decision makers will be if you cannot make decisions for yourself. Putting a good *Estate Solution* in place protects you and the ones you love.

Retirement Issue 5: Income Taxes

The importance of income taxes cannot be overestimated. Choices you make about income, investing, and even estate choices can have profound implications to how much of your wealth you give to the government. I once helped a client reduce her income tax bill by $60,000 per year just by changing how she withdrew money for her living expenses. While not everyone will have such dramatic results, you need to look carefully at your *Tax Solution*.

Step 4: Track Your Progress

Many people mistakenly think that once their Retirement Solutions are completed and executed, the process is over. It is not. Setting up your Retirement Solutions is not a one-time event but an ongoing process.

If I compare the Retirement Solutions process to flying a 747 jumbo jet to Hawaii, you'll get a better idea of what I'm talking about. Even before starting the engines, the pilot knows where he's at and how much fuel is in the tank (step 1). The pilot also knows where he's going (step 2). He has a sound flight plan (solution) for getting the plane from here to there (step 3).

However, once the plane leaves the ground, the pilot's job isn't over. It is just beginning. The pilot must continue to monitor his location, fuel, and course. He must continue to make slight corrections to the plane's direction. He may need to deal with unexpected events, as well. For example, El Nino may throw a hurricane in the plane's path. To compensate, the pilot may need to amend his flight solution. He may need to turn the plane and change his strategy. Through this continual review and adjustment, the pilot will ultimately land the plane in paradise.

In the same way, it is imperative that you continually track your financial progress (step 4). Periodically review where you are, where you're headed, and your strategy for success. Things will change. Your portfolio will change. Taxes will change. Interest rates will change. And, occasionally, even your goals will change. Because everything is moving and changing, you must periodically review where you are to make sure you stay on course. As a practical matter, I recommend that you conduct a review no less than every two or three years. Furthermore, if an unexpected event occurs (e.g., death, disability, sudden inheritance, you should do a review immediately.

Retirement Solutions Are Unique – Three Examples:

Over the years, I have created countless sound Retirement Solutions for my clientele. Each client, and set of solutions, is unique. To help illustrate how Retirement Solutions differ, I have included three examples below.

Case 1: 55-Year-Old – Retire Early

Problem: 55-year-old man was laid off and could only find work far from his home.

Not long ago, a man walked into my office looking tired and worried. He was a 55-year-old aerospace professional who had just been laid off. He had been with the company for over 20 years and had a very specialized skill set. The only job he could find that used his skills was a five-hour drive away from his home.

His wife was a nurse and had worked at the same hospital for years. She did not want to leave her job or move away, so he took the job and rented an apartment five hours away. Every other weekend, he would drive home to visit his wife. He had been living this way for six months when he came to see me. The arrangement was wearing him pretty thin.

He came to me because he was simply shopping around for someone to roll over his 401k. Before arriving at my office, he visited several well-known, brand name national firms. They all asked him the same standard question: "Are you conservative, moderate, or aggressive?" And, of course, they all recommended that he roll his 401k into an IRA with their firms.

I asked him a different question.

"If we could figure out a way to move you back home, would that be important to you?" His reply: "Oh, my gosh, yes! I just didn't think it was possible!"

Solution: Use pension provisions and special tax laws to create an Income Solution that allowed him to retire early.

Without going into detail, I did not roll his 401k into an IRA. Instead, I used special pension rules and tax provisions that allowed him to retire early without any kind of tax penalties. These Retirement Solutions dramatically changed his life.

Case 2: 70-Year-Old Widow – Eliminate Taxes And Increase Safety

Problem: Widow's income was not secure, and she paid high taxes.

Not long ago, a client brought a very nice lady in to see me because of a promise he had made to her late husband. My client had promised that he would make sure this woman's finances were always secure.

When I looked at her entire financial situation, I found that her late husband had left her an extensive investment portfolio, as well as a variety of trusts. When I examined her tax returns, I found she was paying over $60,000 a year in income taxes. When I looked at her investment portfolio, I found that there was a very real possibility that she would run out of money.

Solution: Create sound Portfolio Solution, Income Solution, and Tax Solution using tailored investment vehicles.

I rearranged this woman's portfolio using specific investment vehicles that guaranteed her a lifetime income and provided tax advantages that took her tax bill from $60,000 per year to zero. These Retirement Solutions secured her future.

Case 3: Millionaire Investor – Prevent Large Portfolio Losses

Problem: Investor was tired of large portfolio losses from steep drops in the stock market.

Not too long ago, a 50-year-old man came in to see me. He was relatively wealthy and had several million dollars in investments. His concern was the stock market. He had been through the 2002 and 2008 bear markets. He was tired of losing half his money in market downturns and then having to wait years for his investments to recover. What he wanted was a strategy that would prevent him from losing a lot of money if the market plunged again.

Solution: Implement an active investment Portfolio Solution to curb risk of loss.

In this case, the solution was to use a particular active strategy that had a mechanism for moving his portfolio to cash should the market go into a free-fall.

The specific pension rules used in Case 1 and the tax strategies used in Case 2 are far beyond the scope of this short book. Pension laws and tax laws are just too extensive to list every nuance and strategy. However, in Chapter 10, I do touch on the portfolio strategy used in Case 3. What I want you to learn from these three cases is that well-crafted Retirement Solutions pull all the financial pieces together and move you toward your retirement goals. A highly trained and experienced financial advisor can guide you through that process.

Conclusion

Retirement Solutions are unique. The best Retirement Solutions for you will depend on your resources and your goals. There are four steps to a financially worry-free retirement:

Step 1: Determine where you are financially.

Step 2: Create clear goals.

Step 3: Create solutions for the Five Important Retirement Issues

Step 4: Track your progress.

Get Started Today With Your Free Copy of My Retirement Solutions Questionnaire

Without a doubt, the most important step you will take toward a financially secure retirement is your first one – getting started. To help you get started, I have designed a special Retirement Solutions Questionnaire. This form will help you "get it all together" and move you toward a solid financial path.

When hosting retirement workshops, attendees often comment about how my Retirement Solutions Questionnaire completely transformed the direction of their retirement. I frequently hear, "I really loved your workshop and the things I learned. However, the best part of the workshop was the Retirement Solutions Questionnaire. It helped me get everything in one place. I knew I had this investment here and that investment there, but I had never taken the time to list

---

all of my resources together. Moreover, the questions made us think about what we expect from our retirement, our investments, and our financial professional. Your Retirement Solutions Questionnaire made all the difference. It's great! Thank you!"

For those reading this book, I am making my Retirement Solutions Questionnaire available to you free of charge. Simply call 800-747-7384 to order your free copy. Enjoy.

Michael Dallas, CFP® ♦

Chapter 3

"Will My Money Last?"

Retirees spend a lot of time talking about net worth, portfolio values, and return on investments. In all honesty, these items are merely a means to achieving what you really want – an enjoyable retirement. For this, you will need a consistent stream of spendable cash. I saw a T-shirt one time that expressed it well: "Happiness is a positive cash flow." In this chapter, I will show you how the four steps we discussed in Chapter 2 will move you toward a lifetime of happiness.

No One-Size-Fits-All Solution

It is important to note that the strategies I present in this chapter are only examples. Don't mistake any of them as being the one right answer. Each person reading this book has unique resources, goals, and temperament; therefore, each person will have a unique income strategy for achieving his or her life goals. My intent in this chapter is to present several typical examples. I have intentionally left out complicated details, such as estate planning and qualified versus nonqualified accounts (e.g., IRAs vs. non-IRAs). The combination of strategies that you use is not nearly as important as creating workable Retirement Solutions.

Retirees' Two Fears

Most retirees face two fears: the fear of losing their principal in the short term and the fear of outliving their money in the long term. Both fears are understandable. When employed, most people are not overly concerned about their investments. They feel good when they go up and a twinge of pain when they go down. But for the most part, they just give their statements a quick glance and then just put them away. However, at retirement, retirees become very sensitive to their investments since they are dependent on the performance for their living expenses. A significant loss of principal may mean the difference between staying comfortably retired and needing to go back to work.

Many retirees today will spend more years in retirement than they worked in their careers. Since you probably will be retired for several decades, you need to be sure that you make provisions to increase your income in the future. Think back to 1975. How much income did you need to live? You need far more money for living expenses today than you needed back then. If history is any teacher, that trend can be expected to continue. In fact, even at a "low" inflation rate of just 4 percent, you will need twice as much money in 20 years to have the same standard of living you enjoy today.

During our working years, inflation isn't such a big deal. Employment income generally increases faster than prices rise. However, after retirement, it is another matter altogether. It is up to you to give yourself inflationary raises along the way. We all know retirees who did not prepare for inflation. The older they get, the more destitute they become. Getting squeezed by rising costs is not inevitable. It can be avoided.

Developing Retirement Projections

The biggest question on every retiree's mind is, "Do I have enough money to retire?" Or, stated another way, "How can I be sure my money will last?" Numerous variables make this question difficult to answer – variables such as changing income needs, inflation, Social Security benefits (which increase with inflation), pension benefits (which usually don't increase with inflation), changing interest rates, and uncertain stock market returns.

Finding workable Retirement Solutions requires a gathering together of all these factors. You should put good solutions into place as soon as possible. It is much easier to make small adjustments now than face painful choices later (e.g., running out of money or going back to work). One way to evaluate whether your Retirement Solutions work is by creating mathematical simulations of the future, called *projections*.

There are several approaches to creating projections. They all have one goal in mind – to determine whether a retirement solution is sound. A financial projection combines complex factors and sketches a possible picture of the future.

Projection Methods

Before I outline the various ways of creating projections, it is worth noting that projections should be used with caution. There's an old saying in the computer world, "Garbage in, garbage out." If your projection assumptions are faulty, your results will be useless or possibly even misleading.

There are three broad approaches to creating projections:

- Historical backtesting method
- Monte Carlo projection method
- Point projection method

Each has strengths and weaknesses. While none provide the one right answer, some are better than others. Since creating a good projection is the starting point of your income and investing strategy, it is important to understand how each method works.

Historical Backtesting

The *historical backtesting* method takes you on a tour of the past. It creates projections by using actual historical numbers and applying them to your unique situation. In essence, it asks what would have happened had you retired at different points in history. For example, a backtest may start in 1927. The calculation assumes that you retire in that year and then applies the historical interest rates, stock market returns, and inflation rates to your personal situation. After it evaluates that scenario, the projection then steps to the next year (1928) and assumes you retire then. The projection continues to step through history year by year. It assumes you retire at each point in history and then determines the success or failure of your portfolio. It then generates a report showing how often you would have succeeded or failed in your retirement. This type of projection is extremely interesting and is useful for seeing how history would have treated you in the past.

However, as you might have guessed, this type of analysis has limitations. The largest shortcoming with this method is change – we live in an entirely different world than our parents and grandparents. Over the last century we've seen two World Wars, the Great Depression, and real personal incomes rise four-fold. Communication and travel have made the world much smaller, as a growing population has made it more crowded. Everything, including the investment world, has changed.

Using historical numbers to create projections requires you to understand that modern investments differ from those of the past. For example, a growth mutual fund 60 years ago probably contained baby food, television, and car manufacturers. Growth funds today contain companies that produce software, biotech, and semiconductors. Nevertheless, historical backtesting can be very useful by illustrating how well your income strategy might have performed in the past.

Monte Carlo Projection

Another popular approach is called the *Monte Carlo projection* method. In essence, this type of projection "rolls the dice" to choose random numbers for each year's returns and for inflation. Like historical backtesting, this method runs many scenarios and then reports how often the projections succeeded or failed. If constructed correctly, I believe that a Monte Carlo approach can be useful. However, I have found that many simulations of the market do not mathematically represent the real world. The software frequently neglects historical relationships, such as the effects of inflation on the stock market and interest rates, or the relationship between one year's inflation rate to the next. Unfortunately, when Monte Carlo models neglect important relationships, they provide little useful information.

Point Projection

The easiest and most common method of running projections is known as a *point projection*. This type of projection simply takes your assumptions about the future and puts them together into a simple spreadsheet. The key to successfully using this type of calculation is having realistic (and perhaps conservative) assumptions about the future. Since point projections can be easily used, let's take a closer look at them.

Point Projection Assumptions

When creating projections, our assumptions fall into two categories: those that we can control and those that we cannot control. The factors that cannot be controlled include inflation, interest rates, and stock market returns. The variables that can be controlled include how much you save, when you retire, how much you spend, and how your portfolio is invested. From there, you can see how various decisions (such as how much you spend) affect your future security.

Inflation

Of all the factors affecting retirement, inflation is probably the most dangerous. It destroys more retirements than any other single item. What makes inflation so dangerous is that it erodes retirement income slowly and silently. Like the steel girders of a bridge being rusted away, inflation slowly destroys the strength of your savings and fixed pensions until your retirement collapses.

When creating projections, be sure to account for the continual increase of prices. Since World War II, there have only been a couple of years that the United States did not experience inflation. That tells us that the chance of inflation continuing into the future is a virtual certainty. For optimum protection, build a retirement solution that will give you raises over the course of your retirement.

So what number should you use for inflation – 3 percent, 4 percent, 5 percent? Historically, inflation has run a little over 5 percent since World War II. However, during the 1990s, inflation moderated considerably and began running in the 2 to 3 percent range. I believe that this change is the result of fundamental changes in the way the Federal Reserve manages the country's money supply.

When I create projections, I usually assume a 4 percent inflation rate. This number is lower than the long-term historical norm but higher than our recent experience. For the foreseeable future, I believe that inflation will probably run close to 3 percent. Using an inflation number higher than I expect gives my projections some fudge room. Wouldn't it be better to have a happy surprise (lower inflation than expected) than an unhappy one (inflation higher than projected)? Whatever you do, don't ignore inflation.

Interest Rates

Everyone who's ever put money into a CD, money market, fixed annuity, or bond knows that interest rates continually change. They go up. They go down. They never stay the same. Even so, when you create projections, you have to make an assumption about how much your interest rate investments will earn. In your projections, it is important to use an interest rate that reflects the type of fixed investments you own.

Stock Market Returns

Of all the assumptions in making projections, predicting the stock market is the most difficult. While the market provides higher returns than fixed investments over the long term, it has much more volatility and potential for loss in the short term. Historically, stocks have averaged around 12 percent annual returns. Some years the stock market has returned more than 50 percent; in other years, it has lost more than 50 percent.

Added to this uncertainty is a concept I will discuss further in Chapter 8 – the Perspiration Cost. If an investor is prone to jump out of the market during bad times and into the market during good times, the long-term returns will suffer.

To complicate matters, the 1980s and the 1990s consistently produced high stock market returns. After each of the rare down years during this period, the market quickly rallied and soared to new heights. During this unprecedented period, many investors lost their long-term focus and began having unrealistic expectations of the stock market. With the stock market soaring, investors began expecting high returns every year.

Similarly, the sharp downturn in the stock market between 2000 and 2002 as well as the 2008 crash caused many investors to become pessimistic. During these slumps, investors began moaning that they expected substantially lower market returns indefinitely.

I believe that neither view is correct. We shouldn't expect high returns each year nor should we expect ongoing doom and gloom. To create useful projections, we need to be realistic about the market's potential risks and rewards.

Since stock market returns are the most uncertain portion of your projections, I like to use a number that is substantially lower than historical norms. I often use an assumed stock market return of 9 percent. While this rate is much lower than historical norms, it allows the projections to contain a margin of safety. I've seen people create projections using expectations of 12 percent to 20 percent. Should the market not produce these returns, their security falls apart. To me, depending on high market returns for your security spells danger.

Playing "What If"

When creating any type of projection, you need to ask yourself, "What if I changed this?" or "What if I changed that?" In financial-speak, this type of calculation is known as a *sensitivity analysis*. By asking "What if?" in your projections, you can explore the impact that different decisions may have.

Altering Your Projections

If, after running a projection, you find that your money is estimated to run out too quickly, you can take the following actions:

- Increase your preretirement savings.
- Extend your retirement date.
- Increase your investment returns.
- Decrease your postretirement spending.

Increase Your Preretirement Savings

Savings have the most value when they have time to grow. Most people at or approaching retirement do not have the luxury of long saving periods. Therefore, increasing savings amounts before retirement usually has a very small impact in making portfolios last.

Extend Your Retirement Date

Of all the resources we possess, time is our most valuable asset. Before deciding to delay retirement, I usually recommend that soon-to-be retirees closely examine and prioritize their goals. It is possible that changing or even eliminating less important goals can mean the difference between retiring now or working another 10 years.

Increasing Your Returns

As a general rule, increasing portfolio returns means increasing investment risk. Since retirees depend on savings for income, it is usually not a good idea to take on excessive risk. If your projections show a shortfall using a sound investment portfolio, I don't recommend addressing the problem by trying to substantially increase your portfolio returns. Taking on excessive portfolio risk could spell disaster for your retirement.

Decrease Your Spending

The most effective method to make your retirement last longer is to decrease living-expense needs. A small change in spending now has an enormous effect on how long your portfolio will last. Even a small decrease in spending may mean the difference between the portfolio running out or lasting a lifetime.

It is also important to realize that the living expense draws on your portfolio probably will change during your lifetime. In addition to needing more money to meet higher prices, your spending patterns will change as well. I've found that young retirees generally spend a substantial amount on fun items like boats, RVs, and travel. I've found that in real terms, retirees tend to spend less the older they get. If you think that your spending will change over time, you can include these modifications in your projections. For example, your projections might include extra vacation spending for the first 15 years after retirement.

Creativity and Imagination

Sometimes a little creativity and imagination, in relation to your life goals, can make your retirement dreams come true. The Hendersons are a fantastic example of how this can assist in making a wonderful retirement. When the Hendersons were about to retire, they told me they wanted to live in the mountains and travel part of the year. After running their projections, we found that purchasing a cabin in the mountains would substantially impair their long-term security. The big expense would probably cause them to run out of money.

Undeterred, Mr. and Mrs. Henderson became very creative. After some good detective work, they took a caretaker position at a beautiful mountain home in Colorado. For nine months during the year, they simply looked after and maintained the mountain mansion. During the other three months, they traveled. By being creative, the Hendersons were able to retire early and achieve their life goals. Before deciding to extend your retirement date, carefully consider your life goals and alternative strategies for achieving them.

Point Projection Example

In Illustration 1 on the next page, I have included a simple example of a point projection.

In this case, we have a portfolio of $500,000. This number is listed in the box at the top, next to the word "Investments." This $500,000 portfolio will be allocated 60 percent to growth (i.e., equity) investments such as stocks, stock mutual funds, and stock variable annuity funds. The other 40 percent of the portfolio will be allocated to fixed investments (i.e., interest rate investments) such as bonds, bond funds, and fixed annuities. For projection purposes, let's assume the equity investments earn 9 percent. Let's also assume that the fixed investments earn 5 percent. Given this allocation, with these assumed returns, our overall blended return will be 7.4 percent.

Next, we have a column on the right titled "Living Exp" (for living expenses). In this case, the couple needs $60,000 per year for living expenses. Notice that the living expense number increases each year for inflation. For example, if we assume a 4 percent inflation rate, they will

	Investments	500,000	Report Date	1/1/2013
	Growth Alloc	60%	Grwth Rate	9.0%
	Fixed Alloc	40%	Fixed Rate	5.0%
	Inflation Rate	4.0%	Blend Rate	7.40%

Year Number	Year	End of Year % Value	End of Year Buying Power	End of Year Nominal Value	Portfolio Cash Flow	Living Exp	Pension	Her SS	His SS
					In / (Out)	(60,000)	25,000	6,000	12,000
						4.00%	0.00%	4.00%	4.00%
						1/1/2013	1/1/2013	1/1/2013	1/1/2013
						12/31/2099	12/31/2099	12/31/2099	12/31/2099
				500,000					
1	2013	100%	500,000	520,000	(17,000)	(60,000)	25,000	6,000	12,000
2	2014	100%	499,075	539,800	(18,680)	(62,400)	25,000	6,240	12,480
3	2015	99%	497,232	559,318	(20,427)	(64,896)	25,000	6,490	12,979
4	2016	99%	494,645	578,478	(22,229)	(67,470)	25,000	6,747	13,494
5	2017	98%	490,758	597,146	(24,139)	(70,199)	25,000	7,020	14,040
6	2018	97%	486,173	615,230	(26,105)	(73,007)	25,000	7,301	14,601
7	2019	96%	480,679	632,608	(28,149)	(75,927)	25,000	7,593	15,185
8	2020	95%	474,660	649,188	(30,234)	(78,905)	25,000	7,891	15,781
9	2021	93%	466,934	664,735	(32,492)	(82,132)	25,000	8,213	16,426
10	2022	92%	458,700	679,134	(34,792)	(85,417)	25,000	8,542	17,083
11	2023	90%	449,547	692,206	(37,184)	(88,834)	25,000	8,883	17,767
12	2024	88%	440,037	703,835	(39,595)	(92,278)	25,000	9,228	18,456
13	2025	86%	428,464	713,653	(42,265)	(96,093)	25,000	9,609	19,219
14	2026	83%	416,519	721,508	(44,956)	(99,937)	25,000	9,994	19,987
15	2027	81%	403,628	727,146	(47,754)	(103,934)	25,000	10,393	20,787
16	2028	78%	390,475	730,412	(50,542)	(107,918)	25,000	10,792	21,584
17	2029	75%	374,993	730,764	(53,699)	(112,427)	25,000	11,243	22,485
18	2030	72%	359,204	727,993	(56,847)	(116,924)	25,000	11,692	23,385
19	2031	68%	342,423	721,744	(60,121)	(121,601)	25,000	12,160	24,320
20	2032	65%	325,382	711,807	(63,346)	(126,208)	25,000	12,621	25,242
21	2033	61%	305,880	697,405	(67,077)	(131,538)	25,000	13,154	26,308
22	2034	57%	286,039	678,253	(70,760)	(136,800)	25,000	13,680	27,360
23	2035	53%	265,143	653,853	(74,590)	(142,272)	25,000	14,227	28,454
24	2036	49%	243,875	623,920	(78,319)	(147,598)	25,000	14,760	29,520
25	2037	44%	220,187	587,362	(82,728)	(153,897)	25,000	15,390	30,779
26	2038	39%	196,013	543,789	(87,037)	(160,053)	25,000	16,005	32,011
27	2039	34%	170,701	492,511	(91,519)	(166,455)	25,000	16,646	33,291
28	2040	29%	144,764	433,127	(95,829)	(172,613)	25,000	17,261	34,523
29	2041	23%	116,674	364,138	(101,040)	(180,058)	25,000	18,006	36,012
30	2042	18%	87,806	285,003	(106,082)	(187,260)	25,000	18,726	37,452
31	2043	12%	57,698	194,768	(111,325)	(194,750)	25,000	19,475	38,950
32	2044	5%	26,542	92,873	(116,308)	(201,868)	25,000	20,187	40,374
33	2045	0%	-	-	(122,465)	(210,665)	25,000	21,066	42,133
34	2046	0%	-	-	(128,364)	(219,091)	25,000	21,909	43,818
35	2047	0%	-	-	(134,498)	(227,855)	25,000	22,785	45,571
36	2048	0%	-	-	(140,257)	(236,081)	25,000	23,608	47,216
37	2049	0%	-	-	(147,532)	(246,474)	25,000	24,647	49,295
38	2050	0%	-	-	(154,433)	(256,333)	25,000	25,633	51,267
39	2051	0%	-	-	(161,611)	(266,586)	25,000	26,659	53,317
40	2052	0%	-	-	(168,265)	(276,093)	25,000	27,609	55,219

Illustration 1

need over twice as much money in year 20 to enjoy the same standard of living as they have today.

To the right of the "Living Exp" column are the income columns. These columns show the money that will be coming from a pension and from Social Security. You'll notice their Social Security benefits increase each year but the pension does not. This is because Social Security increases each year for inflation, while the pension amount stays the same.

To the left of the "Living Exp" column, you'll find a column called "Portfolio Cash Flow." These numbers are the difference between the checks coming in and the living expenses going out. In other words, this is the amount that will have to be drawn from the portfolio.

The next column to the left is titled "End of Year Nominal Value." These numbers indicate the estimated value of the portfolio from year to year. This number is calculated by adding the estimated earnings on the portfolio (i.e., "Blended Rate") and subtracting the portfolio draws (i.e., the amount they withdraw from their investments). Given the assumptions, this is the value the portfolio is estimated to be each year.

The next column to the left, titled "End of Year Buying Power," adjusts the portfolio value by inflation. It indicates whether you're getting ahead of or behind inflation. For example, in year 20 of your retirement, the nominal value of this portfolio is estimated to be $711,807 but the buying power is $325,382. While you may have $711,807 in your investment account, it will only allow you to buy what $325,382 buys today. As this example illustrates, it is possible that the nominal value can increase while buying power decreases.

The final column, "End of Year % Value," shows how the estimated future buying power compares to your original amount invested. In 20 years, the buying power is estimated to be $325,382. As indicated by "End of Year % Value," this amount is 65 percent of the buying power with which you started ($500,000).

If you follow the "End of Year Nominal Value" and "End of Year Buying Power" columns down the page, you'll notice that they become zero in year 33. This means that, given the stated assumptions, the portfolio runs out of money. If this was your projection example, you would have to anticipate paying your bills with nothing more than your Social Security benefits and your pension at that point. This result could be okay or not okay depending upon age. If you're 80 years old, this projection shows your money lasting until you're over 113 years old.

But what if you're much younger? Then, running out of money 33 years from now may be unacceptable. Your projections need to fit your goals and your unique point in life.

Rerun Projections Periodically

Projections are not something you do once. You should rerun them at least every two to three years. Not only will they help create solutions at the beginning of retirement, they can also help with staying on track. Over time, everything changes. Needs and goals change. Portfolio values change. The investment environment changes. It is important to refresh your projections to make sure your Retirement Solutions remains sound.

Conclusion

The question everyone asks is, "Will my money last?" While difficult to answer, retirees can estimate an answer by using mathematical simulations called *projections*.

By using projections, retirees can put good solutions into place and can make small adjustments now rather than face painful choices later (such as running out of money or going back to work).

While there are several approaches to creating projections, they all have advantages and disadvantages. By using projections carefully, a retiree can sketch a possible picture of the future and answer that all-important question related to their retirement plans. ◆

Chapter 4

Investing Basics

Savings Accounts vs. Investing

In Chapter 1, I discussed the dramatic price increases that have occurred over time. In 1975, a gallon of gas was 59 cents. Bread was 75 cents. A new home could be purchased for $40,000. A pension of $1000 per month seemed sufficient for many people. Needless to say, 40 years of constant inflation have squeezed fixed-income retirees.

So what's the answer for those living on fixed resources? Where does a retiree look for income investments?

Historically, retirees who put all their life savings in bank accounts (e.g., checking accounts, savings accounts, certificates of deposit) have two guarantees: (1) the guarantee of principal (e.g., FDIC insurance) and (2) the virtual guarantee of systematically losing to inflation. Because inflation continually dissolves the value of your dollars, good investment strategies are needed to keep you ahead of inflation. To beat the inflationary monster, you will need something more than bank accounts. You will need a sound portfolio of investments.

Your Portfolio

In the financial world, a collection of investments is known as a *portfolio*. These instruments include securities such as stocks, bonds, mutual funds, variable annuities, and fixed annuities. One of the first steps toward creating a retirement solution is to list all your investments and their values. You need to know what investments you have in your portfolio.

Constructing A Portfolio

Years ago I went scuba diving on the island of Roatan, Honduras. In the town called West End, there lived a curious lady named Valerie who owned an even more curious hotel. Valerie's Hotel was unlike anything the word "hotel" might bring to mind. Her establishment reminded me of the scrap-wood forts I used to build as a boy. Valerie had strung together a random collection of box-like structures up the side of a steep hill. Bedrooms and cubbyhole sleeping areas were spread throughout in Swiss Family Robinson style.

Out of profound curiosity, I asked her how she had arrived at such an interesting arrangement. "Well," she admitted with a smile, "whenever I save up enough money, I go buy lumber. Then I start hammering." She went on to tell me about some of her "learning experiences," such as the time one of the structures collapsed. She said that she didn't realize she needed strong beams to support the weight of the second story. She assured me that she had learned her lesson and wouldn't be making that mistake again. It never occurred to Valerie that her randomly built compound was extremely dangerous.

I believe that Valerie's Hotel was a death trap. Not only was the compound haphazard, the wood structure was also vulnerable to fire. If a blaze started anywhere in her hotel, the thick, black smoke of burning lumber would make it virtually impossible for guests to find their way out of the tinderbox maze. Although ambitious, Valerie's inexperience in building construction left her completely oblivious to the dangers to which she had exposed herself and her guests.

Fifteen years later, I revisited Valerie's Hotel. While fire had not taken the structure, it nevertheless had become an abandoned heap. The haphazard roof had allowed water to permeate the entire structure, and Valerie's efforts had turned into a pile of rotting lumber. It was a complete loss.

I find that many people construct their portfolios much like Valerie constructed her hotel – randomly. They have no overriding strategy or direction and are often unaware of the hazards they are creating. Like Valerie, these folks usually construct their portfolios as they go along. If an investment sounds good, they nail it on. If a magazine article extols a particular investment, they put some money there. If they see someone on television recommending another investment, they put some money in that. After continually nailing on different investments, they own maze-like portfolios constructed at random.

Instead of random investing, you should approach your portfolio as if you were building a new house. If you have ever built a new home, you know that every aspect of construction, from the number of stories to the style of the faucets, is carefully considered. Nothing is left to chance. Construction gets underway only after thousands of decisions are made and the plans are drawn.

Likewise, a portfolio should be a product of deliberate thought, with every aspect clearly thought out ahead of time. Only after you understand what your end result will be, should construction begin.

The first step in constructing your portfolio is to answer these questions:

- What type of returns do you want?
- What type of risk are you willing to take?
- What type of investments would you like?
- What guarantees are important to you?
- When will you need cash and how much?

- What strategies would be appropriate to increase returns and reduce risk?

Just like building a home, trade-offs must be made. For example, we would all like to build a large mansion that costs only one dollar. In all seriousness, we know that isn't realistic. Similarly, we would all love to earn 50 percent annual returns on our investments without any risk. That probably isn't going to happen either. Wise investors work within the constraints of what is possible and then make decisions based on that information. Whether constructing a house or an investment portfolio, risk must be balanced with returns and costs with benefits.

Today's Financial Renaissance

Many people don't realize that we are quite literally living in an investment renaissance – an exciting era of unprecedented innovation in the investment world. No area of the financial world is left untouched. Everything, from mutual funds to derivatives to insurance products, is improving and changing. New investments and investment strategies become available every day. The rate of change in the financial world shows no sign of slowing.

In addition to this financial renaissance, we are at the same time living through an unprecedented communications revolution. The Internet now gives individual investors direct access to the financial world. Information and tools, once the exclusive domain of the Wall Street elite, are now freely available to anyone. Instant communication allows us to invest and bank from anywhere in the world. Over the next decade, technology will continue to change the way we handle our finances.

While the investing revolution is adding many new benefits, it comes at a price. Today's investors face a daunting selection of invest-ment alternatives. With literally hundreds of thousands of investment choices, how do you even begin to create an investment portfolio? You start with the basics.

Back to the Basics

As Americans, we live in the most fantastic country in the world. From its founding, the United States has always sought to protect and nurture wealth-creating institutions. This emphasis on wealth creation has led to our extraordinary economic and financial success.

In light of this fact, I find it amazing that in this most capitalistic of countries, many people are oblivious to how the capital markets work and how wealth is created.

If money and finance seem mysterious to you, don't worry. The fundamentals of capitalism are not that hard to understand. Capitalism depends on two institutions: the capital markets and businesses. The capital markets connect those with money (investors) to those who create wealth (businesses). Ultimately, the financial success of every American depends on these two institutions. They provide our jobs, the goods we buy, and the returns we make on our investments. As prudent investors, we need a basic understanding of how the capital markets and businesses work. To illustrate these fundamental concepts, let's look at a very simple business – Jason's Lawn Care.

Last summer, young Jason needed spending money. After careful thought, he decided to mow lawns around the neighborhood. On a warm Saturday afternoon, he knocked on doors in his neighborhood and found several enthusiastic customers. Just as he was about to leave the garage with the family lawn mower, his dad stopped him. "Where do you think you're going with the lawn mower?" his dad asked.

"I'm going into business," Jason replied. "Last year, Craig mowed lawns for the people in his neighborhood, and he made a ton of money!"

Realizing that this was a good opportunity for Jason to learn the basics of how a business works, his dad consented to the idea with one condition – the family's lawn mower and tools would not be donated to Jason's new business. He would need to buy his own tools and equipment. Right away, Jason had to face the number one challenge that all businesses face – raising money or *capital*. Jason would have to locate funding to start the operation of his new business.

Together, Jason and his dad made a list of supplies and equipment needed for the business. By purchasing a used mower, old gas cans, and a second-hand weed trimmer, they estimated that the business needed $500 cash to start operations. Unfortunately, Jason didn't have $500. Like all new cash-strapped businesses, Jason needed to raise the money. But how?

Jason's dad suggested that he speak to his Uncle Mitch. When approached by his nephew, Uncle Mitch committed to loan Jason half the amount ($250). In return, Uncle Mitch expected to be paid back in monthly payments, with interest. In other words, Uncle Mitch became a lender in the business. His agreement was to be paid principal and interest every month until the note was repaid.

Later that day, Jason was still pondering how he would raise the other $250 when his Aunt Lil stopped by the house. After hearing Jason's story, she made him an offer. She would give Jason $250 for a 25 percent interest in his business. For every dollar that Jason cleared after gas and interest expense (to Uncle Mitch), he would return 25 cents to Aunt Lil. Jason agreed. Unlike Uncle Mitch, Aunt Lil held an ownership interest in the business.

Notice that both Uncle Mitch and Aunt Lil each had an interest in Jason's new business. Uncle Mitch held a *loanership* interest, while Aunt Lil held an *ownership* interest. In general, Uncle Mitch's interest was more secure than Aunt Lil's. It didn't matter if the business makes a profit or not; Uncle Mitch would expect to be paid. On the other hand, Aunt Lil's return was based on the success of the business. If Jason became lazy, the business would suffer and Aunt Lil might lose her entire investment. On the other hand, if Jason got inspired and mowed from dawn to dusk, Aunt Lil could make a much higher return on her investment. While Aunt Lil's ownership interest in the business was much riskier, it had a much higher potential return than Uncle Mitch's loanership interest.

Ownership vs. Loanership

Even though there are countless investments available today, the investment world can be broken down into two broad categories: *ownership* and *loanership*. We can either loan money to different entities and earn an interest rate or we can own business entities and participate in their success. Just like Jason's lawn-mowing business, loanership investments tend to be more secure, while ownership investments tend to provide higher returns. Let's briefly discuss the different types of loanership and ownership investments.

Loanership

The following investments are loanership-type investments:
- Certificates of deposit
- Interest rate annuities
- Bonds
- Bond mutual funds

Certificates of Deposit

Most people understand *certificates of deposit (CDs)*. They work very simply. When you buy a certificate of deposit, you're loaning money to a bank. A specified interest rate is paid over a specific period of time. If you meet the qualifications, the Federal Depositor Insurance Corporation (FDIC) guarantees your principal investment. Unfortunately, this guarantee comes with a price; historically, CDs have not paid attractive rates of return.

If you choose to park money in a CD, don't select it by rate alone. If the rate seems too high, there's a reason. The bank is probably in trouble. Even though your principal is guaranteed, your interest is not. Many investors have answered ads in the newspaper offering super-high CD rates only to be disappointed. Some have faced the trauma of the bank folding. Several weeks later, they receive their money back from the FDIC – without interest. If an interest rate sounds too good to be true, it probably is. When investing in CDs, don't just look at the rates; make sure that the bank is solid as well.

While historically poor investments, CDs make an excellent place to temporarily store money. For example, Diane has put aside $10,000 that she will use to purchase a new car next year. Since it will be only 12 months until she makes the purchase, she needs an investment that will protect her principal. A CD is an ideal parking place.

On the other hand, CDs generally are not good long-term investments. Looking at the historical, after-tax return of CDs, we find that they barely keep pace with inflation. Over time, retirees who put all their money in CDs find themselves squeezed by rising prices. Over the short term, this is not a problem. But since retirees need income for decades after they retire, rising prices will eventually destroy their standard of living. Instead, retirees should look to a well-diversified portfolio of investments. The higher dividends and long-term growth potential of a well-diversified portfolio can provide rising income and growth of principal. Certificates of deposit are best used for short-term needs, not long-term goals.

Interest Rate Annuities

Interest rate annuities are another type of loanership investment. These investments go by a variety of names, such as *fixed annuities, single premium deferred annuities,* or *deferred annuities.* When you invest in an interest rate annuity, you are loaning money to an insurance company. Like certificates of deposit, interest rate annuities pay a specified interest rate for a specific period of time. Instead of these types of investments carrying federal insurance, many states provide investors with a guarantee.

For the conservative part of a portfolio, interest rate annuities are often a good alternative to CDs. Like CDs, this type of annuity provides guaranteed principal. And historically, interest rate annuities usually pay higher interest rates than CDs with the added benefit of tax deferral.

(To learn more about interest rate annuities and how to choose them, go to Chapter 5.)

Fixed Indexed Annuities (a.k.a. Equity Indexed Annuities)

Fixed indexed annuities (which used to be called *equity indexed annuities*) represent one of the hottest selling vehicles today. However, I advise investors to approach these with extreme caution. If you would like to learn more about why I refuse to offer these to my clients, go to Chapter 5 and look under the heading *Annuity Type 2: Fixed Indexed Annuities.*

Bonds and Bond Mutual Funds

Of all the loanership investments, *bonds* and *bond mutual funds* probably confuse people the most; however, they're not really that complicated. In essence, a bond is a loan that can be bought or sold. Like CDs and interest rate annuities, the borrower's (i.e., bond issuer's) credit quality can vary. Unlike CDs and interest rate annuities, the market price of bonds can fluctuate. To learn more about bonds and bond mutual funds, go to Chapter 6.

As you saw earlier with Jason's lawn-mowing business, Uncle Mitch's loanership investment offered a smaller return for a smaller amount of risk. The same rule applies to the loanership investments listed above. While they offer a degree of safety from loss of capital, their smaller returns offer little hedge against inflation. For that kind of protection, you must look at ownership.

Ownership

Ownership investments are just as easy to understand as loanership investments. These securities include stocks, real estate, and private businesses. Unlike loanership investments, they pay no interest. Instead, as an owner, you participate in the fortunes of the companies.

Investing in individual stocks is an extremely involved and diverse area of investment. Hundreds of books have been written on the subject. If you want more information on how to invest in individual stocks, visit your local bookstore or library or Google "stock investing." You will find everything from sound stock investing advice to get-rich-quick schemes.

For most investors, I recommend against investing serious money in individual stocks and, instead, use a portfolio of mutual funds. Because mutual funds generally are diversified, they can quickly and easily add a tremendous amount of safety to an investor's stock portfolio. In Chapter 7, we will look at several types of mutual funds. (Later, in Chapters 8, 9, 10, and 11, we will bring the investments together and look at a variety of investment strategies.)

Conclusion

As we've learned, history shows that investors who rely solely on bank interest rates will most likely lose their savings to the corrosive effects of inflation. Rising prices continually squeeze fixed incomes until they reach the breaking point. Beating this inflationary monster requires earning higher rates of return. You will need to be a prudent investor. You need to create a sound portfolio of investments.

Fortunately, we are living in an exciting era of financial opportunity and innovation. New investments and investment strategies are being developed daily. Unfortunately, progress comes with a price. In today's world of high technology and financial development, we face a daunting selection of investment choices. Investors often feel overwhelmed.

However, if you start with the basics, you can make sense of the investing world. Investments can be broken down into two categories – *loanership* and *ownership*. Loanership investments pay investors an interest rate. These investments include CDs, fixed annuities, and bonds.

Ownership investments allow investors to participate in the profits of businesses. Stocks are the most popular type of ownership. Instead of owning individual stocks and bonds, many investors use mutual funds to achieve instant diversity. ◆

Chapter 5

Interest Rate Annuities

Annuities

I n the financial world, the word "annuity" is probably one of the most misunderstood investment terms. Myth and confusion surround the word like a thick cloud. However, once people realize the tremendous benefits certain types of annuities can provide, they often exclaim, "that just seems too good to be true!"

While there are many types of annuities, I believe that the most overlooked annuity is the guaranteed, fixed-interest annuity, often referred to as a *CD-type annuity*. These annuities not only provide safety of principal, they also can provide a guaranteed interest rate that is very attractive. For people who want to keep their money safe and earn an excellent rate of interest, CD-type annuities can be a wonderful way to invest.

In addition to simply earning a good interest rate, annuities make several powerful strategies possible. For example, people who have non-IRA investments and who would like to lower their taxes can use a powerful income strategy known as the *combo strategy* to provide a good monthly income while at the same time slashing their current income tax bills. In fact, by using a typical combo strategy, most investors can reduce the current income tax on their interest income up to 80 percent.

In the next few pages, I will dispel the myths surrounding annuities and show you how they can help you increase your interest income, reduce your current income taxes, and enhance your financial security. I want to help you learn how to safely earn more interest income using annuities. The path I will take is to briefly describe the types of annuities that are available and then focus only on those that provide excellent interest rate income and safety of principal. The first step toward that goal is for you to understand that the word "annuity" applies to a variety of investments and not one particular investment. After that first small step, you are ready to discover how annuities can help you secure your financial future.

What are Annuities?

Many people are surprised to learn that the word "annuity" does not describe a particular investment but rather a whole host of investments that are very different from one another. One type of annuity has returns based on how well the stock market performs. Another type of annuity looks like a pension (providing monthly payments for the remainder of a person's life). A final type of annuity looks like a time deposit, which gives an investor safety of principal and a specified interest rate.

Since these various types of investments all have the word "annuity" attached to them, many people confuse one with the other. When they hear something negative about one, they apply it to all types of annuities. For example, people often tell me that someone advised them against CD-type annuities because they have high costs. In fact, CD-type annuities do not have any additional costs associated with them at all. Unlike bonds, stocks, mutual funds, and some other types of annuities, CD-type annuities have no internal fees or add-on commissions that would lower an investor's return. With CD-type annuities, the interest rate an investor locks in is the interest rate he will receive. Unfortunately, because several types of investments share the word "annuity" in their names, people confuse them with one another.

Types of Annuities – The Four Categories

There are four broad categories of annuities:

- Variable annuities
- Fixed indexed annuities
- Immediate annuities
- Interest rate annuities

Annuity Type 1: Variable Annuities

The term *variable annuity* is misleading. I believe that a more descriptive term for variable annuity would be "mutual fund annuity," since variable annuities closely resemble mutual funds. The Securities Exchange Commission's brochure *Variable Annuities: What You Should Know* (http://www.sec.gov/investor/pubs/varannty.htm) states, "The investment options for a variable annuity are typically mutual funds that invest in stocks, bonds, money market instruments, or some combination of the three." Since variable annuities have mutual fund investment choices, they allow investors to enjoy many of the advantages of mutual funds with the benefits of annuities.

Since variable annuities are more like mutual funds, I won't discuss them in this chapter. To learn more about variable annuities, go to Chapter 7.

Annuity Type 2: Fixed Indexed Annuities

After the stock market and interest rates declined sharply in 2001-2002, *fixed indexed annuities* (FIAs) skyrocketed in popularity. In fact, these annuities represent one of the hottest selling vehicles today.

(Side note: There has been a relatively recent change in terminology. Until a few years ago, "*fixed* indexed annuities" were known as "*equity* indexed annuities." For a variety of reasons, including a lot of bad press, the industry changed the generic name from "equity" to "fixed." If you encounter the term, "equity indexed annuities," just know that it is the same thing.)

I am not a fan of FIAs and advise investors to approach these contracts with extreme caution. I believe that Rebekah Barsch, vice president of investment products at Northwestern Mutual, said it best. In the December 14, 2005, Wall Street Journal article, *Why Big Insurers Are Staying Away From This Year's Hot Investment Product*, she said, "[fixed indexed annuities] are so complicated that I think it is a stretch to believe that the agents, much less the clients, understand what they've got. The commissions are extreme. The surrender periods are too long. The complexity is way too high."

Not everyone dislikes fixed indexed annuities. Many insurance companies and insurance agents dearly love these contracts.

Why Insurance Companies and Agents Love The Fixed Index Annuity (but You Probably Shouldn't)

The promise of the sales pitch is tempting: "Participate in stock market returns without downside risk." Phrases such as "no risk," "can't lose," and "safe" echo from the walls of restaurants and hotel meeting rooms enticing investors to get out their checkbooks. In fact, the story is so compelling that hoards of investors already have taken the plunge and purchased FIAs. However, before you follow the scrambling mob over the edge, you need all the facts. In particular, you need the informational tidbits frequently left unsaid by the salespeople. You need to know why insurance companies and insurance agents love fixed index annuities. Once you understand that, you can make an informed choice about whether one is right for you.

Let's start with the easy part. Why do insurance agents love fixed indexed annuities? Very simply: FIAs pay huge commissions. I commonly see policies offering to pay agents 10 percent or more. In the financial world, this is an enormous commission. A financial advisor would generally have to work years managing his clients' fee-only accounts to earn that much. I know of several insurance agents who were able to retire after selling FIAs for just a couple of years.

With such a huge commission potential, it's no wonder that we see agents spending large sums on advertising. Local newspapers commonly sport full-page newspaper ads portraying insurance agents as "senior specialists" and "financial planners for retirees." Television and radio ads talk about the wonders of investing in the market with "no risk." Fancy invitations mailed by the thousands invite retirees in for a free meal and presentation. When you encounter these ads, just know that these are insurance agents selling fixed indexed annuities.

To an insurance company, fixed indexed annuities represent a huge money-making opportunity with limited risk of loss. And if the market conditions turn against the company, it can reduce its losses by changing the terms of your contract. You heard me correctly: The insurance company can arbitrarily change the terms of your contract. In the insurance world, this is called a *moving part*. This means that you may end up earning far less money than you anticipated.

What is a moving part? Want to see an insurance agent die on stage? During the question and answer time at any FIA seminar, ask the agent to explain what is meant by the term "moving parts." Then ask if he has any fixed indexed annuities without moving parts. His face will ashen, then "Plop!" he will fall over dead. Agents selling fixed indexed annuities don't want to talk about moving parts. If forced, most agents will admit to knowing about them but will try to minimize their importance to you. In my opinion, the single most important fact about fixed index annuities is that they all contain moving parts.

A moving part is a provision of the contact that can be changed by the insurance company arbitrarily. This change affects how your return is calculated and therefore changes the returns on your FIA. Depending on the annuity, a company may change factors such as participation rates, cap rates, or spread/asset/margin fees. For example, you may start your contract with a maximum rate of 10 percent but then find yourself several years down the road getting a tiny fraction of that (e.g., 1 percent).

By including moving parts in the contract, the insurance company eliminates a significant amount of its risk. Being able to change your contract arbitrarily allows the insurance company to earn a profit no matter what happens to interest rates or the stock market. If the cost of providing your participation rate goes up, the insurance company simply lowers your returns. Since fixed indexed annuities are generally long contracts (ten years or more), you must "trust" the insurance company not to use the moving parts to change the way your returns are calculated.

A potential abuse of moving parts is the ability to increase corporate profits at the client's expense. The concept is simple. If an insurance company wants to increase profits, it would simply use the moving parts to lower the amount it paid you. Less money for you, more money for the insurance company. I'm not suggesting that any company has done this or would ever do this. I'm just pointing out that contracts that can be changed arbitrarily have the potential to be abused.

My experiences with trust me contracts have not been pleasant ones. After my research showed that fixed indexed annuities represented a trust me proposition (the client is locked in for 10 years and the insurance company can change the contract at will), I refused to offer them.

Here is an article by the regulatory agency FINRA cautioning investors about fixed indexed annuities:

http://www.finra.org/investors/protectyourself/investoralerts/
annuitiesandinsurance/p010614

Annuity Type 3: Immediate Annuities

An *immediate annuity* simply provides an investor with a string of payments (usually monthly) for a specified period of time. The payments could be made for a specific known period of time, such as five years, or for an undetermined period, such as a person's remaining life. When an immediate annuity is for a known period of time, it is a *period certain annuity*. When an immediate annuity is based on a person's lifetime, it is known as a *life annuity*. A cross between the two – someone's lifetime with a guaranteed minimum time – is known as a *life annuity with a period certain*.

Period Certain Immediate Annuities

Immediate annuities that have a specified period are known as *period certain immediate annuities*. This type of annuity pays a fixed monthly payment for a specific period of time. After all payments have been made, the payments cease. If you die before all the payments are made, they would continue to your heirs. Conceptually, a period certain immediate annuity is like a loan you've made to someone who is paying you your principal and interest each month until your principal is completely repaid.

For example, a 5-year period certain immediate annuity would pay you a monthly income for exactly 60 months. Once the payments start, you cannot stop or change them. If you died before all 60 payments were received, any remaining payments would be sent to your heirs each month. After 60 months, your payments would cease.

Life Immediate Annuities

Life immediate annuities, also called *life annuities*, are immediate annuities that will pay you lifetime payments. They can be based on one life (called a *single-life immediate annuity*) or on two lives (called a *joint-life immediate annuity*). They can even contain a guaranteed minimum number of payments in the event of an untimely death.

Single-Life Immediate Annuity

A *single-life immediate annuity* or *single-life annuity* simply pays you a fixed payment until you die. After that, the payments stop. Your heirs receive nothing more. It is easy to see that if you live a long time, you win. If you live a short time, the insurance company wins. While these annuities contain risk for the heirs (i.e., when the annuitant dies, nothing is paid to the heirs), single life annuities are a popular choice for people who want to be absolutely sure they don't outlive their income.

Joint-Life Immediate Annuities

A *joint-life immediate annuity* or *joint-life annuity* is based on two lives. The payments continue until both people (i.e., joint annuitants) are deceased. Since the income continues as long as either person is alive, this type of annuity often is used by married couples who are concerned about providing income to a surviving spouse.

With a joint-life annuity, you can even specify the percentage that the survivor will receive after the first spouse dies. For example, a husband and wife may invest in a joint-life annuity that provides $1000 per month in income with a 50 percent benefit to the surviving spouse. After one spouse dies, the surviving spouse would receive $500 per month (50 percent of $1000) for the remainder of his or her life.

Life Immediate Annuities with a Period Certain

When you invest in a life annuity, you can add a period certain feature, as well. For example, if you invested in a life annuity with a 10-year period certain, you would receive payments for the rest of your life – no matter how long you lived. However, if you died two years after you started the annuity, your heirs would receive payments for 8 more years (for a total payment period of 10 years). By adding a period certain to a life annuity, you can reduce the risk to your heirs while guaranteeing a lifetime income for yourself.

Annuity Type 4: Interest Rate Annuities

I've saved one of the best types of annuities until last – the *interest rate annuity*. This type of annuity provides safety of principal and a specified interest rate. I believe that interest rate annuities represent one of the best opportunities for people who want to earn interest while keeping their money safe.

In most interest rate annuities, you simply put your money in and earn interest. At the end of the term, you have access to your principal and interest without penalties. If you wish, most interest rate annuities will allow you to take your interest out each month as income. Some annuities have other flexible features as well. Many will allow you to take a portion of your principal each year without penalties or will waive early surrender charges in certain circumstances such as a nursing home stay.

Interest rate annuities come in two general types. One has a rate that can change. The other locks in your interest rate for the entire term. Let's take a closer look at each type.

Floating Rate Fixed Annuities

Annuities that have rates that float or change during their terms are known as *floating rate fixed annuities* (or *floating rate annuities*). They usually quote a *first year rate*, a *base rate*, and a *minimum guaranteed rate*. To understand what each of these terms mean, let's look at an example.

Suppose an annuity had a first year rate of 7 percent, a base rate of 5 percent, and a minimum rate of 3 percent. As the name implies, you would receive 7 percent interest during the first year, but in year two you would earn a different rate. If the interest rates in the market had not changed during that first year, you would receive 5 percent the second year (the base rate). However, if interest rates in the market rose (i.e., the base rate rose), you would receive more than 5 percent the second year. If interest rates declined (i.e., the base rate fell), you would receive less. No matter how far interest rates fell, the least amount of interest you would receive in any year would be 3 percent (the minimum guaranteed rate).

Many people invest in floating rate annuities when they think that interest rates will be higher in the future. Unfortunately, most floating rate annuities rely on the annuity companies' discretion to determine what rate they will pay each year. Since an annuity company earns more money by paying you less, you can see the company has a very real incentive to pay you as little interest as possible. My experience is that many people often end up disappointed with floating rate fixed annuities. While they often start out with an attractive rate, they frequently end up getting paid an interest rate that is not competitive.

A Better Way – CD-Type Annuities

My favorite type of interest rate annuity is one that guarantees the interest rate for the entire term. Because the rate is guaranteed, these annuities are often referred to as *CD-type fixed annuities* or *CD-type annuities*. CD-type annuities are very easy to understand. You invest your money, and you earn a guaranteed interest rate. At the end of the term, you have access to your principal (and accrued interest) without any penalties.

I believe that CD-type annuities represent one of the best interest rate investments available. They pay an attractive interest rate and offer other attractive benefits as well. To understand CD-type annuities better, let's look at some of the common uses, benefits, and provisions of this investment type.

Who Uses CD-Type Annuities?
Great for Retiree Income

Since CD-type fixed annuities provide safety of principal, a competitive interest rate, and other valuable benefits, they are a great choice for the safe portion (low risk) of a retiree's investment portfolio.

Great for IRAs and Long-Term Goals

Younger investors often use CD-type annuities to fund their long-term dreams and goals. Many investors don't want to invest in the stock market. For them, finding a good interest rate investment can be difficult. With safety of principal and excellent interest rates, younger investors might find CD-type annuities an excellent choice to meet their investing goals. (However, keep in mind that annuity gains distributed out of the annuity before age 59 ½ have a 10 percent tax penalty.)

Features of CD-Type Annuities
No Extra Fees

CD-type annuities have no additional fees or add-on commissions. The interest rate you lock in is the interest rate you will receive.

High Level of Safety

CD-type annuities are backed by insurance companies, and in many states the funds are guaranteed. For the highest levels of security, I recommend that investors always choose CD-type annuities that are rated highly.

Safety Feature 1: State Oversight and Insurance

Your state's insurance commission or board regulates and oversees the insurance companies doing business in your state. They require insurance companies to maintain reserves equal to the withdrawal value of your annuity. Furthermore, most states require additional levels of capital surplus to further increase investors' security.

In addition to oversight, each state protects its policyholders by providing a safety net often referred to as a *state guaranty association*. All 50 states plus the District of Columbia and Puerto Rico have insurance associations that would pay the claims of financially impaired companies. Your state specifies what types of insurance and annuities are covered and the dollar amount of that coverage.

For example, in Texas, fixed annuities are guaranteed by the Texas Insurance Guarantee Fund. For specifics on this guarantee, you can order the brochure titled *If My Insurance Company Fails* from the following address:

Texas Life, Accident, Health,
and Hospital Service Insurance Guaranty Association
301 Congress, Suite 500
Austin, TX 78701
800-982-6362
512-476-5101

You can also view the brochure directly at the following Web address:

http://www.tdi.texas.gov/pubs/consumer/cb006.html

Safety Feature 2: Choose a Company With High Ratings

In addition to state oversight, there are several rating companies that evaluate the financial quality of each annuity company. The most widely recognized rating service is A.M. Best. I recommend that investors interested in having the highest level of safety in their portfolios use only companies rated in the top four ratings by A.M. Best: A++, A+, A, A-.

It is important to note that, like CDs, you should not choose an annuity by rate alone. Again, if the interest rate seems too high, there's a reason. To avoid problems, make sure the insurance company is sound. The most popular ratings services are A.M. Best, Standard & Poor's (S&P), Moody's, and Fitch.

You can review A.M. Best ratings of any insurance company free of charge by logging onto the following Web address:

http://www.ambest.com

To view the ratings, you will need to subscribe to the A.M. Best online service. The subscription is free.

I use a handy service called *The Insurance Forum*. Each September this organization compiles a *Special Ratings Issue* with four ratings for each insurance company. If you would like a comprehensive look at insurance company ratings, you can order this inexpensive newsletter (the 2012 *Special Ratings Issue* was $25) at the following address:

The Insurance Forum

PO Box 245

Ellettsville, IN 47429-0245

812-876-6502

http://www.theinsuranceforum.com/pages/ratings.html

Guaranteed Interest

CD-type annuities are a wonderful source of guaranteed interest. From the day you invest, you know exactly what your interest rate will be. Most CD-type annuities will allow you to withdraw your interest as monthly income. On the other hand, if you would rather reinvest, CD-type annuities provide compounded, tax-deferred interest.

Interest Can Be Withdrawn As Income

Most CD-type annuities allow investors to distribute the interest on a monthly basis, though a few do not. If taking out the annuities' accrued interest is important to you, make sure your CD-type annuity allows penalty-free distribution of the earned interest.

Interest Can Be Reinvested

Virtually all CD-type annuities allow investors to reinvest their accrued interest. As with all types of annuities, your interest accrues with tax advantages. You owe no income tax on your interest until you actually take it out of the annuity. This ability to defer taxes indefinitely allows investors to control and often eliminate their income taxes on that annuity.

Reinvested Interest is Compounded

When you reinvest your interest in a CD-type annuity, it is compounded. (You earn interest on your interest.) Since various CD-type annuities have different compounding periods (e.g., some compound monthly, some quarterly.) many investors use a number called the *annualized return* to make an "apples-to-apples" rate comparison between the annuities.

The annualized return indicates the amount of interest that will accrue from the beginning of the year until the end. For example, a $100,000 account that is reinvesting interest will be worth $105,000 at the end of the first year on a CD-type annuity that has a 5 percent annualized return. At the end of the next year, the account would be worth $110,250 ($105,000 + 5 percent). And so on.

Other Benefits

Many CD-type annuities have other useful features, as well. Two popular features are *annual free withdrawal waiver* and *nursing home waiver*. These features provide flexibility through penalty-free access to funds.

Free Withdrawal Waiver

Some CD-type fixed annuities allow a portion of the principal to be withdrawn each year without penalties. This amount is often referred to as the *free withdrawal amount*. This feature allows investors a way of accessing cash in case a need or emergency arises. With this type of annuity, the free withdrawal amount is often 10 percent per year. For example, if your annuity is worth $10,000 at the beginning of its term, you would be able to distribute $1000 during the year without a penalty. If this feature is important to you, make sure your annuity offers it.

Nursing Home Waiver

A few CD-type annuities will waive surrender charges if you need to stay in a nursing home. This feature is commonly called a *nursing home waiver.* The terms on this feature vary widely from annuity to annuity and state to state. If this feature is important to you, make sure you understand the terms your policy offers in your state. A nursing home waiver can be very helpful if you need access to your funds in the event a nursing home stay becomes necessary.

Early Withdrawal

As with most time-related interest rate investments, CD-type annuities have surrender adjustments if they are liquidated early. The first type of adjustment is the *surrender penalty.* It is simply an early withdrawal charge. The second type of early withdrawal adjustment is known as the *market value adjustment* or *MVA.* Unlike the surrender penalty, the MVA may be in your favor or not in your favor. To understand early withdrawal adjustments, let's take a look at each.

Surrender Penalties

Surrender penalties are easy to understand. Like many time investments, an early liquidation of your CD-type annuity may incur a penalty. The surrender schedule is usually printed plainly in the sales literature and in your annuity policy. Often, the surrender penalty declines with each passing year. For example, an annuity may have a 5 percent penalty the first year, a 4 percent penalty the second year, and so on.

Market Value Adjustment (MVA)

The *market value adjustment* or *MVA* is probably one of the more confusing elements of fixed annuities. An MVA is nothing more than an adjustment (positive or negative) that is applied when an account is liquidated early. It is designed to help the insurance company coordinate the value of the underlying investments it makes when it funds your annuity (i.e., bonds, loans.) with the early liquidation proceeds of the annuity.

The way an MVA works is simple. If you make an early liquidation of an annuity that has an MVA, you may have some money added to your liquidation value or you may have some money taken away. Whether money is added or subtracted depends on whether the interest rates in the market are higher or lower than when you first invested in the annuity. If interest rates in the market are higher, the adjustment is negative (money is taken away). Similarly, if interest rates in the market are lower, the adjustment is positive (money is added).

For example, suppose you purchased an annuity with a market interest rate of 6 percent. Over the next year, the market interest rates dropped to 4 percent. If you liquidated your annuity (before your MVA period expires), your MVA would be positive. That is, money would be added to your early liquidation proceeds since interest rates were lower than when you placed the investment. (Of course, any surrender penalties would still apply.)

For most CD-type annuities, the interest rate guarantee period and the MVA period expire at the same time. However, a few annuities will have an MVA period that is longer than the interest rate guarantee period. I highly recommend that you avoid these types of annuities. Choose only annuities in which the MVA period expires when the interest rate guarantee expires.

Since the MVA feature allows insurance companies to pay more interest, they have been a boon to investors who want higher interest rates. However, you need to understand what an MVA is and how it can affect your investment should you liquidate your annuity early.

State-by-State Approval

Every state has an insurance board that is responsible for deciding which annuities are available to its residents. Some annuity boards (e.g., New York, Washington) approve very few annuities. Others allow their citizens much more choice.

Furthermore, each state's insurance board places different requirements on the annuities that are available. As a result, some annuities may not be available, may have special terms, or may have a special interest rate guarantee that only applies to your state. When shopping for a CD-type annuity, be sure to find out the availability and the variations that may apply to you.

Tips for Shopping

As we discussed, choosing the right CD-type annuity is relatively simple. I recommend that you:

- Choose CD-type annuities – those that have a surrender period and a MVA period that are not longer than the interest rate guarantee period.
- Choose a high-quality annuity – one that possesses one of the top four ratings by A.M. Best.
- Check to see if the annuity is available in your state and what variations may apply.
- Decide which benefits are important to you – these might include a nursing home waiver and/or annual free withdrawal.
- Select the annuity that has the highest interest rate with the benefits you want – generally, the fewer extra benefits an annuity has, the higher the interest rate.

An excellent way to easily find and order top-rated CD-type annuities that meet these criteria is to go to my website:

http://annuity.MichaelDallas.com

The reason I created this site was to make it easy for people to find CD-type annuities. Since these vehicles carry low commissions, many insurance salespeople will not present them. This fact makes it hard for the general public to find and shop for CD-type annuities. By posting them in an online list, I help people find and shop these wonderful interest rate opportunities.

All the annuities on my website meet the criteria I discussed above. Finding the annuities that are available in your state is easy. If you select your state in the box at the top of the list, the list will display only those annuities that are available in your state. To learn which benefits are provided with each annuity, you can simply click the "more info" button. A screen describing each annuity will appear. For most annuities, the company brochure is also available for viewing.

Once you've selected a CD-type annuity, you can either call my toll-free number or use the *Secure Order Form* to order the paperwork. Once we receive your order, the paperwork for your new annuity will be sent to your home by overnight Federal Express. After it arrives, simply authorize the paperwork and forward it directly to the insurance company in the enclosed, prepaid Federal Express shipping envelope. It is quick and easy. Best of all, you are in control.

There are no additional fees, loads, or charges to you for this service. The annuity company pays for processing your order.

My annuity website allows people to find and order great CD-type annuities without the interference of a high-pressure salesman. People can examine various CD-type annuities in peace. Best of all, if they have questions, they can call my toll-free number for friendly, professional help.

Annuity Strategies

CD-type annuities can be used in a variety of strategies. Some strategies are designed to reduce or eliminate taxes. Others are designed to provide the highest possible monthly income. While another is designed to do both – lower taxes and provide monthly income. Let's look at a few ways CD-type annuities are used.

Objective 1: Take Monthly Interest Income

The most common use of CD-type annuities is to provide strong, monthly interest income. For this goal, you simply find an annuity that guarantees the highest available rate and pays out monthly income. Each month, your interest will arrive by mail or will be deposited directly into your bank account. At the end of the term, your entire principal is available to you without penalties.

Objective 2: Reduce Your Tax Bill

There are two strategies that are commonly used to reduce income taxes on interest income. The first is simple – straight reinvestment. Taxes are deferred as the CD-type annuity grows. The second strategy, the *combo strategy*, allows an investor to protect his principal, take a monthly income, and slash his taxes. Let's look at each strategy.

Tax Reduction Strategy A: Straight Reinvestment

If you don't need the interest income for living expenses, the simplest strategy is to simply reinvest your interest. As long as you leave your interest in the CD-type annuity, you owe no taxes. In fact, you won't even receive a 1099 tax form at the end of the year.

Tax deferral is a powerful strategy for enhancing your financial security. Think of tax deferral this way – the money you would have sent to the government in taxes stays in your account instead and earns interest for you.

For people who pay tax on their Social Security retirement benefits, the tax savings can be even greater. Since deferred annuity interest is not used in the IRS's calculation (to determine how much of their Social Security benefits are taxable), many people can lower or even eliminate the income tax on their Social Security benefits by moving a portion of their interest income portfolio to CD-type annuities and reinvesting the interest.

Tax Reduction Strategy B: Combo Annuity – Take Income and Reduce Your Taxes

Not everyone has the luxury of being able to reinvest. Many people need income from their investments to meet their living expenses.

Nevertheless, they would still like to lower their income taxes. For these people, a little known strategy can work financial miracles. The strategy is often referred to as a *combo strategy* or *split annuity strategy*. Once you understand the strategy, you will wonder why no one ever told you about it before.

As the names imply, this strategy uses two annuities – one CD-type annuity and one period certain immediate annuity. In the combo strategy, your principal is preserved by the CD-type annuity and your income is created by the immediate annuity. In most cases, you can create an income stream that is 75 to 80 percent tax-free.

To know whether a combo strategy will work for you, answer the following questions:

- Do you pay income taxes?
- Are you taking interest income from non-qualified (e.g., non-IRA) investments?

If your answer to each question is 'yes,' a combo strategy may help you put more money in your pocket. To view a current example of a combo annuity strategy, go to:

http://annuity.MichaelDallas.com/combo.asp

After you enter in your state, age, and investment amount, the page will calculate and display the highest paying annuities that we offer, your monthly income, and your tax savings. If you have questions about the combo strategy, don't hesitate to call me.

The combo strategy can be a great way to create sound income, preserve your principal, and lower your taxes.

IRA and Rollover Protection

Many people use CD-type annuities to provide safety of principal and sound interest rates for their IRA and employer rollovers. Because many people want a portion of their retirement savings to be protected against the ups and downs of the stock market and to earn an excellent rate of interest, CD-type annuities are a popular choice in retirement accounts.

Medicaid Protection Strategy

Many people use annuities in strategies that protect their assets in the event of a nursing home stay. These strategies are commonly called *Medicaid annuity strategies*.

To understand Medicaid annuity strategies, you need to have a brief understanding of Medicaid. Very simply, Medicaid provides medical benefits (in this case, nursing home benefits) to those who have very few assets. For people who are not wealthy but have some savings, a nursing home stay often depletes their life savings before Medicaid will help. To protect their limited assets, many people turn to Medicaid protection strategies. One popular strategy is to buy a so-called *Medicaid annuity*.

It is important to realize that there really is no such thing as a Medicaid annuity. There are simply annuities that, in some states, may preserve some of your assets for your heirs. Even though Medicaid is primarily funded by the federal government, each state modifies the program to suit its needs with different rules for receiving Medicaid benefits. Therefore, the information here is extremely general and should not be used in designing a specific strategy. If you want to pursue any kind of Medicaid strategy, I highly recommend you get a competent elder-law attorney to advise you.

In the simplest terms, Medicaid provides nursing home benefits to those without available assets. To determine whether you have assets available for nursing home care, Medicaid looks at your sources of income and your investments. However, Medicaid treats different types of assets in different ways. Some are *includable* and some are *excludable* in the qualifying calculation.

Those who use a Medicaid annuity strategy attempt to convert includable investment assets into excludable assets. If properly designed, some immediate annuities are excludable. There are a couple of strategies to use depending on marital status and other factors.

For example, people often purchase a special type of immediate annuity that not only pays the annuitant lifetime payments but also has a lump sum death benefit for the heirs (of the unused principal, if any exists). Since the principal of the annuity is not available to the annuity holder once they are in a nursing home, it is counted as excludable (in some states) and the payments usually go to the nursing home facility (or Medicaid) to pay for the nursing home care. At the annuitant's death, the balance of the annuity is paid to the heirs as a lump sum. The hope is that none of this money will go to Medicaid.

Another strategy has one spouse (the one trying to qualify for Medicaid benefits) invest his or her portion of their estate into a period certain annuity (e.g., 5-year payout). As strange as it sounds, in some states these annuity payments are excludable.

The idea of all these strategies is that since the asset value and payments are excluded from Medicaid's calculation, Medicaid benefits will be received while preserving some of the estate for the heirs and surviving spouse.

Pension Alternative Strategy

At retirement, many people are offered pension choices from their employers. These choices often include the following:

- Monthly payment for their life – A pensioner receives monthly payments for his entire life. At his death, the pension payments stop. The heirs receive nothing.
- Monthly payments for his life and his spouse's life – As long as either is alive, payments will continue to the pensioner and/or the spouse. The percentage a surviving spouse receives can often be chosen, as well. For example, if a pensioner chose a spousal benefit of 75 percent, his surviving spouse would receive 75 percent of

the pension after the pensioner's death. Once the spouse dies, the payments would stop.

- Lump sum payment – Often, a pension will allow a lump sum choice instead of life payments. Since the lump sum is usually large, it represents the amount of money the pension has set aside to pay for the pensioner's lifetime benefits. By taking the lump sum, the pensioner gains much more control over his financial future. To avoid immediate taxation, the lump sum is usually rolled into a self-directed IRA and invested.

Many people like the idea of lifetime income and often take one of the life annuity choices instead of the lump sum. However, if the retiree is clever, a lump sum payment often can create lifetime payments that are much higher than the choices offered by the pension.

A frequently used strategy to increase lifetime income is to take the lump sum and invest the money in a life annuity. A life annuity works just like the employer pension. Though if you shop around, a life annuity can often offer a higher monthly payment. If you are facing a pension choice and would like to see if you can increase your monthly amount, simply go to:

http://annuity.MichaelDallas.com/lifeannuity.html

After you enter your age, state, gender, and investment amount, the page will display your payment choices. If you want to compare other types of annuities such as joint life annuities, just call my toll-free number for a quick quote.

Conclusion

There is no question that the word annuity is frequently misunderstood and misinterpreted. However, once you understand the outstanding benefits some types of annuities can provide, you can use them like an expert to create sound lifetime income with safety of principal.

One of the most overlooked annuities is the guaranteed fixed-interest annuity known as the *CD-type annuity*. These annuities provide safety of principal and an attractive guaranteed interest rate. For those who want to keep their money safe while earning an excellent rate of interest, CD-type annuities can be a great choice.

Annuities can enable investors to use powerful tax saving strategies. In addition to straight tax-deferral, investors can use the *combo strategy*. This technique allows investors to create a good monthly income while drastically reducing their income tax bills. A typical combo strategy can reduce an investor's investment income tax bill by up to 80 percent.

With a little understanding, you can use annuities to increase your income, decrease your taxes, and enhance your financial security.

Other Annuity Terms

Below are some annuity terms that you may hear but were not specifically addressed in this book.

- *Fixed Annuity* - A common term used for interest rate annuities.
- *Tax-deferred annuity* or *deferred annuity* – While all annuities add the benefit of tax deferral to nonqualified accounts, people usually use these terms when referring to interest rate annuities. These annuities may have a guaranteed rate for the entire term (i.e., CD-type annuities) or an interest rate that changes (i.e., floating rate fixed annuities).
- *Single premium deferred annuity* (SPDA) – This term is used to describe interest annuities that usually allow only one contribution or a *single premium.*
- *Flexible premium deferred annuity or flex annuity* – These terms usually apply to interest rate annuities that allow more than one contribution over time. ◆

Chapter 6

Bonds and Bond Funds

Bonds

O f all the fixed investments, bonds probably confuse people the most; however, they're not really that complicated. In essence, a *bond* is a loan that can be bought or sold. Like CDs and fixed annuities, the borrower's (bond issuer's) credit quality can vary. Unlike CDs and fixed annuities, the market price of bonds can fluctuate. The two factors that most affect the market price of bonds are credit worthiness and market interest rates. Let's examine how each factor affects the market price of bonds.

Credit Rating

Like CDs and fixed annuities, you want to be aware of the borrower's credit worthiness. If someone were to tell you that she had "triple-A credit," you would know she has the ability and the habit of paying her debts on time. In that same way, a bond's credit rating reflects the borrower's ability to repay the bond's principal and interest. The higher the rating, the more likely the bond will be repaid. On the next page, I've listed part of the rating schedule for the two most popular bond-rating services – Moody's and Standard & Poor's.

Moody's	Standard & Poor's
Aaa	AAA
Aa	AA+
A	A
Baa	BBB
Ba	BB
B	B
Caa	CCC
Ca	CC
C	C

Moody's: Aaa/Standard & Poor's: AAA

Bonds that are rated Aaa are judged to be of the best quality. They carry the smallest degree of investment risk and are generally referred to as *gilt edged*. A large, exceptionally stable backer protects interest payments and assures the principal is secure. While the various protective elements of Aaa bonds are likely to change, changes that can be visualized are most unlikely to impair the fundamentally strong position.

Moody's: Aa/Standard & Poor's: AA+

Bonds that are rated Aa are judged to be of high quality by all standards. Together with the Aaa group, they comprise what are generally known as *high-grade bonds*. They are rated lower than the best bonds because margins of protection may not be as large as in Aaa securities, fluctuation of protective elements may be of greater amplitude, or there may be other elements present that make the long-term risk appear somewhat larger than the Aaa securities.

Moody's: A/Standard & Poor's: A

Bonds that are rated A possess many favorable investment attributes and are considered as upper-medium grade. Factors to assure security to principal and interest are considered adequate, but elements may be present that suggest a susceptibility to impairment some time in the future.

Moody's: Baa/Standard & Poor's: BBB

Bonds rated Baa are considered as medium-grade obligations (i.e., they are neither highly protected nor poorly secured). Interest payments and principal security appear adequate for the present, but certain protective elements may be lacking or may be characteristically unreliable over any great length of time. Such bonds lack outstanding investment characteristics and, in fact, have speculative characteristics, as well.

Moody's: Ba/Standard & Poor's: BB

Bonds rated Ba are judged to have speculative elements; their future cannot be considered as well assured. Often the protection of interest and principal payments may be very moderate and thereby not well safeguarded during both good and bad times over time. Uncertainty of position characterizes bonds in this class.

Moody's: B/Standard & Poor's: B

Bonds that are rated B generally lack characteristics of a desirable investment. Assurance of interest and principal payments or of maintenance of other terms of the contract may be small over any long period of time.

Moody's: Caa/Standard & Poor's: CCC

Bonds rated Caa are of poor standing. Such issues may be in default or there may be present elements of danger with respect to principal or interest.

Moody's: Ca/Standard & Poor's: CC

Bonds rated Ca represent obligations that are speculative in a high degree. Such issues are often in default or have other marked shortcomings.

Moody's: C/Standard & Poor's: C

Bonds rated C are the lowest rated class of bonds, and issues so rated can be regarded as having extremely poor prospects of ever attaining any real investment standing.

In general, AAA bonds are considered highly likely to pay all payments and principal on time. On the other end of the scale, it is very probable the C-rated bonds won't pay their principal or interest on time – if at all. In between is a sliding scale between these two extremes.

Since AAA bonds carry a high probability of repayment, why would anyone want to own anything else? The answer is, of course, the interest rates. Lower-rated bonds pay higher rates of return. In essence, investors are compensated with higher interest rates for taking higher risk. So which is better, high-rated bonds or low-rated bonds? The answer is, both. The best strategy for your bond portfolio is diversity. Having some higher-rated bonds adds security of principal, while owning some lower-rated bonds provides a higher income.

Interest Rates (Market Risk)

The most confusing aspect of bonds is the relationship between interest rates (in the market) and the price of bonds. Just remember, when interest rates in the marketplace go up, the market value of bonds goes down. When interest rates in the market go down, the market value of bonds goes up. It is a mathematical certainty.

How does this work? Let's look at a hypothetical example. Imagine that interest rates in the market are such that 30-year U.S. Treasury bonds pay 8 percent. I purchase a $1000 bond directly from the U.S. Treasury. For 30 years, Uncle Sam will pay me $80 per year ($1000 x 8 percent). At the end of that time, Uncle Sam will repay my $1000. Nothing about this arrangement will change. However, the price for which I can sell my bond on the open market will continually change.

For example, suppose that 12 months after I purchase the bond, interest rates rise to 10 percent. I decide to sell my bond at that time. It just so happens that you are in the market to purchase a bond. I offer to sell you mine. Would you pay me $1000 for my 8 percent bond? Of course not. Why would you buy an 8 percent bond from me when you can go to the U.S. Treasury and buy a 10 percent bond for the same price? Does this mean that my bond is worthless? No. It is worth something more than $0 and something less than $1000. To find a price for my bond, we would use some financial math. We would figure out what price you could pay for my bond and still earn a 10 percent return. For example, we might decide that my bond was worth $833. At that price, I am selling it to you at a *discount* or less than the maturity value of $1000.

Notice that nothing about the terms of my bond has changed. I am still getting $80 per year. If I held my bond for 30 years, I would be repaid my $1000 principal. What has changed is the market value of my bond – the price for which I can sell it before maturity. Since interest rates in the marketplace rose, the market value of my bond dropped.

Now let's suppose that over the next year, interest rates in the market drop to 6 percent. Do you think I would sell my 8 percent bond for $1000? No way. Since you can only get 6 percent on a new bond, I'm going to want more than $1000. I would sell it to you at a *premium* or more than the maturity value. Again, we'll use math to decide what price you can pay for the bond and still earn a 6 percent return. This inverse relationship between interest rates and the prices of bonds in the marketplace is known as *market risk*.

It is important to note that interest rate fluctuations affect long-term bonds much more than short-term bonds. Think of it this way. You might be willing to pay me a $100 premium on my 30-year bond ($1100 total) to receive 30 higher-interest payments. However, you probably would not pay me $100 premium for a 2-year bond since you would only receive two higher-interest payments. This is why longer bonds can sell at much higher premiums or discounts. In other words, longer-term bonds have a much higher fluctuation in their market values than short-term bonds. If you want to lower the volatility (fluctuation in value) of your bond portfolio, invest in shorter-term bonds.

Interest Rate Risk

From time to time, someone in my workshop will say to me, "I'm not worried about market risk. I'm going to buy a 30-year bond, take the interest, and hold it to maturity. I'll get my money back, so I won't have any market risk." He is absolutely correct. Since he's holding the bonds to maturity, he won't have market risk. However, he's taking on other types of risk instead. For example, suppose that the week after he purchased the bonds, interest rates doubled and stayed high for 29 more years. He would be losing unearned interest each and every year. This lost earning potential is known as *interest rate risk*. It is the risk of locking in a low interest rate for a very long time.

Inflation and Bonds

Inflation also poses risk for these long-term bondholders. Suppose that 5 years into their 30-year bond portfolio, inflation rose dramatically. By the end of the term, inflation would have destroyed the buying power of the principal.

In general, I shy away from bonds that have a maturity date greater than 15 years. They have substantially more risk without paying much more interest. Furthermore, there's no way to predict inflation decades down the road. I believe that a shorter, more flexible bond portfolio is preferable to a longer, riskier bond portfolio.

Bond Mutual Funds

By far the most popular way to own bonds is through mutual funds. Bond mutual funds provide investors with an instant portfolio of bonds. (If you're unsure exactly what a mutual fund is, just skip ahead and read Chapter 7 on mutual funds and variable annuities. Then come back to learn about bond mutual funds.) Because a bond mutual fund may own hundreds of different bonds and can be liquidated easily, it has distinct advantages over individual bonds. Bond funds provide instant diversity, easy reinvestment, flexible income choices, and easy repositioning (or liquidation).

Because of limited resources, most individual investors cannot afford to extensively diversify their bond holdings. Their portfolios just aren't large enough to buy too many different issues. On the other hand, typical bond funds own dozens if not hundreds of different bond issues. By purchasing bond funds rather than individual bonds, investors can achieve a much higher level of diversity with very little effort.

Likewise, when investors own individual bonds, reinvestment of interest presents a problem. Every time an interest payment is made, the bond investor needs to shop around for more bonds to buy. With a bond fund, reinvestment is not a problem. By merely checking a box on your fund application, the dividends (interest payments) are instantly reinvested into more shares.

Taking income from a bond mutual fund is easy. With individual bonds, distribution amounts are usually limited to the interest payments. If an investor wanted to take more than the interest payments, he would need to liquidate some of the bonds. Bond funds make taking distributions much easier. Because shares can be liquidated at will, an investor can create a systematic distribution of any amount he likes – whether it is more or less than the interest payments.

Finally, bond funds allow a tremendous amount of flexibility and liquidity. When liquidating, bond funds are much easier to handle than individual bonds. A portfolio of individual bonds would need to be sold one by one, while a bond fund can be liquidated or repositioned with a simple phone call. Investing in bond funds provides investors with the advantages of bonds and the flexibility of a mutual fund.

Nevertheless, bond funds often cause investors more concern than individual bonds. Bond funds report the value of the bonds they hold each month. This makes it easy for bond fund investors to clearly see how changing interest rates affect the value of their funds. In a time of rising interest rates, this can be disconcerting. For example, in 1994, interest rates rose sharply. Many investors who held individual bonds weren't concerned; since no one sent them a notice, they were unaware that the market value of their bond portfolios had dropped.

On the other hand, bond mutual fund investors received statements from their mutual fund companies with up-to-date market values. Unlike those who hold individual bonds, bond fund investors could easily see the market value of their investments falling. Because bond funds regularly report their values, I've found that investors tend to be more psychologically sensitive to interest rate changes when they hold bond funds than when holding individual bonds.

Credit Quality

Like individual bonds, credit quality plays a big role in determining how much interest a bond fund pays. Funds holding lower-rated bonds pay more interest than funds holding higher-rated bonds.

Finding the credit quality of a bond fund is easy – just ask or look. A quick call to your mutual fund company will reveal the quality mix of your fund. If you want to look at the credit quality of several funds, a mutual fund evaluation service (e.g., Morningstar, ValueLine) can make your search quick and easy. These services will usually list the percentage of the portfolio in each credit classification such as AAA or BBB.

Think back to the late 1980s and early 1990s. Remember junk bonds? You haven't heard anything about these investments for a long time, have you? Do you think they're gone? They're not. They're still here. They've just been repackaged in a politically correct wrapper. Today, junk bonds are known as *high-yield bonds*.

While I believe high-yield bonds can be an excellent way for investors to add attractive income to a diversified portfolio, I strongly recommend that investors avoid buying individual junk bonds and instead use high-yield bond mutual funds. The diversity and professional management of a mutual fund make owning them much safer than owning individual high-yield/junk bonds.

The need for diversity in high-yield bonds cannot be overstated. Think about it this way. If you buy five individual junk bonds and one of them sours, that single failure can significantly impact your bond portfolio. But if an individual bond sours inside a large, well-diversified, high-yield bond fund, it will make very little impact on your portfolio.

Furthermore, bond fund managers have extensive resources to research the companies and municipalities that issue the bonds. Because of their experience, research, and resources, prudent bond fund managers can uncover hidden opportunities, such as low-rated bonds with excellent prospects.

Because the risk of loss is high, I recommend that you avoid individual high-yield bonds. When investing in bonds rated on the low end of the scale, always use mutual funds. I believe that the diversity and professional management of the fund will add value and safety to your holdings.

Duration

Like bonds, bond mutual funds are sensitive to changes in market interest rates. Some bond funds are more sensitive than others. In general, bond funds that hold "longer bonds" (those that have maturities farther in the future) will be more volatile than those funds holding "shorter bonds" (those with shorter maturities). The number that measures this sensitivity is called *duration*. To find a bond fund's duration, just call the mutual fund company and ask for it. The fund's service representatives will quote a number in years. Focus on the number and mentally replace the word "years" with the word "percent." For every 1 percent change that market interest rates change, the bond fund's value will change by the duration (in percent).

For example, suppose you called your bond fund company and asked for your fund's duration. You learn that the duration is five years. By replacing the word "years" with the word "percent," you would think about the duration as 5 percent. If interest rates in the market rise one percentage point, the value of your bond fund will fall by 5 percent.

Let's put some numbers to this. If you had $100,000 invested in the fund, and interest rates rose by 2 percent (e.g., from 8 percent to 10 percent), your fund's value would fall by 10 percent (two times the duration), or $10,000. In other words, a 2 percent increase in interest rates would cause the bond fund to drop in value from $100,000 to $90,000. Likewise, if interest rates in the market fell by 3 percent, the bond fund's value would increase by 15 percent (three times duration), or $15,000 (from $100,000 to $115,000). By learning your fund's duration, you can measure how sensitive it is to changes in market interest rates.

Average Weighted Maturity

Don't confuse duration with *average weighted maturity*. Like duration, this number is a measure of volatility. Technically, average weighted maturity is the length of time until the average bond in a bond mutual fund will mature. The longer the average weighted maturity, the greater the price volatility. Sometimes you have to settle for using average weighted maturity instead of duration because it is the only volatility number available. But when duration is available, I prefer to use it instead.

Conclusion

Even though bonds and bond mutual funds tend to be widely misunderstood, they really are not that hard to understand. A bond is an

IOU that can be purchased or sold between investors. By understanding the factors that affect the value and the interest earning potential of bonds, investors can use the power of bonds to weave a strong investment portfolio. ◆

Chapter 7

Mutual Funds and Variable Annuities

O f all the innovations in the history of finance, none has changed the face of investing more than mutual funds and variable annuities. These investments have brought the benefits of the capital markets and professional management within easy reach of the common man. Over the past 30 years, these vehicles have been responsible for adding unprecedented wealth to the American public. It is both unfortunate and remarkable that many people have little or no concept of how these two investment types work. Myth and folklore surround them. Let's take a closer look at mutual funds and variable annuities to see what they are, how they work, and hopefully, dispel the myths.

Mutual Funds
What Is A Mutual Fund?

If you're not sure what a mutual fund is, don't be embarrassed. There are scores of people who hear about mutual funds, and perhaps even invest in them, and yet aren't sure what they are. Simply put, a mutual fund is an instant portfolio of stocks and/or bonds. To illustrate, let's create a mutual fund together.

Let's pretend that you and I and eight other friends decide to open a mutual fund of our own. After some discussion, we decide that our new fund will invest in medium-sized companies involved in producing high-tech products like microchips and computers. After forming the mutual fund company, we each put in $10,000 in exchange for shares in the fund. After a quick vote, we decide that you should be our fund manager. It is now your responsibility to take our $100,000 (10 x $10,000) and invest it in the stock market. As shareholders of the mutual fund, we will all participate equally (according to the number of shares we each own) in the risk and the rewards.

Share Price, Dividends, and Capital Gains

As shareholders in the fund, we share the dividends, interest, and capital gains of the portfolio. For example, suppose that the total value of the fund's stock portfolio increases sharply. Our share price will advance, as well. Likewise, when the stocks in the portfolio pay dividends, these payments are passed on to us as mutual fund dividends.

While most people understand how share price increases and dividend payments work, capital gains distributions are often confusing. However, once you understand that a mutual fund is nothing more than a portfolio of investments, capital gains distributions are easy to comprehend. When the fund manager buys and sells securities (in this case, stocks), each trade produces a taxable gain or a tax loss. For example, suppose you (as the fund manager) purchased IBM shares at $80. Later, you sold the shares for $100. At the sale, there is a taxable gain of $20 per share. To pass this gain onto us (the shareholders), you will declare a capital gains distribution at the end of the year. It will then be our responsibility (as shareholders) to pay the tax on this transaction.

Open-End vs. Closed-End Funds

A year goes by. All our friends hear about the wonderful job you have done as manager. They also want to invest in our fund. They give you their money, and you issue new shares to them. Since our fund allows new investors to join and add new cash, it is considered an *open-end mutual fund*. By remaining open to new investors, it can grow larger and larger. Open funds are the most common type of mutual fund.

On the other hand, some mutual funds are not open to new contributions of cash. These funds are known as *closed-end mutual funds*. If you want to own shares in a closed-end fund, you have to purchase them from current owners. To facilitate the buying and selling of its shares, closed-end mutual funds shares are traded like stocks on the stock exchanges.

Exchange Traded Funds – ETFs

Over the past couple of decades, a new mutual fund structure has taken the investing world by storm. These vehicles (i.e., investment types) are known as *exchange traded funds* or *ETFs*. ETFs are essentially the next generation in mutual funds. They are designed to give us the benefits of open-end funds and closed-end funds while avoiding the unique drawbacks of each.

To understand why ETFs have become so popular, you first need to understand the problems unique to each open-end and closed-end mutual fund.

The main problem with open-end funds is liquidity. All shares of open-end mutual funds are bought or sold once per day at the day's closing price. For example, if you want to buy XYZ Growth Fund today, your purchase will occur at the end of the day at the market closing price. Forget buying the fund at 10 AM and then selling the fund at 1 PM. You always buy it or sell it at the market closing price for that day.

On the other hand, closed-end funds are completely liquid. They trade all day long on the stock exchange. You can buy and sell them minute by minute if you wish. However, closed-end mutual funds have their own unique problem. Unlike open-end mutual funds, the shares of traditional closed-end funds can be selling for more or less than the investments they contain (i.e., the fund's portfolio of investments). When the shares sell for less than the portfolio value, it is known as a *discount to net asset value* or *discount to NAV*.

Since the discount to NAV can get bigger, it can significantly affect investment returns. For example, let's say that the portfolio of investments within the ABC Closed End fund goes up in value by 10 percent. Unfortunately, this rise doesn't necessarily mean that the price of the ABC Closed End fund shares will go up by the same percentage. If the discount gets bigger during this period, we will see a much smaller increase in the value of the fund's share price (e.g., 7 percent). In the financial world, we say that the fund is *inefficient* because it does not transfer the entire return to us. Because the discount to NAV affects investment returns, it adds an extra element of risk that open-ended mutual funds don't have.

So wouldn't it be great if we could have a type of fund that enjoys the benefits of each – the liquidity of a closed-end fund and the efficiency of an open-end fund? Introducing exchange traded funds! ETFs trade all day long (like a stock or traditional closed-end fund) but with values that track very close to the NAV.

How does an ETF accomplish this? Without getting too far into the weeds, an ETF will have a provision that allows large investors (who can buy millions of dollars of the fund at one time) to trade large blocks of the fund back to the issuer at NAV. This provision creates an environment where large investors are always looking to buy fund shares at a discount and sell them back to the issuer at NAV. This market activity has the effect of forcing ETFs to trade extremely close to their NAV. If this is confusing, don't worry about it. Just remember that ETFs are designed to provide very efficient and liquid vehicles for investing.

The Deception of Mutual Fund Ratings

Of all the financial information available, by far the most misused and misunderstood are so-called mutual fund ratings. Many investors regularly consult ratings services to help them make their mutual fund choices. In fact, studies indicate that over 90 percent of all new mutual fund purchases go into funds that have the top two ratings by the most popular ratings service – Morningstar. This result implies that many investors rely heavily on Morningstar ratings to make their mutual fund decisions. Unfortunately, these investors are deceived. At best, mutual fund ratings are useless. At the worst, these ratings are misleading and harmful.

What ratings am I referring to? In almost every public library in the United States, you will find thick reference books filled with mutual fund information. These publications are commonly referred to as *mutual fund ratings services*. These services can be an excellent source of information because they provide a quick way to compare existing funds. From this compilation, you can discover a wealth of information, from historical returns to manager background to a fund's objectives.

Included with the useful information are what the publishers refer to as *fund ratings*. Different services use different symbols to indicate their ratings. The most popular publisher, Morningstar, uses stars (one star being the lowest rating and five stars being the highest rating), while other ratings services use indicators such as numbers or letters. The ratings imply that high-rated funds are high quality while low-rated funds are low quality. As you will see, the ratings can be deceiving.

Rating vs. Ranking

In my opinion, the term "rating" is misleading. A rating implies quality or a lack thereof. A more accurate term for these values is "ranking." At first, the difference between a rating and a ranking may not be apparent. But the difference is enormous.

To understand the difference, let's look at a true rating – bond ratings (see Credit Rating in Chapter 6). As I explained in Chapter 6, bond ratings measure the credit quality of bonds on a scale between AAA and C. A triple-A bond is very high quality, while a C-rated bond is very low quality. If you invest in a triple-A bond, your chances of getting all your payments on time and your principal back at maturity are considered high. On the other hand, if you purchase a C-rated bond, you have a very high probability of not getting your money back. In a very real and practical way, a bond rating indicates a bond's quality.

Unlike bond ratings, mutual fund ratings do not measure quality. Instead, they rank relative past performance. While this may seem like a useful measurement, it is not. Ranking is a poor indicator of whether a mutual fund will perform well in the future. Here are three reasons why:

1. Rankings fail to communicate how much better or how much worse a fund has performed than other similar funds.
2. Rankings frequently compare dissimilar funds.
3. Past performance does not indicate future returns; last year's winners are often this year's losers.

The best way to visualize how rankings work is to imagine a college classroom with five students. At the beginning of the first-period class, the teacher announces there will be a test. He further states he will be using a ranking system to grade the papers. The highest grade will receive an A. The second highest grade will receive a B. Third highest will receive a C. And so on. After grading the papers, the teacher finds that one student scores 90 percent. This student receives the A. The second highest score of 80 percent earns a B. The third highest score of 70 percent earns a C. The fourth ranking score of 60 percent earns a D. Finally, the fifth score of 50 percent receives an F. At this point you might think that the teacher's system works just fine. The bell rings. The students change classes.

During the next period class, the teacher makes the same announcement. He administers the same test. This time the top score was a perfect 100 percent. This sterling paper receives the A. Another student scores 99 percent. That paper receives a B. A third scores 98 percent and earns the C. The fourth scores 97 percent for a D. The last student scores 96 percent, earning an F.

The limitations are obvious. The rankings tell us nothing about how much better the best paper is from the worst. Notice that in the second-period class, the A score of 100 percent is only slightly better than the F score of 96 percent. If you were the parent of this failing college student, you would not be happy. You might strongly encourage the student to party less and study more.

Like the second-period class tests, a relatively slim performance difference between the high scores and the low scores frequently occurs within mutual fund ratings. Don't take my word for it. Prove it to yourself. Log onto the Internet, or go to the library and obtain several mutual fund reports from a mutual fund ratings service. Select a particular peer group (fund groupings) and choose a variety of ratings from the top to the bottom. Ask a friend to help out by writing down the last five year-over-year returns for each fund without listing their names or their ratings. For example, the first fund might be "Fund A: 2008: -35 percent, 2009: 20 percent, 2010: 10 percent, 2011: 2 percent, 2012: 10 percent." The second fund might be "Fund B: 2008: -38 percent, 2009: 25 percent, 2010: 9 percent, 2011: 5 percent, 2012: 14 percent." From this raw return information, try to figure out which are the high-rated funds and which are the low-rated funds. I think you'll be surprised at what you find. You probably won't be able to discern the high-rated funds from the low-rated funds.

Misclassification

Another problem with mutual fund ratings is that they often compare incomparable funds against each other. They are comparing apples to oranges. Making matters worse, mutual fund companies often aid in the confusion. Consider this humorous example.

Imagine a couple with one child in the third grade. Their goal in life is for their son to be number one in his class – to have the very top ranking, we might say. In order to achieve this goal, they do all the things they should; they help him with homework, work with flash cards, and help him with his spelling. But, alas, it is not to be. To their horror, their son is merely average. He's just a regular kid. He earns good, but average, grades. He's not the top student in his class.

The parents are distressed. They spend days discussing this dilemma. Finally, they hit upon an idea. They decide that if they move their son down a grade – to the second-grade class – he will be the top student. Sure enough, after moving him back to a lower grade level, their son is now number one. They have achieved their goal.

While this example may sound ridiculous, mutual funds often employ a similar strategy. How? Remember, I stated earlier that most of the cash flowing into mutual funds goes into funds that carry high ratings (the top two ratings of the most popular mutual fund ratings service). Mutual fund companies and fund managers know this. Since their income is directly related to the number of dollars in their funds, they have a very big incentive to get high ratings; they need high ratings to get investors to put money into their funds. A common strategy for acquiring better ratings is misclassification.

To understand how misclassification works, you need to understand a little bit about how the ratings are assigned in the first place. Publishers of mutual fund ratings do not dump all mutual funds into one big heap and then rank them. Instead, they first sort the funds to be rated into *peer groups* (groups of supposedly similar funds). The publishers then use proprietary formulas to rank the funds in each group. Like the parents who put their third-grader in a second grade class, mutual funds try to get their fund put in the most advantageous peer group.

An old misclassification strategy is for a fund company to name a fund one way and to invest the portfolio another. For example, a fund company might name a mutual fund, The World's Greatest Value Stock Fund when, in fact, the fund is almost completely invested in growth stocks (rather than value stocks). If growth stocks do well and value stocks perform poorly (like 1998 and 1999), this misnamed growth fund will be rated very highly against its value fund peers.

Unfortunately for the fund companies, most ratings services uncovered this trick several years ago. Instead of just looking to the name and stated objectives, ratings services often look at the fund's portfolio before making its peer classification. Simply misnaming a fund doesn't always work any more.

Style Drift

To get around this new scrutiny, fund companies frequently use *style drift*. Style drift simply means that a mutual fund starts out with one style and, over time, drifts into another style. For example, suppose that a fund manager manages a balanced fund. Balanced funds are typically invested half in stock and half in bonds. Over the next year, this balance fund manager buys lots of stock while selling most of the fund's bonds. At the end of the year, instead of being half stock and half bond, the fund is 90 percent stocks and 10 percent bonds. The balanced fund has become a growth fund. The style of the fund has drifted from balanced to growth.

A clear, real-world example of style drift occurred in 1998, 1999, and early 2000. During most of those years, most value funds (funds that invest in undervalued stocks) underperformed their growth fund cousins. However, some value funds allowed their portfolios to drift into holding a considerable amount of growth stocks. Because these meandering funds contained a large portion of growth stocks, they earned higher returns and thus higher ratings during this period than their value-oriented peers. Because of the high ratings these funds earned, many investors abandoned their high-quality value funds and moved their money into those funds that held more growth stocks. Unfortunately, between 2000 and 2002 their moves cost them dearly when growth stocks plunged sharply.

Ratings Are Based on Past Performance

Think about mutual fund ratings another way. Do you really think that the publishers of mutual fund ratings services know which mutual funds will perform best in the future? Of course not! At best, their ratings can only look at the past. There is a saying in the investment world that, "Last year's winners are this year's losers." Likewise, every mutual fund prospectus in the world contains the statement, "Past performance is not indicative of future results." This statement is in there for a reason. No one knows the future, not even mutual fund ratings publishers.

In the end, mutual fund ratings fail to deliver help to investors. To be useful, mutual fund ratings would need to help investors accomplish two things:

- Increase returns
- Decrease risk

Unfortunately, publishers' mutual fund ratings have never been able to prove their ratings do either one. And, believe me, they have tried.

Research Proves Mutual Fund Ratings Don't Work

Over the years, scholars have closely studied whether mutual fund ratings actually deliver on their implied promise of helping investors increase their returns or reduce their risk. Over and over again, professionals and scholars find inconsistencies with the ratings. They also fail to find any statistical evidence that the ratings provide any useful help to investors.

For example, in his December 29, 1997 Forbes article, *No Stars for Morningstar*, Mark Hulbert points out an obvious logical problem with the ranking these mutual fund ratings create. He states that, "Morningstar gives nearly half the domestic equity no-load funds it evaluates a four- or five-star ranking (Morningstar's grades for above-average). Only a quarter received a one- or two-star ranking (Morningstar's grades for below-average)." He goes on to say that, "Morningstar's mutual fund ratings remind me of the children who live in Garrison Keillor's Lake Wobegon: They are all above average."

Another comprehensive study completed in September 2000 by professors Christopher Blake at Fordham University and Matthew Morey of Pace University concludes that, "You would be misguided to use (the stars) if you were trying to pick funds that were going to have superior performance in the future. (Morningstar ratings should not be viewed) ... as predictors of the future."

The weightiest criticism comes from Nobel Prize winner William F. Sharpe of Stanford University. In January 1998, Dr. Sharpe published his now famous scholarly study of the Morningstar star ranking system. He concluded, "(Morningstar's star ranking system is not) ... an efficient tool for choosing mutual funds within peer groups when constructing a multi-fund portfolio – the ostensible purpose for which Morningstar's rankings are produced."

Over the past decade, criticism of the star rating system continues to flow in. In Tom Nugent's December 5, 2003, National Review Online article, *The Real Fund Scandal*, he points out that Morningstar's star ranking system performed poorly during the stock market downturn between 2000 and 2002. He quotes Warren Bitters, a professional evaluator of mutual funds who conducted a study of Morningstar rankings as stating, "Morningstar ratings were very poor predictors of future performance, at least at this key market turning point." He found that from March 2000 to March 2003, five-star rated funds (Morningstar's top funds) experienced an average mean investment loss of nearly 60 percent. The one-star rated funds (the lowest Morningstar rating) experienced a much lower decline of less than 11 percent. In other words, Morningstar's "worst" funds outperformed its "best" funds by almost 50 percentage points.

In June of 2010, Vanguard published a well-received study that concluded, "We also find that a given rating offers little information about expected future relative performance; in fact, our analysis reveals that higher-rated funds are no more likely to outperform a given benchmark than lower-rated funds…"

Not to be discouraged, Morningstar presented a "new and improved" rating system in the back end of 2011 which used "gold, silver, bronze, neutral, and negative" as rating indicators instead of stars. Morningstar claimed this system would avoid "recency bias" by keeping a long-term perspective and by not being influenced by "what investors are buying and selling." How did the new Morningstar ratings system do in 2012? Not well at all.

In a February 2013 blog post, *Wall Street Rant*, the author looked at the performance of the new system. The research found that the new and improved system didn't help investors any better than the old star system (which means not at all).

Multiple Interests Keep Ratings Alive

So if scholars have proven over and over that mutual fund ratings (e.g., Morningstar's rating system) do not help investors, we are left with several pressing questions. Why do ratings persist? Why don't publishers of mutual fund ratings simply drop the rating? Why don't we hear more criticism about the mutual fund ratings from mutual fund companies and investment professionals? Again, the answers are simple: Everyone in the investment community has a vested interest in keeping mutual fund ratings alive.

Ratings Publishers

Ratings publishers realize their ratings are a very popular part of their publications. People flock to the library and the Internet to view the Morningstar ratings. Can you imagine what these people would do if tomorrow morning they opened the publication or logged on to their website and found no ratings? They would be lost. There would be nothing to tell them which are "good" funds and which are "bad" funds. If the ratings disappeared, most of these folks would quickly abandon the Morningstar publication for another. Publishers are in business to sell subscriptions – period. Printing a rating, no matter how dubious, is a large part of selling their publications. Publishers are not about to abandon their ratings anytime soon.

Mutual Fund Companies

What about the mutual fund companies? Why don't they object to the ratings? The answer is advertising. Think about it. Each page in a mutual fund ratings service is free advertising for the mutual fund. This gratuitous advertising has become so valuable that many mutual fund companies wouldn't exist without it. It is important to realize that there are thousands of mutual funds on the market today. Because of the sheer number of funds, publishers pick and choose which funds will appear in their pages and which will not. If a fund company was to contest a publisher's ratings, it could easily mean the end of this free advertising.

In addition to receiving free advertising, mutual fund companies also use the publishers' ratings as evidence of superiority. We've all seen mutual fund ads in magazines and newspapers proudly displaying a list of funds next to their high ratings. These ads imply that because the funds have high ratings, they are superior in quality. Between the free advertising and the perceived credibility that high ratings carry, mutual fund companies have every reason to keep the fund rating scheme going and absolutely no incentive to dispute them.

Investment Professionals

What about investment professionals? Why don't they object to the ratings? Alas, most financial professionals have neither the time nor energy to dispute the ratings. And even if they did, most investors don't want to hear the truth – that their main method of choosing mutual funds is seriously flawed. They prefer to ignore the facts and continue reading the stars. Because of this resistance from investors, many financial professionals prefer to go with the flow and use the ratings in their presentations. It is easier all the way around.

In the end, few people have a reason to expose mutual fund ratings for what they are – useless at best, harmful at worst. On the contrary, mutual fund companies, investors, and financial professionals have a vested interest that they continue. So what should you do? Don't use mutual fund ratings. They won't help you.

The Search for Good Information

If you simply ignore the mutual fund ratings, you will still find much good information in the mutual fund ratings publications. They provide an excellent way to view many funds at once. For example, you can view annual returns, top holdings, and sector weightings of many funds by simply flipping the pages. This information gives you a general idea of how different mutual funds are performing. But don't stop with the mutual fund ratings book. Go to the fund companies and explore the funds further. Get the prospectuses. Read them. Learn what type of stocks and bonds are in the funds. Learn how the managers make their decisions. Make sure each fund meets your objectives. The more you know about your funds, the more comfortable you will be.

Meanwhile, whatever else you do, ignore the so-called ratings. They don't help and could lead you into making unwise decisions.

Variable Annuities

I live in the Dallas-Fort Worth Metroplex. A decade ago, there were two gentlemen in my area who gave a great deal of attention to *variable annuities*. One was a broker who hosted a popular weekly radio show. He believed that everyone in the world should invest in variable annuities. On the other end of the spectrum was a journalist who wrote for a large, well-known newspaper. This journalist believed no one should ever put one dime into a variable annuity. While both eventually progressed to other ventures, the controversy over variable annuities continues. As with most subjects regarding investing, the truth falls somewhere between the two extremes. Variable annuities can be a great tool in which to meet certain investment goals, but they are not for everyone in every situation.

Mutual Fund Annuities

I believe the term "variable annuity" often misleads people. I've had many people tell me, "I have a variable annuity. Last year, it paid 6 percent interest. This year, it is paying 5.5 percent interest." They think that because the interest rate on their fixed annuity fluctuates, it is a variable annuity. It is not. These folks do not have a variable annuity. They have a fixed annuity with a fluctuating interest rate.

I believe that a more descriptive term than "variable annuity" would be "mutual fund annuity." Variable annuities more closely resemble mutual funds than fixed annuities. The Securities Exchange Commission's brochure *Variable Annuities: What You Should Know* (http://www. sec.gov/investor/pubs/varannty.htm) states, "The investment options for a variable annuity are typically mutual funds that invest in stocks, bonds, money market instruments, or some combination of the three." Since variable annuities have mutual fund investment choices, they allow investors to enjoy many of the advantages of mutual funds with the benefits of annuities.

Popular Funds and Managers

Many variable annuities contain large collections of popular funds and fund managers. If you have a favorite mutual fund, you can probably find its twin in a variable annuity. For example, suppose you like a fund that we'll call the XYZ Growth Fund. You could probably find the same manager managing an identical fund (often with the same name) in a variable annuity. Along with that fund, you might find 20, 30, or even more well-known funds managed by popular managers.

In addition to providing a full range of fund investments, variable annuities add benefits that are important for many people. They can add tax-deferral, spousal protection, protections against market declines, and guaranteed lifetime income. Of course, these benefits are not free. But for some people, the benefits of a variable annuity can be well worth the investment. Let's look at the specific upsides and downsides of variable annuities.

Variable Annuities Add IRA-Type Benefits To Nonqualified Accounts

For nonqualified accounts (accounts that are not an IRA, 403(b), 401(k), etc.), variable annuities can add many IRA-type advantages. Like an IRA, variable annuities add tax deferral, estate-planning tools, and (in some states such as Texas) creditor protection.

Tax Deferral

When most people think of variable annuities, they think of tax deferral. Indeed, tax deferral is one of the most valuable benefits for nonqualified variable annuity accounts. By putting money into a variable annuity, you can avoid taxation on your dividends and capital gains. Like an IRA, the only time you pay taxes on the gain is when you take your money out.

If you've ever owned a mutual fund in a regular, nonqualified account, you know that year-end often brings tax surprises. That's when most mutual funds declare their capital gains distributions. For those investors who own variable annuities, capital gains season is a nonevent. In fact, variable annuities don't even report capital gains or dividends to the IRS.

Likewise, transfers between variable annuity mutual funds are free from tax implications. If you've ever transferred money from one regular mutual fund account to another, you received a "gift" from your fund company at the end of the year – a IRS Form 1099. In a regular mutual fund, transfers between funds are taxable events. If you have a gain in the fund, you must pay your tax. The Form 1099 lets you and the IRS know that a taxable event has occurred. Not so in a variable annuity. Like an IRA, you can move money from one investment choice to another without any tax implications – no Form 1099, no taxes.

Estate-Planning Tools

Another IRA-type benefit of variable annuities is probate avoidance. Like an IRA, variable annuities always pass to the named beneficiary. For example, suppose Todd had his daughter, Kim, listed as the beneficiary on his variable annuity. However, his will lists his son, Mark, as the beneficiary. When Todd dies, the variable annuity will go to Kim. Variable annuities (with named beneficiaries) completely bypass the probate process. They direct the assets quickly and efficiently to the named beneficiaries on the annuity itself.

Likewise, many variable annuities allow you to proscribe how the assets are to be paid to your heirs. For example, suppose Cecil is going to leave a variable annuity to his three grandchildren – Johnny, Jill, and Timmy. Johnny and Jill are very good with money, but Timmy is not. If Timmy received a lump sum of money, he would spend it before the sun set. Cecil would prefer that Timmy receive monthly payments instead of a lump sum. With some variable annuities, Cecil can provide lump sums for Johnny and Jill and a monthly payment for Timmy. This strategy is often an economical alternative to using expensive trusts. By using an appropriate variable annuity, you don't have to hire an attorney or trustee to carry out your wishes.

Creditor Protection

In some states (such as Texas), variable annuities provide excellent creditor protection. Like an IRA, creditors cannot get access to variable annuities. It is easy to see why high-risk professionals like pediatricians and surgeons enjoy variable annuities.

Over the past few years, courts have held that medical professionals retain a lifetime of liability – even after retirement. Lawsuits continue to be filed for medical treatments given decades before. Unfortunately, malpractice insurance often terminates at the doctor's retirement. Without this insurance, retired doctors are fully exposed to litigation. Because judgments cannot get at the assets of a variable annuity in Texas, many doctors in that state protect their serious money by using variable annuities. Their investments remain protected even after they quit practicing and retire.

Variable Annuities Add Benefits for All Accounts

A common misconception about variable annuities is that they only provide benefits for nonqualified (e.g., non-IRA) accounts. This is not true. Variable annuities can add benefits to all accounts – nonqualified as well as qualified. The two most popular benefits that can be added are *death benefits* and *living benefits*. Because they add valuable asset protection, these two features often help investors sleep better at night.

Heir Protection

This feature is commonly called a *death benefit guarantee*. Very simply, it guarantees that your heirs will get back no less money than you put in. For example, suppose you put $100,000 into a variable annuity. You allocate the money into a very aggressive stock fund. The next day, the stock market crashes. Your $100,000 investment is now worth $80,000. You're so upset that you have heart attack and die. Your heirs will get the greater of your account value or what you put into the variable annuity. In this case, $100,000.

Many times, variable annuities will offer enhancements to the heir protection. A common enhancement is a *step-up*, or increase in the benefit each year. For example, a $100,000 annuity that has a 6 percent step-up will guarantee that your heirs receive no less than $100,000 the first year, $106,000 the second-year, $112,360 the third year, and so on. The heir protection increases each year. Death benefit guarantees are excellent ways to provide protection for a spouse. If something happens to one spouse, the death benefit guarantee helps ensure that the survivor has a place from which to draw income.

Remarkably, investors don't have to pass any health exam to get the guarantee. An investor can be totally uninsurable for life insurance yet get the death benefit guarantee on a variable annuity. Without going into specifics, this quirk allows for some very clever strategies in some situations.

Living Benefits (Principal Guarantees)

The main drawback to a death benefit guarantee is the "death" portion of the guarantee. Somebody has to die for the benefit to become active. Most people (including me) do not relish the idea of dying as a way of protecting assets. That's why *living benefits* on variable annuities have become so popular. These innovative features help investors feel more secure by providing long-term protection against uncertainty.

Living benefits come in two general types – a *principal guarantee* and an *income guarantee*. It is important to realize that you can guarantee one or the other but not both.

Principal Guarantee

The living benefit that guarantees principal is often referred to as an *accumulation benefit*. This feature simply provides that at the end of a specified period of time, you will have a guaranteed lump sum. A typical accumulation benefit guarantees the 10-year value of the account. For example, suppose an investor put $100,000 in the annuity and invested it aggressively. Unfortunately, the market performed poorly and actually lost money. At the 10-year anniversary, the account was worth $90,000. At that point, the insurance company would "repair" the account by adding $10,000. As long as the investor leaves the money invested for 10 years, the risk of loss is mitigated.

This type of guarantee can give investors comfort during a rough market. For example, think about the stock market between 2000 and 2002. During those three years, the stock market suffered tremendously. The Dow Jones Industrial Average dropped around 40 percent while the NASDAQ dropped nearly 80 percent. Many investors abandoned their Retirement Solutions, jumped out of their portfolios, and lost a lot of money. By abandoning their investments, many investors missed the massive market recovery in 2003 and 2004.

I believe that had these investors used variable annuities with guarantees instead, they would have stuck to their investment strategies and succeeded. It is easier to stick with a portfolio during rough times if your principal is protected. If the market recovers, you'll prosper tremendously. If it doesn't, you'll at least not lose anything.

Income Guarantee

The second type of variable annuity living benefit is an income guarantee, which is often referred to as a *guaranteed withdrawal benefit*.

This annuity feature has become very popular because it guarantees retirees what they ultimately want most – guaranteed lifetime income. But hold on to your hat, this feature is going to take a little more explanation.

To illustrate the guarantee, I want to compare it to something you probably already know – mutual fund investing. Imagine that a retiree (let's call her Jane) has a portfolio of $500,000 invested in regular mutual funds. To meet bills, Jane must take $25,000 per year from the portfolio. A couple of years after retirement, the market crashes. Her $500,000 portfolio drops in value to $250,000. Over the next few years, the market stays down and doesn't recover and Jane runs out of money. When her funds run out, her income stops.

Had this been a variable annuity with a guarantee withdrawal benefit, Jane's income would continue for the rest of her life – even if her account value drops to zero. In essence, the benefit guarantees that she will always have income no matter what happens in the market.

Now let's suppose that instead of a market crash, we had a market boom. Jane's variable annuity rises from $500,000 to $1,000,000 in value. In that case, her income will double. Her guaranteed income will rise from $25,000 to $50,000 per year. Her guaranteed income can go up but not down.

The amount of the guaranteed income depends on several factors including the age of the investor, how long the money is invested before the income starts, and the terms of the contract. There are significant variations between annuities in how the income is calculated, so be sure you do comparison shopping. An annuity that may be right for one investor might not be best for another.

Potential Drawbacks to Variable Annuities

I can hear some of you saying, "Wow! Variable annuities are fantastic! Like mutual funds, I can invest any way I want. I can add tax deferral. I can switch funds and rebalance without taxes. I'm protected from creditors (in some states, anyway). My heirs are protected against market loss. My downside risk is protected with living benefits. So, what's the catch?"

As with most things, there are benefits and costs to variable annuities. The two main potential drawbacks to variable annuities are tax treatment and internal costs.

Tax Treatment

Ironically, one of the advantages of variable annuities is also one of its disadvantages. While variable annuities add IRA-type benefits, they also add IRA-type tax treatment. Like an IRA, any gains are taxed as regular income and like an IRA, heirs don't receive a step-up of tax basis at your death. I will explain each in a moment.

Capital Gains Rates vs. Regular Income Rates

Earlier, I discussed the fact that variable annuities add the benefit of tax deferral to your nonqualified accounts; whenever a dividend or a capital gain is paid by a fund in a variable annuity, there are no taxes due. Likewise, when you move money from fund to fund, these transactions are not taxable events, either. However, the trade-off for adding tax deferral to nonqualified accounts is in the different tax treatment of capital gains and accumulated dividends.

Under the current tax code, capital gains receive special tax treatment – they are taxed at 20 percent (or 10 percent for those in the 15 percent tax bracket). Like an IRA, variable annuities do not enjoy this special capital gains tax treatment. Instead, any increase in the value of your annuity is taxed at regular income tax rates when you take the money out.

The same disadvantage applies to qualified dividends. Under the current tax code, investors can pay 0 to 20 percent on qualified dividends depending on their tax bracket. When the dividends are paid in a variable annuity, they don't receive this preferential tax treatment.

To illustrate the difference in tax treatments, let's look at the brother and sister investors of Randy and Sue.

Randy puts $10,000 in a regular mutual fund. Each year, the fund declares a $1000 capital gain. (Assume that Randy reinvests the gain back into the fund.) Since this fund is nonqualified [not an IRA, 401(k), or 403(b)], Randy will have to declare the $1000 capital gain each year on his income tax return. Because capital gains receive a special tax rate of 20 percent, Randy will pay the government $200 each year in capital gains tax.

After five years, Randy's fund has grown to $20,000. He decides to sell. Since he will already pay tax on $5000 in capital gains, these are added to his original investment to calculate his tax basis. When he sells the fund, he will owe capital gains tax on the difference between his tax basis and the proceeds. In this case, he will owe capital gains tax on $5000. ($20,000 proceeds minus his $15,000 tax basis; his tax basis is calculated by adding his original $10,000 investment to five years of declared capital gains [5 x $1000 = $5000]). Since capital gains rates are 20 percent, Randy will owe another $1000 in tax. Over the five years, he will pay 20 percent tax on $10,000 in gains or $2000 total in capital gains tax.

On the other hand, Sue puts $10,000 in a variable annuity. Like Randy's fund, over the next five years, the funds in her variable annuity declare $1000 per year in capital gains. Since variable annuities are tax-deferred, Sue will pay no tax on these capital gains. Like her brother, at the end of the five years, her account is worth $20,000. She decides to liquidate her account, as well. In Sue's case, she will owe regular income tax on the $10,000 increase in value.

The differences between Randy and Sue are when the taxes are owed and what rates are used. Randy owes capital gains tax each year they are declared. Sue owes regular income tax only when she decides to liquidate. While Randy enjoys a lower tax rate, he has much less control over timing his taxes than Sue. In fact, Sue didn't have to liquidate her account. She could have left her money in the account indefinitely and continued to pay no tax.

Think about this, too. Each year, Randy paid money out of his pocket in taxes, but Sue did not. She could have used her extra $200 each year to make new investments. These $200-per-year investment contributions would have further improved Sue's financial situation.

Tax Basis Step-Up vs. Inherited Tax Basis

If you hold regular, nonqualified accounts, upon your death that account will receive what's commonly called a *tax basis step-up*. Instead of your beneficiaries inheriting your tax basis, any gains on these accounts are forgiven.

(As illustrated with the example in the previous heading titled, *Capital Gains Rates vs. Regular Income Rates,* your basis is "your own money" in the investment and is not subject to tax when you sell it. Your basis includes your original investment, plus contributions, plus reinvested dividends and capital gains, less adjustments for withdrawals.)

For example, suppose you own $10,000 worth of IBM stock. You purchased this stock long ago at a cost of $1000. If you sold the stock today, you would owe capital gains tax on the gain of $9000 ($10,000 sales price – $1000 cost). However, if you died today, your heirs would inherit the stock, and their basis would be today's value. In essence, the unrealized gain on the stock is forgiven; your heirs could sell the stock tomorrow (after your death) and owe no capital gains at all. At your death, your heirs receive a new, higher tax basis.

On the other hand, heirs to qualified accounts [e.g., IRA, 401(k)] and variable annuities inherit the deceased's tax basis. For example, suppose you own a variable annuity worth $10,000. If your tax basis is $1000, the basis your heirs inherit will be $1000, as well. If you died today and your heirs liquidate the variable annuity tomorrow (after your death), they will owe regular income tax on the $9000 gain. For many people, losing the tax basis step-up is not a problem. Many investors would rather maximize their current safety and income today than the size of their heirs' after-tax inheritance tomorrow.

Nevertheless, if maximizing your heirs' inheritance is important, many variable annuities have a special feature just for you. Some variable annuities provide a death benefit guarantee that adds a tax protection feature. For example, suppose your heirs inherited your variable annuity that had a gain of $100,000. If you had chosen an annuity with a 40 percent tax protection feature, your heirs would receive an additional $40,000 to help handle their tax bill. As I mentioned before, since each annuity is different, be sure you understand the benefits.

Note: Variable annuities do not change the tax treatment on IRAs. The possible tax advantages and disadvantages of variable annuities only apply to nonqualified accounts (e.g., non-IRAs). Putting a variable annuity in an IRA or other qualified account does not change the tax treatment of these accounts at all.

Higher Internal Costs

Like mutual funds, variable annuities have what are commonly called *internal fees*. These fees are charged by the mutual fund and variable annuity companies to pay for their services. As the name implies, these fees are charged "internally." You will never see the fees deducted from your accounts. Instead, they are taken out of the investment portfolio before the account values are reported. As might be expected, since variable annuities provide more benefits, the internal fees are generally higher than straight mutual funds.

As a rule of thumb, variable annuities have annual charges that are between 1 and 2 percent more than regular mutual funds. For example, mutual funds often have internal fees that run around 1 percent per year. Typical variable annuities may have internal fees that run between 2 and 3 percent per year. Adding living benefits and death benefits can increase these costs another .75 to 1.25 percent. Before investing in a variable annuity, be sure you understand the total costs.

Variable Annuities often Provide Performance Enhancement

There's no doubt that internal fees can impact your overall returns. However, there are other factors that offset the higher costs. As I discussed earlier, one factor is tax deferral. By deferring taxes as long as possible, an investor can use the money that otherwise would have gone to pay taxes to earn greater income.

The factor that often offsets the costs is the ability to invest more aggressively. Instead of using fixed (lower returning) investments to reduce your downside risk, you may instead use the living or death benefits provided by the variable annuity. For example, instead of investing in a regular, balanced mutual fund, an investor may decide to invest in a variable annuity equity fund protected by a principal guarantee. This strategy, properly executed, may allow the investor to take advantage of the higher potential returns of an all-stock fund while still reducing the risk to his retirement.

Using a variable annuity guarantee can be an excellent strategy for getting higher returns and protecting the aggressive parts of your portfolio. Just be sure you understand the terms of your variable annuity, know about any additional costs of the benefits you want, and have a well-organized plan for how the annuity fits into your Retirement Solutions.

How to Choose a Variable Annuity

You should look at three things when choosing a variable annuity:

• Make sure the insurance company is strong.

- Make sure the annuity you choose provides the benefits you want and need.

- Choose an annuity that contains investment choices you want.

Choose a Strong Company

People commonly ask me, "If the insurance company has problems, what will happen to my investments?"

With variable annuities, you need not worry. Variable annuity mutual funds are segregated and separate from the assets of the insurance company.

Even though your investments are segregated, you rely on the insurance company to provide additional features such as the death benefit guarantee or living benefits. Therefore, carefully choose the company with which you invest. Extremely large, financially sound companies are the best choice. Should you need to exercise a living or death benefit, you want a powerful company from which to collect. Luckily, researching insurance companies is extremely easy. Company size and financial ratings can be retrieved from services such as Standard & Poor's, A.M. Best, Moody's, and Fitch. With so many large, financially sound insurance companies, there is absolutely no reason to choose anything but a very high-quality company.

Get the Benefits You Want

Every company offers a unique package of benefits. Make sure the variable annuity that you choose provides the benefits you want. For example, if an increasing death benefit is important to you, make sure the annuity you choose contains it. Likewise, if living benefits are important to you, make sure the company you choose provides that. Since every company's offerings are different, examine them closely. Make sure you get the benefits you want.

Choose an Annuity With Fund Choices You Want

Once you find a company you like, take a look at the fund choices. Today, you can easily find variable annuities that provide 20, 30, or more fund choices. Make sure these choices include a variety of good funds.

You should also be aware that many annuities limit your fund choices when you choose a living benefit. For example, one annuity company might require that you keep 30 percent of your portfolio in bonds. Another company might limit your choices to a handful of predetermined fund portfolios, while another company might require that they make all of the portfolio decisions altogether. These investment restrictions can severely impact your overall performance, so choose your variable annuity carefully.

Conclusion

We live in a golden age of investing. The relatively recent innovations of variable annuities and mutual funds have changed the face of investing forever. No longer are the capital markets the exclusive domain of the rich and powerful. Through these vehicles, the world of stocks and bonds belongs to us all. As a result, the capital markets have been responsible for distributing an unprecedented amount of wealth to the American public. As prudent investors, we need to understand these investments and learn to use them skillfully. ◆

Chapter 8

Investment Costs

There's probably no subject in investing that receives more attention than investment costs. Books, articles, and investment gurus devote an enormous amount of time and published pages discussing ways to incrementally increase returns by reducing costs. The typical discussion addresses explicit costs such as the expenses fund managers and brokers charge for giving advice, processing transactions, and managing portfolios. In this chapter, we will talk about all of these costs. However, I find it interesting that in the midst of all this advice, one of the biggest investment costs goes largely unnoticed. I believe that investors lose more money to *this* cost than any other. It is a cost that you should avoid, so we will talk about it as well.

Commissions

In the beginning, the only financial professionals available to the public were brokers. These people simply sold securities (such as stocks) and charged a commission for each trade. From these commissioned beginnings, the investment world was built. Even today, commissions remain very popular. When talking about commissions, I like to lump them into three basic structures:

- Front-end commissions
- Surrender-period commissions
- Advisory fees and level commissions

Front-End Commissions

The most well-known type of commission is referred to as a *front-end commission*. Very simply, this is a commission charged when the investment is made. With a front-end commission, you will see an immediate reduction in your account's value. Stocks and certain mutual funds often carry this type of charge. On a stock, the commission is simply added to the cost of the trade. If you buy $10,000 of a stock and the commission charged is $500, your broker will want $10,500 from you to settle the trade. Simple enough.

With mutual funds, this type of commission is known as an *A-share commission*. Instead of a commission being added to the trade, your value immediately drops by the commission amount. For example, suppose you invest $10,000 in an A-share mutual fund with a 5 percent commission. If you examine your account immediately after your investment, you will notice that your account value has dropped in value to $9500. That immediate dip is due to the front-end commission.

Surrender-Period Commissions

The next type of commission is known as a *surrender-period commission*. Many investments such as certificates of deposit, fixed annuities, variable annuities, and B-share mutual funds may carry what are commonly called *surrender periods*. If your money stays in the investment for a specified period of time (the surrender period), no penalty is incurred. On the other hand, if your money comes out early, a penalty is deducted. This penalty period is designed to keep investors committed to their investments long enough for the investment provider (e.g., mutual fund company, bank) to recover its sales costs. In general, surrender-period mutual funds usually have higher internal costs than their front-end cousins. Even so, many people prefer surrender-period investments because there is no initial drop in their account value. All their money goes to work right away.

Advisory Fees and Level Commissions

Since advisory fees and level commissions share many of the same characteristics, I'll discuss them together. Unlike front-end commissions and back-end commissions (commission types that pay the advisor a big fee up front and little thereafter), advisory fees and level commissions pay an advisor a consistent annual fee, as long as the advisor–client relationship exists. Typically, these fees run around 1 to 2 percent per year.

Over the past few years, these arrangements have become extremely popular for three reasons:

- They are often better at matching the professional's compensation with the services rendered.
- They are better at aligning the goals of the investor and the investment advisor.
- They free the investor from up-front fees or back-end penalties.

In the old days of finance, commissions were king. Brokers spent countless hours making cold calls trying to sell stocks, bonds, and mutual funds. As a reward for their efforts, they were paid commissions. However, in the new world of investments, service is king. People no longer want to just be sold an investment. People want someone with knowledge, experience, and training to look over their entire financial picture to help them chart a course for success. People want a long-term advisory relationship with an experienced financial professional.

A level commission often frees professionals to provide better ongoing service for existing clients. It is easy to see why. Common sense tells us that a financial professional cannot service an account forever if it produces no income. As you might suspect, financial professionals who charge only transaction commissions usually need a continual stream of new clients to stay in business. Unfortunately, as the client base bulges, the clients often suffer. Transactional professionals eventually have to divert their time, effort, and resources away from servicing existing clients to that of acquiring new ones.

Advisory fees and level commissions solve this problem by matching the compensating fees with the services rendered. Investors prefer this structure because they have no up-front or back-end commissions. Financial advisors prefer this arrangement because it frees them from continually seeking new clients. Instead, they can focus on providing existing clients with the best service and advice possible.

The main difference between advisory fees and level commissions is how they're charged. Typically, advisory fees are charged directly to an investor's account, while level commissions are paid from the investment's internal costs or hidden costs (e.g., 12b-1 fees[*]). Investors who use the advisory fee approach see a charge from their account when the fees are paid. Investments that use level commissions show no visible advisory charges. Since these fees are deducted from within the fund itself, the investors never see a direct charge to their statement. Neither is better or worse than the other. They are simply two approaches to the same objective.

Internal Costs

As I discussed in earlier chapters, the fund approach (i.e., using mutual funds and variable annuities) provides wonderful benefits to investors such as instant diversification and accounting simplicity. As you might guess, mutual fund and variable annuity companies charge for their services. Collectively, their charges are known as *internal costs*. Typically, these charges never show up on your statement. Like the name

---

[*] 12b-1 fees: This term refers to a regulatory provision that allows mutual fund companies to collect an internal fee so they can promote and sell their funds.

implies, they are internal to the funds. The companies simply deduct the charges before they report your account balance. Even though you don't see these charges, they do affect your investment returns.

Many financial gurus rail against internal fees and advise their followers to choose only cheap investments. I believe this is poor advice. Instead of choosing investments because they're cheap, I recommend choosing investments because they provide a good value.

As we all know, getting something cheap isn't necessarily synonymous with a good value. When you shop for an automobile, you're probably not looking for the cheapest car possible. Instead, you search out the one that will provide the quality and features you want at a good price. You're shopping for the best value for your investment.

In the same way, when you're shopping for investments, first decide which benefits and services you want and need. For example, do you need an investment that provides a principal protection strategy? Do you want guaranteed income? Do you want investment advice? Once you decide what features and services you need, only then can you compare the different investments and choose the one that will give you the best value.

The "Perspiration Cost"

As I mentioned at the beginning of the chapter, the biggest cost investors pay is little discussed. I call it the *Perspiration Cost*. Without question, investors pay more in Perspiration Costs than all the other costs and fees combined. The tragedy is that this cost can be completely avoided. Let's look at the Perspiration Cost and how you can keep it from ruining your investment returns.

For over a decade, a research firm named Dalbar, Inc. has conducted a study that compares the actual return of individual investors with the market indexes. Over and over the research has concluded that, on average, individual investors severely underperformed the markets.

The latest study, conducted in 2011, looked at the previous 20-year period. During that time, the S&P 500 advanced at an average annual compounded return of 8.2 percent. The study also found do-it-yourself no-load investors earned an average annual rate of return of 3.17 percent. In other words, these investors would have been better off keeping their money in money market accounts. They would have earned more money without assuming any of the risk. Where did most of the market returns go? Perspiration Cost.

So why do I call this the Perspiration Cost? When an investor looks at his portfolio and starts to perspire, the next decision will in all probability cost a lot of money. An example best illustrates the principal.

Let's look at Bob and his portfolio. Bob has a simple portfolio with two mutual funds, Fund A and Fund B. After the first year of investing, I received a phone call from Bob. "Michael," he said, "I was just looking over my portfolio, and I see that you were right on target with Fund A. Man, has it soared or what! I can't believe how much money I've made on that investment! On the other hand, I was looking at Fund B. It hasn't lost any money, but compared to Fund A, it hasn't done well at all. Michael, I think we should ...." What do you think Bob said next? "Michael, I think we should move all of Fund B into Fund A."

Bob is by no means unusual. It is in our nature to want to move toward success. Most all of us are a little bit greedy. Herein lies the problem. Bob looked at his portfolio and started to "perspire" with greed. He began thinking, "Oh man! If I had put all of my money in Fund A, think of how much more money I would have right now!" Unfortunately, when you look at your portfolio and start to perspire, that's when you're about to make a bad investment decision.

So now let's assume that, against my warnings, Bob moved his assets from Fund B into Fund A. Over the next year, Fund A lost money while Fund B grew. At the end of the next year, I received another call from Bob. "Michael, you know what? You were right. Last year, when

I said that we should move everything to Fund A, I was wrong. I made a mistake. Now I wish I had not moved my money. Look at how much money I've lost! I'm so tired of losing money. You know what I think we should do? I think we should ...."

Again, Bob looked at his portfolio and started to perspire. This time, instead of perspiring with greed, he's perspiring with fear. He started thinking, "Oh my goodness! If this fund continues to go down, I'll lose everything. I could be ruined! I better cut my losses here." For most people, the emotion of fear is more powerful than their feeling of greed. When the market becomes volatile, people pay tremendous amounts of money in Perspiration Costs. They panic and jump ship at just the wrong time.

Of all the costs investors pay, the Perspiration Cost is the highest. It is not uncommon for an investor to lose more to Perspiration Cost in one year than to all the other combined costs he would pay over his entire lifetime!

So how can you avoid the Perspiration Cost? In a nutshell, you need to do two things. First, create a sound Portfolio Solution outlining the way in which your portfolio will be managed. It will describe the type of investments and the investment strategies to be used in your portfolio.

For example, your Portfolio Solution may prescribe that your portfolio consists of 60 percent equities (stocks). Once your Portfolio Solution is firmly in place, let it guide your decisions. Whenever you are tempted to move out of an investment, stop and ask yourself why. Is it because the portfolio needs to be changed to preserve its diversity? Or is it because you're perspiring (by being greedy or fearful)? By creating a sound Portfolio Solution and sticking to it, you will remove the emotion and the emotional cost – the Perspiration Cost – out of your portfolio.

In Chapter 11, we will look at investment strategies. In that chapter, we will discuss the link between investment strategies and investment costs. We will also look at why we should consider the Perspiration Cost when evaluating our investment strategy.

Conclusion

Investment costs include anything that reduces the expected returns of a portfolio. These include commissions, fees, and internal costs. When you evaluate all these costs, confirm that they are providing good value in terms of benefits and services.

The single largest and most destructive cost of all – the Perspiration Cost – goes largely undiscussed. Fortunately, there are ways of reducing and even eliminating the Perspiration Cost from your retirement solution. ◆

Chapter 9

Diversification

When making investment decisions, you need to keep one thing in mind – all investments are risky. Period. *Any* money you have is *always* experiencing some sort of risk.

When talking about risk, I always think about a certain client of mine. She said that in the 1970s her father didn't trust the banks. To keep his money safe, he kept his life savings of seven thousand dollars in a plastic Gatorade can in the pantry. (This is the equivalent of $40,000 today.) One weekend, her mother cleaned out the pantry and threw away the can. Weeks later, when the woman's father noticed that the can was missing, it was too late. The father's safe money strategy ended in a total loss.

I can hear some of you thinking, "But what if I put all my money in federally guaranteed certificates of deposit? Since they're guaranteed, there's no risk. Right?"

Wrong. CD investing has risk, too. While you may not lose any principal, you assume the risk of having your buying power erode over your retirement. Think about it. Could you live on the same income you lived on 20 years ago? Probably not. It is also unlikely that in 20 years you'll be able to live on your present income. To protect your future, you need a strategy for increasing your income. Historically, CDs have not done that. After taxes, these "safe" investments lag behind the rising cost of living. Your losses may not be as quick as losing it in a Gatorade can, but over time you will lose value, just the same.

Asset Allocation

Very simply, *asset allocation* is a way of spreading your investments between different investment types. In other words, asset allocation keeps you from putting all your financial "eggs" in one investment "basket."

Market investments (e.g., stocks, bonds, real estate) generally "travel in groups." For example, in 1998 and 1999, the stock prices of companies involved in the "growth" areas of the economy (computers, communications, biotechnology, etc.) skyrocketed. Between 2000 and 2002, these same stocks plunged sharply. Since similar investments often rise or fall together, financial people categorize investments by lumping them into groups. These groups are known as *asset classes*.

Asset Classes

Each asset class contains different risk and return potential. In general, the higher the potential return, the higher the potential risk. To see how risk and return are measured, let's look at two familiar groups of investments – certificates of deposit and stocks.

Answer the following questions:

Certificate of Deposit

1. What is the highest recorded 6-month CD rate? _____
2. What is the lowest recorded 6-month CD rate? _____
3. What is the difference between the highest and lowest 6-month CD rates? _____
4. What is the average historical 6-month CD rate? _____

Standard & Poor's 500 Stock Index (S&P 500)

5. What is the highest 1-year return on the S&P 500? _____

6. What is the lowest 1-year return on the S&P 500? _____

7. What is the difference between the highest and lowest S&P 500 returns? _____

8. What is the historical average return on the S&P 500 stock index? _____

Answers:

1: 18.0% (August 1981); 2: 0.6% (June 2012); 3: 17.4% (18.0 – 0.6%); 4: 5.8% (from Federal Reserve records); 5: 45% (1954); 6: -39% (2008); 7: 84%; 8: 12%

From this example, you can see that (on average) 6-month CDs have returned less than 6 percent while the S&P 500 stock index has returned 12 percent. Historically, stocks have enjoyed higher returns than CDs. The conclusion is pretty clear: If you're looking for good, long-term growth, stocks perform better than bank investments.

Notice that even though CDs don't have negative returns, their returns vary from year to year. Over time, you cannot be certain about what returns you will receive on CDs. In the financial world, this uncertainty about returns is known as risk and can be measured.

However, we don't get higher returns without higher risk. In the example above, we find that the difference between the highest and lowest returns on CDs is 17 percent. Compare that to the S&P 500 Index, which has a whopping 84 percent spread between the highest and lowest return. The greater variation of stock returns means that stock investments have more risk than CDs.

In Illustration 2, I've included a chart showing five more asset classes: small company stocks, large company stocks, long-term government bonds, intermediate-term government bonds, and short-term government bills. Next to each I've listed the compound annual rate of return and its risk as measured by its standard deviation. I've also included a chart showing each group's annual returns from 1926 through 2012.

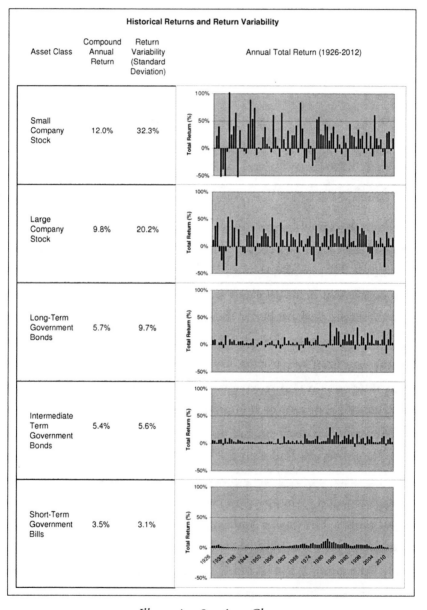

Illustration 2 – Asset Classes

Stocks

In the graphs, notice the two stock groups – small company stocks and large company stocks. While both groups represent stocks, the return bars on the small company stocks reach higher and lower than the bars on the large company stock graph. Some even reach all the way to the top and bottom. These graphs visually illustrate that the variability of returns (risk) is higher for small stocks than for large stocks. In other words, from year to year, the potential gains or losses on small stock investments are greater than that for large stocks.

In these samples I've listed a number tagged "return variability." Mathematicians know this number *as standard deviation.* It is a mathematical measurement of risk for each investment. While there are many ways to mathematically measure the variation risk of an investment, standard deviation is one of the more common. An in-depth description of standard deviation is beyond the scope of this book. Nevertheless, you don't need to be a mathematician to appreciate this concept. Just remember, the higher the standard deviation, the higher the risk. By looking at the standard deviation number, we can see that small company stocks bear more risk than large company stocks.

Bonds

Continuing on to the bonds, the numbers show that they have less risk than the stocks. However, a closer look at the charts shows that the risk varies depending on the maturity length of the bonds. The longer-term bonds have more volatility than the shorter-term bonds.

Likewise, when we look at the annual compounded return of each investment group, we find a general truth: Investments that provide higher returns generally carry higher risk. This is not an accident – it is a social phenomenon. Over the long term, investors will put their money into riskier investments only if they receive higher returns. These charts reflect that trend.

Asset Classes

As I discussed before, the term asset class represents categories into which financial professionals group investments. Even though there are no hard and fast rules on how to group investments, there are some generally used categories. Below, I've listed a couple of asset classification systems.

This system categorizes stocks by size and growth vs. value styles:

United States Stocks

    Small-Size Company Stocks

        Value Stocks

        Growth Stocks

    Medium-Size Company Stocks

        Value Stocks

        Growth Stocks

    Large-Size Company Stocks

        Value Stocks

        Growth Stocks

This system categorizes stocks by sector:

Utilities

Consumer Staples

Consumer Discretionary

Healthcare

Energy

Technology

Material

Financials

Industrials

Foreign stocks can be categorized by these methods as well as by region and whether the country is *developed* (e.g., Europe) or *emerging* (e.g., China).

Likewise, interest-bearing investments can be categorized in various ways.

Loanership
> Money Markets
> Certificates of Deposit
> Fixed Annuities
> U.S. Government Bonds
>> Long-Term Bonds
>> Medium-Term Bonds
>> Short-Term Bills
> Corporate Bonds
>> High-Quality Bonds
>>> Long-Term Bonds
>>> Medium-Term Bonds
>>> Short-Term Notes
>> Medium-Quality Bonds
>>> Long-Term Bonds
>>> Medium-Term Bonds
>>> Short-Term Notes
>> High-Yield Bonds (Low Quality)
>>> Long-Term Bonds
>>> Medium-Term Bonds
>>> Short-Term Notes
> Municipal Bonds
>> High-Quality Bonds
>>> Long-Term Bonds
>>> Medium-Term Bonds
>>> Short-Term Bonds
>> Medium-Quality Bonds
>>> Long-Term Bonds
>>> Medium-Term Bonds
>>> Short-Term Bonds

High-Yield Bonds (Low Quality)
Long-Term Bonds
Medium-Term Bonds
Short-Term Bonds
Foreign Bonds (Government and Corporate Bonds)

Diversification

Once you understand the concept of asset classes, you can use this knowledge to evaluate your diversification. In any given year, some asset classes will do better than others. By diversifying your portfolio between different asset classes, you will reap the higher potential long-term rates of return provided by the capital markets while substantially reducing your risk.

Since most investors use mutual funds, it is important to understand that each mutual fund has its own asset allocation. To determine the overall allocation of your portfolio, you need to dissect each of your mutual funds and then add up the parts.

For example, suppose an investor has a very simple portfolio. The portfolio is evenly divided between mutual fund A and mutual fund B. Mutual fund A is allocated 50 percent to large growth stocks and 50 percent to large value stocks. Mutual fund B is allocated 50 percent to large growth stocks and 50 percent to long-term government bonds. This investor's overall portfolio allocation is 50 percent large growth stock, 25 percent large value stock, and 25 percent long-term government bonds.

Think Ahead

Without proper evaluation, finding and managing your portfolio's allocation can be complicated and time-consuming. The only way to take control of your portfolio's allocation is to determine the overall design of your portfolio before the first investment is made.

Many investors do not realize that mutual funds often contain a complicated mix of asset classes. The more complicated the funds, the harder it is to determine how a portfolio is allocated.

A couple of years ago, a man asked for my assistance in evaluating his portfolio. Even though he assured me that he was well-diversified, I was unprepared for what I found. When I examined his holdings, I learned that he had over 50 different mutual funds. Because he had so many mutual funds (each with a different allocation), it was almost impossible to determine his overall allocation.

When I asked him how he came by so many different funds, he told me the story of each. A guy he saw on television managed one. A newspaper journalist recommended another. A fellow worker recommended another. And so on. Because his portfolio had so many funds and was built in such a willy-nilly fashion, he had no way of determining his overall allocation. He had no idea how much of his portfolio was in large company stocks, small company stocks, or foreign stocks. There is no doubt that he would have been much better off owning only a few well-chosen mutual funds. He would have had plenty of diversity and better control

Selecting a Portfolio

In my opinion, the process that most investment companies use to help retirees create an investment portfolio is not thorough enough. The usual process begins and ends with evaluating what is called *investing temperament*. Investing temperament is how the investor "feels" about having losses and gains in his portfolio. In creating Retirement Solutions, I believe that we need to go deeper. We need to take a financial look at how we will achieve retirement goals.

For example, when you get help from most firms – whether from a well-know national brokerage firm or a do-it-yourself mutual fund company – the process is similar. The company asks you a series of questions which basically boils down to the single question: "Are you conservative, moderate, or aggressive in your investment strategy?" You choose one and the company presents you with a boilerplate portfolio recommendation. I believe this process often results in a portfolio of investments that may not be right for the investor.

I believe that in addition to determining an investor's temperament, a financial analysis should be conducted to make sure the investment portfolio works financially. You want to make sure the investment mix is not too conservative – the returns not meeting the retiree's needs. You also want to make sure the portfolio is not too aggressive – exposing the retiree to risks that could destroy his retirement.

Conclusion

Asset allocation is an easy-to-understand premise: Since similar investments provide comparable returns and experience comparable risk, they can be lumped together into groups called *asset classes*. The two broadest asset classes are loanership (interest-type investments) and ownership (stock-type investments). Within these classifications, investments can be further subclassified. Since asset allocation allows you to easily control returns and risks, it simplifies investment decisions.

When creating a retirement solution portfolio, asset allocation provides a starting point in evaluating potential risk and returns of your Retirement Solutions. ◆

Chapter 10

Win By Not Losing – Asymmetric Investing

L et me ask you three questions. First, are you worried the stock market might experience a sharp decline in the future? Second, are you worried that the stock market will continue to stagnate? Third, would you feel better if you used an investment strategy that could not only protect you against a drop in the market but could also perform well in a languishing market?

If you answered "yes" to these questions, then this chapter is for you. The strategy in these pages has been extremely effective over the past decade at mitigating losses during market free falls and creating outstanding returns in a flat market.

Let me explain a little bit about what Asymmetric Investing is, how it works, and how to use it.

First, let's talk about symmetric and asymmetric or symmetry vs. asymmetry. When we say something is symmetric, we mean there is an equality about it. For example, Illustration 6 shows two figures. The figure on the right is symmetric. If we draw a line down the middle, each side would look like a reflection of the other. The figure on the left is asymmetrical. There is no line we could draw in the figure to make the two halves look the same. As you can see, the idea of symmetric and asymmetric is easy to understand.

Asymmetric Figure   Symmetric Figure

Illustration 6 – Symmetric and Asymmetrical

Symmetric and Asymmetric Games

Likewise, sporting games can be symmetrical and asymmetrical. I think boxing is a terrific example of a perfectly symmetrical sport. Two men square off and try to beat each other senseless. The symmetry is easy to see; two men facing off mano a mano.

Most sports are not so symmetrical. In my part of the world, football is king. Football is a great example of an asymmetric game. What do I mean? Football is asymmetric because the strategy used by each team changes depending on who has the ball. When a team possesses the ball, it plays offense. The offensive team uses a whole set of strategies designed to get the ball down the field. On the other hand, the defensive team uses a whole other set of strategies designed to prevent the offensive team from scoring. The strategy each team uses during the game will change depending whether it is playing offense or defense.

Symmetric Investing

In the investing world, most portfolio management is symmetric. The most popular symmetric strategy is called *buy and hold*. This strategy is simple: We diversify our portfolio among a wide variety of investment classes and then hold them for the long haul. We "buy" a set of investments and "hold" them. No matter what happens in the market, you hold after you buy. The strategy is symmetric. It doesn't change.

During decades when the market was relatively stable and rising, the symmetric strategy of "buy and hold" proved extremely profitable for investors.

The Lost Decade – Frustrating Symmetric Investors

Since the September 11 attacks on New York City in 2001, the stock markets have suffered two of the four largest declines in modern history. From 2000 to 2002, the markets fell around 40 percent. Then, in 2008, the markets suffered a drop of over 50 percent. These two declines resulted in what is now commonly called *The Lost Decade* in which the stock markets produced little or no returns over a ten-year period for buy and hold investors.

Market Timing – The Most Popular Asymmetric Investment Strategy

There are several types of asymmetric strategies. The concept called *market timing* represents the most popular. Market timing is simply buying low and selling high. When the market reaches a low point, you buy. When the market reaches the top, you sell. Unfortunately, there are insurmountable problems with trying to time the market. The first issue is that you never know when you have reached the bottom or when you have reached the top until after the fact.

The second problem is emotion. The fact is that the emotions of most do-it-yourself investors ruin their returns. As a matter of proof, Dalbar, a well-respected research company has published a number of papers over the past two decades showing most investors ruin their returns by moving money in and out of the markets. In their latest report, Dalbar contrasted the S&P 500's 20-year annual return of 8.2 percent with an average investor return of 3.17 percent. Most investors cost themselves about 5 percent per year trying to time the market.

As we discussed in Chapter 8, I call this effect the *Perspiration Cost*. Simply put, when the market falls, many investors get scared and take their money out of the market. After the market recovers, investors begin to feel better and put their money back in. In other words, they sell low and buy high – just the opposite of what you want to do. The bottom line is that market timing cannot be done reliably and should not be attempted.

So, if we can't implement market timing successfully, does this mean we should avoid using an asymmetric approach altogether. Not necessarily. Some asymmetric approaches have the potential to work extremely well.

The 3F Strategy

One specific Asymmetric Investment strategy has worked very well over the past decade. It's an approach I call the *Three Factor Strategy* or *3F Strategy*, for short. The approach is the result of a lot of smart people doing decades of study in the behavior of financial markets. Consequently, no one person or institution can claim to be the "father" of the approach or the sole practitioner of its implementation. Of all the asymmetric investment approaches I have studied over the years, I believe the 3F Strategy is one of the best. It is supported by research and successful implementation.

Offense and Defense

So how does the 3F Strategy work? Conceptually, the strategy manages your portfolio like a coach manages a football team. As we discussed earlier about asymmetric games, sometimes the team plays offense. Sometimes it plays defense. The question then becomes, how do we know when to play offense and when to play defense in our portfolio?

Momentum

Research has shown the stock market possesses what statisticians call *auto-correlation* or what financial people refer to as *momentum*. This concept simply means that if the stock market has been going up in the past, it is statistically more likely to continue going up in the future. Likewise, if the market has been heading down, statistically, it is more likely to continue going down in the future.

To go back to the football analogy, momentum tells us "who has the ball." If the market momentum is moving in our favor, we have the ball and need to play offense. If the momentum is moving against us, then we don't have the ball, and we need to play defense. Logically, the next question is, "how do we measure momentum?"

Measuring Momentum – The Three Factors

The reason I call this strategy "The Three Factor Strategy" is that it uses three primary factors to measure the direction and magnitude of the stock market's momentum.

The three factors are:

1. price level (whether market prices are relatively high or low).
2. volatility (how much prices are fluctuating).
3. the change in volatility (whether the relative price fluctuations are increasing or decreasing).

By using these three factors, we determine which direction the momentum is moving. For example, in a relatively expensive, volatile market, where the volatility is increasing, the momentum would be against us. Our portfolio would be playing defense. On the other hand, in a relatively cheap market with low and declining volatility, the momentum would be in our favor. Our portfolio would be playing offense.

Implementation – Breaking the Markets Apart

My favorite implementation of the 3F Strategy breaks the financial markets into different groups, then plays offense and defense for each group. Using this scenario, the strategy moves our portfolio in and out of various sectors.

Every one of the 500 stocks in the S&P 500 Index can be classified into one of nine groups called *sectors*. Sectors include technology, utilities, materials, industrials, healthcare, financials, energy, consumer staples, and consumer discretionary.

With implementation of the 3F Strategy, each sector would be evaluated by the three factors for momentum. Our portfolio would then play offense or defense by weighting the sectors appropriately.

What Are the Potential Downsides?

Every investment and investment strategy has pros and cons. So what are the downsides to using the 3F Strategy? First, there are no guarantees. Like any investment prospectus will tell you, past performance does not guarantee future results.

Second, the 3F Strategy requires work to implement. Since it is an active strategy (i.e., the portfolio is being monitored and changes are being made), it requires daily attention to the markets and a good bit of statistical number crunching. As you might guess, this amount of attention incurs higher costs.

The third disadvantage is that in regular (non-IRA) accounts, the 3F Strategy is not as tax efficient as a passive buy and hold strategy. Because the strategy is active, the investments could be sold at any time. As you know, when investments are sold with gains, taxes are due. (Obviously, in IRA accounts, this is not an issue.)

However, even with these disadvantages, in a volatile period such as the past decade, I believe these issues are more than offset by the benefits.

What Are the Potential Advantages?

- The strategy is automatic. It works while you sleep.
- The strategy is completely liquid. It has no surrender penalties or time commitment.
- The strategy does not use options or derivatives.
- The strategy protected investors in 2002 and 2008 downturns.

Conclusion

For investors who are worried that the stock market might experience a sharp decline in the future and who would be more comfortable with a strategy to protect their downside, an active asymmetric strategy should be considered. Even though this type of strategy does incur higher investment costs, the advantages of portfolio protection and peace of mind could be well worth the cost. ◆

Chapter 11

Choosing A Portfolio Solution

Use An Empirical Approach

There are countless investments and investment strategies available today. Not all of them are good or appropriate for everyone. Retirees, more than anyone, should take great care when making investment decisions. Unlike young workers just starting out, retirees cannot start over. They need to preserve what they have. I believe the best way to invest is by using an *empirical approach*.

To illustrate what I mean by an empirical approach, let's use an analogy and step back to the year 1900. The question I propose is, what would you need at the beginning of the 20th century to go into the pharmaceutical business? You would need a few jars, some turpentine, cocaine, opium, and anything else you wanted to put in your so-called "medicine." And without interference, you could stick labels on your jars claiming the concoction cures everything from colds, cholera, tuberculosis, cancer, yellow fever, polio, warts, and everything in between. The fact is that in 1900, customers bought medicine at their own peril. Medicines frequently were ineffective, contaminated, and downright dangerous.

Flash forward to the beginning of the 21st century. Things look a lot different. Today, when a pharmaceutical company brings a substance to market, it has to prove several things.

First, the pharmaceutical company has to prove that the medication doesn't hurt people. Second, it has to prove that the substance is effective and does some good. And third, the company needs to show that the drug is at least as effective as drugs already on the market. The way companies provide this proof is through *empirical evidence*. They do trials and then statistically analyze the results.

I believe that the state of today's financial industry is very much like the pharmaceutical industry of 1900. Anybody with a good idea can pretty much sell anything they want. For this reason, I think we need to be very careful about the investments and investment strategies that we use.

Because we have a "buyer beware" investment world, I believe that investment vehicles and strategies should be selected using four criteria. First, I recommend that strategies be *quantitative* – based on numbers, not feelings, or hunches, or some superstar stock picker. Second, I need to see empirical evidence that the strategy has actually worked. Third, I want a deep understanding of exactly *how* the strategy works. Fourth, I like to see peer-reviewed research by smart guys (i.e., well respected academic researchers) that give credibility to the approach.

The Three General Portfolio Approaches

One of the most truthful posits in the financial world is that there is no free lunch. If you are going to get higher returns, one way or the other you will have to pay for them. The two ways we "pay" for higher returns is either by paying higher fees or taking higher risk.

Let's look at this another way. Here are the three things every retiree wants in his portfolio:

1. Higher returns

2. Lower costs

3. Lower risk

However, the financial world has a sense of humor. The fact is that an investor can have any two of these, but not all three. This fact means that there are three general approaches to retirement investing:

- Approach 1: Higher returns + lower cost = higher risk.
- Approach 2: Higher returns + lower risk = higher cost.
- Approach 3: Lower risk + lower cost = lower returns.

Approach 1: Higher Return, Lower Cost Strategies

Generally, low cost strategies include buy and hold portfolios using low cost stock market mutual funds. The advantage of this approach is that over the long haul, portfolio returns are enhanced by lower costs. The disadvantage is that there are no strategies in place to protect the portfolio in the event the market declines sharply or for an extended period of time.

Approach 2: Higher Return, Lower Risk Strategies

Higher cost strategies include using stock market investments with guarantees or active (asymmetric) strategies. These include variable annuities with lifetime income guarantees or principal guarantees as well as actively managed stock market strategies. Whatever strategy you use, make sure you evaluate it empirically and thoroughly. Just because an investment vehicle has a higher cost doesn't mean you automatically get better protection.

Approach 3: Lower Risk, Lower Cost Strategies

These strategies generally use interest rate investments (i.e., what I call *loanership* investments) to provide relatively stable principal and relatively low costs. The advantage is that costs and risk are low. The disadvantage is that returns are usually low, as well.

No matter how we invest, we are continually moving our investment portfolio between risk, reward, and cost.

Be Ready to Evolve

Over the two decades I have been a financial advisor, the mix of investments and investment strategies that I use with my clients has changed. For example, in the early 1990s, interest rates were relatively high and market returns strong. A typical portfolio was a well-diversified mix of stock market mutual funds and interest rate investments.

As the go-go 90s gave way to the more volatile New Millennium and a Post-911 World, more often I began utilizing variable annuities with guarantees. These strategies provided wary retirees with income security and peace of mind.

After the crash of 2008, interest rates plunged to zero and insurance companies slashed the benefits on their variable annuities. As a result, I did not feel that either of these strategies provided the types of returns or safety that was needed for my clients. I had to rethink my portfolio strategies. I began utilizing asymmetric investment strategies with excellent results to provide higher returns and mitigated risk.

As you can see, the strategies I use evolve as the financial world changes. There are new opportunities but there are also new risks. I believe that the best financial advisors continually monitor the investment world and reevaluate where the opportunities lie for their clients. I fully expect that my recommendations will continue to evolve as the world changes.

TEOTWAWKI

When I was a kid, I stayed up late on Friday and Saturday nights watching old black-and-white horror films on television. After each film, I retreated to my bunk bed, terrified that the evening's monster would somehow find its way into my darkened room. One night, I would be afraid of Frankenstein's monster; the next evening, I feared Count Dracula's pointy fangs.

In the same way, we Americans collectively fear our own imaginary monsters. In the 1960s, we feared that the USSR might bomb us. In the 1970s, we feared that OPEC would deprive us of energy. In the 1980s, we were certain that Japan would soon purchase our more desirable states. In the 1990s, thousands feared impending doom from the Y2K bug. In the 2000s we feared terrorism. So far in the early 2010s, we have been dealing with worldwide debt downgrades and the never-ending European economic crises.

The one thing that is far worse than any of these crises is our own fearfulness. The worst mistakes an investor can make is to act on the belief that the world is about to end. I have seen many people ruin their financial situations preparing for "the end of the world as we know it," also known as *TEOTWAWKI*. The fear of impending disaster diverts people's resources and causes them to make bad decisions.

During my lifetime, there have always been TEOTWAWKI gurus – people who proclaim that the end is near. By manipulating the media's insatiable appetite for an exciting story and preying on people's fear of disaster, these con artists attract many fearful followers. Without fail, these "prophets of doom" have the prescription for our salvation. If we just buy their book and follow their advice, we will survive.

Many times the advice is to purchase a warehouse of supplies, such as blankets, camouflage clothing, guns, ammunition, large amounts of food, and specialty gear such as electrical generators and water purifiers. If the expense of all this junk doesn't financially ruin their followers, their investment advice usually does. Most investment recommendations usually include buying commodities such as gold, silver, or old coins. Close examination reveals that those who follow this kind of advice often lose a lot of money. At the very least, they end up with a bunch of camping gear they don't need and a portfolio full of crummy investments. History's lesson: pessimism doesn't pay.

I remember watching a news show in 1999. The reporter interviewed a family in the midst of making extravagant preparations for the impending Y2K collapse. This family bought all the gear and even built an underground shelter in their back yard. Whatever money they had left was plowed into gold and silver. At the conclusion of the broadcast, the reporter asked, "So what has all this preparation cost? Has it been expensive?" Without thinking, the wife blurted out, "Yes it has. If the end of the world doesn't come soon, we're going to go broke." While most investors are not quite this extreme, there is a parallel path of fear many investors follow.

It may sound paradoxical, but I believe that to be successful in your retirement planning, you need to be optimistic. Being optimistic doesn't mean that you stick your head in the sand and ignore what's going on in the world. There's a huge difference between awareness and stark fear of imaginary monsters. Later in this book, I will discuss the only monster you should fear, and the only time that I believe you should become extremely defensive in your decisions is when a depression is looming. Luckily, depressions are extremely rare and can often be identified before they strike. You can learn the signs and put strategies in place to protect yourself.

Aside from that one circumstance, it is best to remain optimistic in your planning. In my experience, pessimism means trading off choices for damage control and brings with it unattractive rates of return. Optimism, on the other hand, frees you to make good decisions and take advantage of fabulous investment opportunities. I believe that optimism provides rich rewards.

Conclusion

In choosing a retirement portfolio, we need to be careful choosing the investments and strategies we use. First, I recommend that retirees take an empirical, numbers-based approach. Second, retirees need to understand themselves and how they will react to upheavals in the financial markets. Third, retirees need to pursue an investing approach that matches their financial situation and investing temperament. Fourth, we need to continually monitor the changing financial world to identify new opportunities. And finally, we need to remain optimistic. ◆

Chapter 12

Your Financial Advisor

O ne of the most critical decisions you'll ever make in your investing career is choosing a financial professional. A good financial professional can help you create a sound retirement solution. He or she can help you select appropriate investments, lower your taxes, and prepare you for the unexpected. I believe that choosing a good financial advisor can be one of the best decisions a retiree or soon-to-be retiree can make.

However, in the world of investments (or financial planning) there's a great deal of confusion and misinformation. This is certainly true when talking about financial professionals. Areas of confusion include licensing, certification, compensation, and independence. In this chapter, I will unravel the mysterious world of financial professionals.

Do-It-Yourself

When talking about financial advisors, the best place to start is with the do-it-yourself crowd. We all know someone who practices do-it-yourself financial planning. He makes all his own investment decisions, fills out all his own investment forms, and probably even completes his own will and estate-planning documents. While the do-it-yourself approach may be right for some, most investors should avoid it. There are too many things that can go wrong. One imprudent decision or missed opportunity can cost you dearly. A good financial professional can be, literally, worth his or her weight in gold.

A Secure Retirement Gone Wrong

Several years ago Don and Celeste came to me seeking help. Their retirement was in severe trouble. Unfortunately, two decades of inflation and poor decisions had caused major damage to their financial security. At that late stage, the best I could do was to help them patch up a bad situation.

In 1976, Don had retired from a large oil company in Houston where he was an engineer. His retirement package included an annual pension of $10,000 and a $150,000 lump sum rollover. Don and Celeste had achieved what most people would like – retirement at age 50. They were happy.

Like all retirees, Don and Celeste wanted security. As a do-it-yourself financial planner, Don calculated that all he needed to do was invest their money in bank CDs. Between their interest income and the $10,000 pension, he figured that they would have plenty of money for living expenses. He was confident that he had everything under control.

By 1996, things were not going well. Don and Celeste were barely getting by. During the previous 20 years, prices had risen dramatically, while interest rates plunged to 30-year lows. Not only could they no longer afford to travel, they were having trouble paying for the necessities such as groceries, clothes, and utilities. What once appeared to be a secure retirement was no longer adequate.

Don and Celeste are not alone. Many retirees fail to obtain good financial guidance. A good advisor early in their retirement could have counseled them about the ravages of inflation. In fact, with sound Investment Solutions, Don and Celeste would be enjoying more financial security and freedom now than when they first retired. Financial planning is one of those areas in which people get into trouble from dangers they never knew existed. In Don and Celeste's case, they weren't aware that inflation and falling interest rates could impoverish them.

Other issues should be addressed, as well. Besides helping you create an income solution, your professional should help you recognize important income tax issues, estate-planning problems, disability dangers, and issues surrounding other benefits such as Social Security and Medicare. Let's take a closer look at how to find a good financial advisor.

Licenses

A lady once called me on the phone and asked, "Do you have a license?" I replied that I did. She responded, "Well, I'm looking for a planner who doesn't have a license."

The conversation was so odd that I remember it to this day. I couldn't help but wonder whether her doctor, her dentist, and her attorney were unlicensed as well. The fact is that the federal government and every state in the union require licensing of people who handle securities and who provide financial advice.

There are a variety of securities licenses. The securities laws outline two broad categories of licensing – *investment advisory* and *brokerage*. The idea is that an investment advisory license allows a professional to advise clients for a fee while a brokerage license allows a commission to be earned.

The most widely used investment advisory license is the *Registered Investment Advisory* license or *RIA*. The RIA relationship is becoming extremely popular with investors and regulators for good reason. The RIA arrangement tends to be extremely transparent with all fees charged directly to the client. There are no hidden charges, fees, or commissions.

On the brokerage side, the Series 7 is the most comprehensive license. This license allows an investment professional to provide a full range of investments by charging a commission. Professionals with this license can provide advice and service on any listed investments, including stocks, bonds, mutual funds, options, and futures.

Another type of license financial professionals frequently possess is an insurance license. Currently, insurance licenses are issued on the state level only. Having an insurance license allows a financial professional to provide more than just hazard and life insurance to his or her clients. It allows the financial professional to provide investments such as fixed annuities and variable annuities.

Counterintuitively, there is not a single best license. Different types of investments require different types of licenses. Some investment strategies are only available under the RIA license. Other investments require a Series 7 license, and others require an insurance license. To help their clients most effectively, good financial professionals will possess all three licenses – the RIA, the Series 7 license, and the insurance license. By having all three licenses, an investment professional can reach deep into the world of investments to get whatever their client needs.

I believe that being licensed is just the starting point. Don't get me wrong, passing the Series 7 licensing exam is not easy (the failure rate is quite high). Nevertheless, the licensing requirements only set a minimum level of competency. Since the decisions that retirees and soon-to-be retirees make are absolutely critical to their financial security, they should choose a financial professional who is more than just licensed. They need to choose someone with a high level of training and experience. In my opinion, every retiree and soon-to-be retiree needs an experienced Certified Financial Planner™ Certificant.

Financial Planners: Certified vs. Uncertified

Anyone can use the title "financial planner." It requires no training, experience, or licensing. Unfortunately, since there are no restrictions on using the title, the moniker is frequently adopted by those who should not be giving advice. In fact, I recommend that investors be wary of anyone using this term who has no financial planning credentials.

On the other hand, the term, Certified Financial Planner™ Certificant (CFP®) indicates a professional who has extensive experience, knowledge in financial planning, and adherence to a Code of Ethics. To be certified, a professional must have at least three years of financial planning experience, 18 college hours of special training, and pass a grueling two-day exam. (The failure rate for this exam is frequently higher than 45 percent.) Unlike Series 7 and insurance licensing requirements, the Certified Financial Planner™ Certificant certification seeks to set a high standard of mastery in financial planning. Without a doubt, there are many financial planning certifications (and more every day); however, the CFP® certification has become the gold standard in the industry. It is an extremely difficult certification to achieve and the most widely recognized for its excellence. Since this certification is so demanding, those who have achieved CFP® status have committed themselves to a high level of knowledge, training, and ethical standards.

Independent vs. National Firms

Quite frequently I get the question, "It seems like everyone these days is providing financial planning and investment advice. Who should I choose? My bank? A big brokerage firm? Who?"

My answer is very simple: Choose the best independent Certified Financial Planner™ Certificant you can find and avoid the large national firms. To understand why, we need to look more closely at who's who in the investment world. We need to discuss broker-dealers and their relationships to your financial professional.

Broker-Dealers

As I discussed earlier, every financial professional is required to possess a securities license. This license must be placed with a securities firm who will be legally responsible for overseeing the professional's activities and compliance of the securities laws. This securities firm is known as an *broker-dealer*, or *BD*. (The BD probably operates under a Registered Investment Advisory license, as well. But for simplicity, we will call the firm a BD.)

In general, there are two basic types of BDs: large national firms and independently owned private firms. One of the major decisions in every financial professional's career is whether to go *national* or to go *independent*. You would easily recognize the names of most national firms. They advertise heavily in all forms of media – television, radio, magazines, and newspapers. Not an evening goes by that I don't see the ads of several large brokerage houses during my favorite television shows.

To an inexperienced, newly licensed broker, big-name firms offer many advantages. National firms offer support, training, and guidance. Most importantly, because of their heavy advertising and wide name recognition these big companies provide a steady stream of prospective clients. A national firm makes it much easier for a beginning broker to survive the learning curve and become established.

Likewise, many investors feel that choosing a big-name brokerage house enhances their financial security. However, it has been my experience that selecting an investment advisory firm based on name recognition could be a mistake. Advisors at these companies often are forced to put the brokerage firm's corporate objectives ahead of their clients' goals. As an investor, you don't want your advisor's advice to be compromised; you want your goals to come first.

Big Firms' Track Records

Historically, some large firms have been found to give special incentives to their salespeople who push proprietary products such as mutual funds or a stock share offering. For example, national firms may pressure their brokers into moving excess stock inventory or selling their own brand-name mutual funds. While these practices may coincide with their investors' goals, there is a very real possibility they may not. This kind of corporate pressure on brokers can compromise their ability to serve their clients. This is why I believe that every investor should choose a professional who is *independent.*

Independence – The Better Way

Being independent versus nonindependent is a matter of who works for whom. It is an important philosophical difference that can have very real implications for your future. In essence, an independent financial professional has the freedom to work for you. He or she is free from the broker-dealer's corporate objectives and is able to put your goals, aspirations, and dreams first.

So how can you tell if your advisor is independent? Simply ask. "Do you work for a large national firm or are you independent?" Everyone in the financial world knows exactly what this means. If the broker tries to avoid or reconfigure your question, he or she probably works for a large national firm. Independent advisors are very proud of their independence and will be very impressed with your question.

How Advisors Get Paid

The number one question I get about advisors is "How do they get paid?" The reason for confusion in this area is understandable – times are changing. What was once a very straightforward commission-based industry is now complicated with choices from back-end fees to investment advisory fees. The two main ways financial professionals are compensated are:

- Commissions
- Advisory fees

Each has its advantages and disadvantages. Even though there is no one best way to compensate your financial professional, knowing the differences between each will help you make the right decision for you.

Commissions

Historically, the financial world has been closely associated with commissions. Since the early days of the stock market, brokers placed trades for clients – either buying or selling securities – and charged a commission for the transaction. Today, most investors don't want to be sold an investment. They want high-quality advice and help from an experienced professional. Because the demand for ongoing, quality advice is increasing, the way financial professionals are compensated is changing. You can see this change reflected in the new types of commission structures now available. Commissions can be lumped into three basic structures: (1) front-end commissions, (2) surrender-period commissions, and (3) level commissions.

Front-End Commissions

The most well-known type of commission is referred to as a front-end commission. Very simply, this is a commission that is charged when the investment is made. With a front-end commission, you always will see an immediate reduction in your account value. Stocks and certain mutual funds often carry this type of charge. For example, in mutual funds, this type of commission is known as an *A-share commission*. It works like this:

Suppose you invest $10,000 into an A-share mutual fund. If you examined your account immediately after making the investment, you would notice that the value had dropped slightly (often around 4 to 5 percent). That immediate dip is due to the front-end commission.

Surrender-Period Commissions

The next type of commission is known as *surrender-period commissions*. Many investments such as certificates of deposit, fixed annuities, variable annuities, and B-share mutual funds may carry surrender periods. As long as your money is left in the investment for a specified period of time, the account incurs no penalty. If you liquidate early, a penalty is deducted. This penalty period is designed to keep investors committed to their investment long enough for the investment provider (e.g., mutual fund company) to recover marketing costs. In general, surrender-period investments usually have higher internal costs than their front-end cousins. Even so, many people prefer surrender-period investments because there is no initial drop in their account value. All their money goes to work right away.

Advisory Fees and Level Commissions

Since advisory fees and level commissions share many of the same advantages, I'll discuss these together. Unlike front-end and back-end commissions, which pay the advisor a big fee up front and little thereafter, advisory fees and level commissions pay an advisor a consistent annual fee as long as you're a client. Typically, these fees run around 1 to 2 percent per year.

Over the past few years, these arrangements have become extremely popular for three reasons. They are often better at matching the professional's compensation with the services rendered, they are better at aligning the goals of the investor and the investment advisor, and they free the investor from up-front fees or back-end penalties.

In the old days of finance, commissions were king. Brokers spent countless hours making cold calls trying to sell stocks, bonds, and mutual funds. As a reward for their efforts, they were paid commissions. However, in the new world of financial planning, service is king. People no longer want to be sold an investment. They want someone with knowledge, experience, and training to look over their entire financial picture to help them chart a course for success. People want a long-term advisory relationship with an experienced financial professional.

Because of this fundamental change, front-end and back-end commissions often impede the relationship between financial professionals and their clients. From the client's point of view, why should the professional get a large fee up front? After all, most of the services will be provided over the next 5, 10, or even 20 years.

Likewise, a level fee often frees professionals to provide better ongoing service for existing clients. Common sense tells us that a financial professional cannot service an account forever if it produces no income. Financial professionals who charge only transaction commissions usually need a continuous stream of new clients to stay in business. Unfortunately, as their client bases bulge, the clients frequently suffer. Transactional professionals eventually have to ration their services away from servicing existing clients to acquiring new ones.

From the investor's point of view, the main difference between advisory fees and level commissions is how they're charged. Typically, advisory fees are charged directly to an investor's account, while level commissions are paid from the investment's internal costs. Investors who use the advisory fee approach see a charge from their account when the fees are paid. Investments that use level commissions show no visible charges (e.g., 12b-1 fees). Since these fees are deducted from within the fund itself, the investor never sees a direct charge to the statement. Neither is better or worse than the other; they are but two approaches to the same objective.

Fee-Only Planners

There are many planners who advertise as *fee-only*. Since this is a relatively new term, there is quite a bit of confusion over its meaning. Many people think that a fee-only planner charges only hourly fees. Most of the time, he or she does not; the fee referred to is a portfolio advisory fee. To add to the confusion, I see some planners using the term fee-only to describe themselves. They present themselves as *fee-only planners*. In this usage, the advisors are representing themselves as professionals who only work on fees and never use a commission basis for any client. In my opinion, the usage of "fee-only" is mostly just a marketing gimmick. It really doesn't mean much in terms of getting a better advisor. Let's look at why.

Fee-Only Accounts

To add a final complication, the term fee-only also can be used to describe a type of account – a *fee-only account*. As I described earlier, a fee-only account is charged fees and not commissions. Under this usage of the term, a planner may have fee-only clients as well as commission-based clients.

It's also important to note that fee-only accounts don't always work for everyone. For example, many fee-based programs require large account sizes to open. This means that if an advisor only works on fees, he or she may have to turn away smaller clients. I don't believe that anyone seeking financial help should be denied because of account size.

Double Dipping

Several years ago, a couple transferred their account to me from another firm. When I carefully examined their old account, I found that the previous broker had been *double dipping*. Double dipping is an easy term to understand. It means that the broker is getting paid twice. In this case, the unscrupulous advisor had been investing the couple's money in commissioned mutual funds as well as charging them an annual advisory fee. My experience shows that the vast majority of financial professionals practice with high ethical standards, and most would never engage in this type of behavior. Nevertheless, be on the lookout. Make sure you only are being charged one way – either commissions or advisory fees, but not both.

Hourly Fees

Some do-it-yourself financial gurus admonish their followers to do their own financial planning. However, when it comes to the difficult issues, they backpedal and recommend hiring a Certified Financial Planner™ Certificant on an hourly basis. Their advice sounds good in theory. Unfortunately, it usually doesn't work in the real world.

I regularly get phone calls from frustrated do-it-yourselfers trying to find an hourly Certified Financial Planner™ Certificant. After calling everyone in the phone book, they have learned that most planners won't take one-time, hourly engagements. I can understand why. My experience shows that few do-it-yourself investors actually follow through in completing the financial planning process. When the time comes to write a check for the planning service, they seem to lose interest. I doubt that any planner who tried to earn a living from these types of engagements would stay in business very long.

I've also found that hourly fees discourage people from the ongoing advisory process. Many times clients won't call their professionals with questions if they knows they're going to be charged for the time. As a result, many of these investors may make critical decisions without professional help.

Different Situations Require Different Compensation Structures

Like any professional, good financial advisors don't work for free. It is up to you and your advisor to choose the right compensation structure for you. In some cases, commissions may be best. In other cases, advisory fees may be right. There's no one-best method. All compensation structures have their advantages and disadvantages. The most important consideration is that you choose a professional you like and trust. A good professional will provide excellent service no matter which method you agree upon. Just be clear about how that advisor is to be paid. Experienced financial professionals are accustomed to questions about their fees and will openly discuss them with you.

Further Tips For Choosing Your Financial Advisor

Find Someone You Trust

You can have the best financial professional in the world, but if you don't trust him or her, you won't be happy. Your number one job in finding a financial professional is hiring someone you trust.

Find Someone Experienced

In my opinion, nothing sharpens a financial advisor more than experience. As a retiree or soon-to-be retiree, you cannot afford to make serious mistakes. You need someone who knows the tips, tricks, and nuances of financial planning. Without question, you want an advisor who has extensive experience.

Select Someone Who Specializes In Helping People Like You

Since the financial landscape is large, I recommend finding an advisor who specializes in clients with situations similar to your own. For example, the investment needs of retirees and soon-to-be retirees are very different than those of young families. Young families usually have small portfolios and need aggressive, high-growth, high-risk investments. On the other hand, retirees want to preserve their life savings. They often need investments that will generate income while preserving principal. As a retiree or soon-to-be retiree, you need an experienced professional who is familiar with the many complicated issues you'll be facing.

Get Someone Who Provides the Services You Want and Need

Make sure your professional provides the services you want and need. For example, if you want a monthly call, make sure your professional offers that service. Getting the ongoing services you expect will make your retirement much more enjoyable.

Choose Someone Who Has a Reputation
For Excellence and High Integrity

When selecting a financial advisor, choose someone with a good reputation. Ask around. The financial community is a small one. People who practice excellence will be well known. You should accept nothing less than the best.

Ask For References

When asked, every financial advisor should be willing to provide you with a list of clients as references. You can be sure that all these people will only say good things about the advisor. That's why they're on the list. Call them anyway. When you talk to these people, be friendly and find out who they are. You want an advisor who serves the pillars of the community. They hold (or have retired from) good jobs and positions of responsibility. A professional who attracts good people says a lot about his or her character.

How To Choose Your Unofficial Advisors

In the United States, we enjoy the fabulous right to freedom of speech. Nevertheless, every freedom has its price. In the investment world, the price is that anyone can offer financial advice – good or bad – without restriction. As long as a writer isn't getting a fee for specific investment advice or trying to manipulate the financial markets, there are no restrictions, no licenses, and no qualifications required.

I like to call these people unofficial advisors. Included in this group are authors of financial books, writers at newspapers and magazines, and personalities on television and radio. The newest kids on the block are the web authors who publish advice via the Internet. Collectively, these unofficial advisors provide a mountain of recommendations on everything from hot stock picks to IRA investments. Unfortunately, in this vast mountain of information, there is as much dirt as gems. In my opinion, there are many unqualified people offering inaccurate and sometimes harmful financial advice. Be careful.

A Writer's Goals May Not Be Your Goals

Often unofficial advisors try to set themselves apart by claiming that their advice is unfettered by commissions or advisory fees. They argue that they're unbiased writers; their advice is pure. I often see the opposite.

One of the burdens a writer bears is to be successful he or she must attract a large audience. The fact of media life is that the quickest way to attract a large audience is with alarmist statements, controversy, and conflict. Sound advice is often replaced by sound bites.

Ask the Hard Questions

Whenever you take advice from a writer in the media, you need to know his or her training, experience, and background. Don't judge an unofficial advisor by popularity or the scope and reach of his or her media (such as a large regional newspaper). I can easily name several best-selling authors and popular media personalities who every day dole out less-than-sterling advice. There is absolutely no correlation between an author being popular and his or her providing good advice.

I once called the office of a very popular financial columnist. When I asked about his educational background and experience, his assistant became very evasive and wouldn't give me much information. I later learned that he had no financial training whatsoever, nor had he held any position of responsibility in the financial world. Prior to writing his financial column, he had offered cooking advice in a large, northeastern newspaper. In fact, his only investment experience was his own mutual fund account. Yet he was handing out advice through one of the largest newspapers in the United States.

Am I saying that all popular writers and speakers offer poor advice? Not at all. But you need to apply the same tests to your unofficial advisors that you apply to your official ones. What type of training and experience does the advisor have? Is he or she a Certified Financial Planner™ Certificant? What positions of responsibility has he or she held in the financial world? Has he or she ever been responsible for other people's money? I find that the more training, real-world experience, and credentials a person has, the better his or her advice.

How Not to Choose an Advisor

At least once or twice a year I get a phone call that goes something like this: "Hi. I'm looking for a financial advisor. What kind of returns did your clients get in the last one-, three-, and five-year periods?"

While on the surface, this may sound like an intelligent question, in reality it is useless. Every investor is unique. Financial professionals manage a virtually infinite variety of portfolios. No two are exactly alike. Some are aggressive. Some are conservative. Some take income. Some do not. Some are designed with mutual funds or variable annuities. Others have individual stocks and bonds. In fact, this question brings us to what I call "the biggest secret in the world about investment professionals."

The Biggest Secret In the World About Investment Professionals

Are you sitting down? Because I'm about to tell you the "biggest secret in the world about investment professionals." It may shock you to learn that all investment professionals get their investments from . . . the same place. That's right. As Americans, we all live on the same soil, under the same sky. Likewise, we all invest in the same stock markets, bond markets, and interest-rate markets. While there are an infinite variety of investments, they all originate from the same capital markets.

No professional has a special investment or inside information that isn't available to everyone else.

Since all investment professionals invest in the same markets, does that mean all financial professionals are the same? Certainly not. Let's compare financial professionals to artists. Every artist in the world has access to the same paint and the same canvas as every other artist. They all shop at the same art supply stores. None has secret paint or a special canvas that isn't available to everyone else. Does that mean that there's no difference between artists? Of course not. We all know there are huge differences between the inexperienced beginner and the seasoned professional. One sells his work at garage sales to sweaty bargain hunters; the other sells his treasures at extravagant auctions to big city museums. When choosing a financial professional, get an experienced "artist" – someone who has extensive experience and training.

Expectations Gap

My experience has shown that, for the most part, financial advisors and their clients enjoy wonderful relationships. However, from time to time, problems arise. The number one problem investors and advisors experience is what I call the *expectations gap*. What investors expect from their financial professional doesn't match with what they're getting. You can have the best financial professional in the world, but if there is an expectations gap, you (and probably your advisor, as well) won't be happy. It is important that you and your advisor stay in harmony. The better your relationship, the more relaxed and happier you will be in your retirement.

When a gap does occur, it is usually caused by one of two things – either your professional isn't providing the services he or she should or your expectations are unrealistic. To figure out which is correct, let's talk about what you should and what you shouldn't expect from your financial advisor.

Your Financial Advisor
Doesn't Have a Crystal Ball

Several years ago, I took on a new client named Patrick. After spending considerable time over several meetings discussing Patrick's goals and desired level of safety, he and I zeroed in on a well-diversified portfolio that met his objectives. The portfolio would participate in up markets while providing an appropriate amount of asset protection in down markets. Not only did the solution meet his income and safety objectives, it also provided for his other financial goals. It was a sound and appropriate plan. Unfortunately, just after his investments were placed, the stock and bond markets dipped sharply. His portfolio value declined and he became angry.

"Michael, you're a financial advisor; you should have known that the markets were going to drop. That's your job!"

Nothing could be farther from the truth. Expecting your financial advisor to know the future is expecting the impossible. Absolutely no one knows the future, not even me. It is anyone's guess which part of the investment world (e.g., value stocks, growth stocks, bonds) will do best tomorrow, next month, next year, or the next five years, and which will do worst. Any financial professional who states otherwise should change his stationery from financial advisor to spiritual advisor.

I'm not saying that we (as advisors and investors) shouldn't make guesses about the future. In fact, because the future is always foggy, we have no choice but to base our decisions on historical norms, educated guesses, and global trends. But don't mistake norms and trends for certainty. The future is always uncertain. Think about it for a second; if we knew with absolute certainty what tomorrow would bring, we wouldn't need to diversify our portfolios at all. We would need only one investment – whichever one was going to do the best.

Since your advisor cannot see the future, what should you expect? You should expect help in creating and understanding an appropriate

Investment Solutions. What do I mean by that? Your advisor should work with you to create a portfolio that appropriately reconciles your resources with your goals. These portfolio objectives include selecting investment risk, tax avoidance, estate planning, and any other goals you want to accomplish. While your advisor cannot predict the future, he or she can help you prepare for an uncertain future.

You Should Understand
What Your Portfolio Can and Cannot Do

Expectation gaps may occur in the portfolio itself. Often investors set unrealistic expectations about what their portfolio can and cannot do. For example, if a large portion of your portfolio is invested in the stock market, you should expect to lose money occasionally. Stocks are volatile. Sometimes they go down. A financial advisor can help you choose a portfolio designed to minimize your risk and maximize your returns. However, using an advisor does not ensure that your portfolio won't experience a loss during a market decline.

Likewise, if you have a conservative fixed-income portfolio (e.g., bonds and fixed annuities), you should not expect large gains. Understanding your portfolio is not only important to your financial well-being, it is also important to your happiness and peace of mind.

In Patrick's case, he and I needed to spend more time discussing what an advisor could and could not do and what he should expect from his portfolio. Patrick is not unusual. Like most new retirees, creating a financial solution was something new to him. He just needed to adjust his expectations.

Expect Lots of Questions

The objective of a good advisor is to learn about your dreams, your aspirations, and your goals and then help you create a solution for achieving them. Expect a lot of questions. It is his or her job to ask. The more your advisor knows about you, your situation, and what you want to accomplish, the better job he or she can do. Be straightforward and honest. Never lie. If you don't feel comfortable answering a question, just say so. Your advisor is your financial doctor. To help you, he or she needs to know what's going on.

What You Should Expect from Your Advisor

As I discussed earlier, the only thing that differentiates one financial advisor from another is the quality of advice and service. Your professional's advice and service should focus on three areas:

- Putting your goals first
- Educating you about your financial picture
- Providing you with ongoing service

Putting Your Goals First

Your goals should be the focus of your financial solutions. For example, many strategies call for diverting some resources into vehicles like trusts or life insurance to protect heirs against estate taxes. However, not everyone has this goal. Some people have absolutely no concern for their adult children heirs. They prefer to maximize their own security and income while they're alive and let the adult children take care of themselves.

In these cases, the financial advisor should divert no resources to protecting the heirs against estate taxes. All resources should be focused on the investor's security and income. Likewise, you should be the beginning, middle, and end of your Retirement Solutions. While a good financial advisor should call issues to your attention, in the end, only your goals matter. Every recommendation should revolve around your dreams, goals, and aspirations.

Educating You About Your Financial Picture

You should expect your advisor to clearly communicate with you and educate you about financial topics. The more you know, the more comfortable you will be. Your advisor should have a way of educating you about your investments and your financial situation. Different professionals use different methods. Some advisors hold seminars and educational classes for their clients. Others just spend a lot of one-on-one time. Either way, your professional should help you understand your financial situation. The more you know about your own situation, the more comfortable you will be.

Providing Ongoing Service

I believe the most important aspect of an advisor's service is responsiveness. Whenever you call your advisor, you should be able to get prompt, courteous help with your questions and problems. Become acquainted with your professional's support staff. While your advisor is there to give you advice, his or her support staff can often help you with any administrative details such as getting a check or changing your address. Responsive service from your advisor and his or her support staff is a fundamental part of good service.

What Your Advisor Expects From You

Above all, your financial advisor expects two things from you – the truth and clear communication.

The Truth

Just as you expect the truth from your advisor, your advisor expects the truth from you. If you don't feel comfortable answering a question, just say so. But don't lie. Lying not only makes it impossible for an advisor to do a good job, it also raises red flags. In the financial advisory world, a client who doesn't tell the truth means trouble. Experienced financial advisors know that untruthful clients waste time and resources and pose legal risks for them and their staff. As a result, it is not unusual for a financial advisor to invite an untruthful client to move his or her accounts elsewhere. Being truthful is an essential part of the solution process.

Clear Communication

You should maintain clear communication with your financial advisor. Any time you have a question, are concerned, or are dissatisfied, you should call your advisor. That's what he or she is there for.

For example, if you become worried about stock market gyrations, pick up the phone and call. Ask how the current market conditions affect your portfolio. While your professional doesn't have a crystal ball, he or she can explain how the market conditions affect your portfolio and what opportunities the current situation may present. Don't feel like you are being a pest. You're not. That's what your advisor is there for – to answer your questions.

Above all, the one time you always should pick up the phone and call is when you're dissatisfied. If you are unhappy, don't wait. Don't let it fester. Letting your advisor know how you are feeling gives him or her the opportunity to do the job you hired them to do.

Conclusion

I believe that choosing a good financial professional is the best decision a retiree or soon-to-be retiree can make. The financial world is very complicated and confusing. You have a never-ending stream of financial decisions to make. At retirement, you will face a long list of once-in-a-lifetime decisions about your investments, pensions, rollovers, Social Security, and Medicare. After retirement, you must deal with ongoing income decisions, portfolio adjustments, and tax issues. A good financial professional can help you make these decisions and avoid catastrophic mistakes. A good Certified Financial Planner™ Certificant can help you face retirement and fulfill your goals and dreams during your best years. ◆

Chapter 13

Social Security

Without a doubt, Social Security has been a boon for today's retirees. In my experience, I've seen that most retirees could not make the leap to retirement without it. Since this government program plays such a vital part in your financial well being, it is important you understand it.

Because the Social Security Administration is a massive government program providing coverage from worker disability to retirement benefits, the space of this book does not allow me to fully discuss its every detail. That would require a set of books the size of a small set of encyclopedia. Instead, I'll discuss the most important points and often overlooked strategies about a specific program within Social Security – your Social Security retirement benefits.

Who Qualifies

To qualify for Social Security retirement benefits, you must meet two criteria. You need to have enough work history, and you need to be of retirement age. Your work history must include at least 40 credits. A credit is earned for each yearly quarter in which you have earned income taxed by Social Security. You need to have worked at least 10 years at jobs in which you paid Social Security taxes.

Next, you need to be retirement age. Generally, the minimum age is 62. For widows or the disabled, it can be earlier. As long as you meet these two criteria, you qualify for Social Security retirement benefits.

What Earnings are Counted

The biggest myths regarding Social Security relate to how benefits are calculated. A popular misconception is that benefits are calculated using the last three or five years' earnings. This is not true. Benefits are calculated using your highest 30 years of earnings, adjusted for inflation. For example, suppose you had 40 years of earnings. Each of these year's earnings would be adjusted upward for inflation (e.g., according to 2014 inflation charts, if you earned $5000 in 1970, those earnings would be adjusted upward to about $30,000). After adjusting each year for inflation, Social Security takes the top 30 years and applies a benefits calculation. People often ask me if their benefits would be significantly affected by working another year. Since the calculation covers 30 years, the earnings from one more year usually would make little difference in their benefit amounts.

Full Retirement Age Benefits

Most everyone knows that full retirement benefits – those benefits due at Social Security's stated *full retirement age* – start around age 65. However, during Social Security's last reform, the full retirement age changed somewhat. Your full retirement age now depends on the date of your birth. For example, the full retirement age for those born in 1937 or earlier is 65. The full retirement age for those born in 1938 is 65 and 2 months. Those born in 1939 have a full retirement age of 65 and 4 months. And so on until beneficiaries born 1960 or later have a full retirement age of 67. Examine the current schedule below to find your full retirement age.

Year of Birth – Full Retirement Age

1937 or earlier – 65 years
1938 – 65 years and 2 months

1939 – 65 years and 4 months

1940 – 65 years and 6 months

1941 – 65 years and 8 months

1942 – 65 years and 10 months

1943 through 1954 – 66 years

1955 – 66 years and 2 months

1956 – 66 years and 4 months

1957 – 66 years and 6 months

1958 – 66 years and 8 months

1959 – 66 years and 10 months

1960 and later – 67 years

Early Retirement

Even though your full retirement age falls somewhere between 65 and 67 years, you can start your retirement benefits as early as age 62. This is the same for everyone no matter what your full retirement age is (except for widows and the disabled, who have special rules that apply to them).

So, if one can start receiving benefits early, why would anyone wait? People who wait to start their benefits usually do so to get a higher benefit amount. Retirement benefits are reduced for every month you take them before your full retirement age. For example, if Margaret was born in 1937 and she started receiving Social Security retirement benefits at age 62, she would receive 80 percent of her full retirement benefit. Likewise, if Richard, who was born in 1960, started his retirement benefit at age 62, he would receive 70 percent of his full retirement benefit. Those born between 1937 and 1960 are on a sliding scale between these two percentages.

Does that mean you should wait to start your benefits? Not at all. I generally recommend that today's retirees start receiving benefits as soon as possible. The reason is simple. Even though the monthly benefit is greater at full retirement age, you have to give up years of payments. It will take around 12 years of your higher benefit amount to make up for the foregone checks. Assuming your benefits earned interest, you may never financially recover the lost benefits. The bottom line is that if you are retired, it makes good financial sense to start retirement benefits as soon as possible.

Another factor you need to consider is if you qualify for a significant Affordable Care Act (ACA) healthcare subsidy. Since the subsidy is based on your taxable income (i.e., your MAGI), you need to weigh the effect of starting Social Security against the amount your subsidy would be reduced.

Earned Income Limits

The people who probably don't want to start their benefits early are those who want to keep on working past retirement age. These workers may choose to wait to apply for their benefits. The reason is simple. Social Security severely penalizes earnings over a certain amount for those under their full retirement age. The amount that a beneficiary can earn before the benefits are reduced is known as the *earnings limit*. The earnings limit changes from year to year. In the year 2014, someone under full retirement age who was receiving benefits could earn up to $15,480 in wages before his or her benefits would be reduced.

Any earnings over this amount would reduce his or her Social Security benefits by $1 for every $2 earned. For example, if 63 year-old Mrs. Rigby earned $20,000 in 2014, her Social Security benefits would be reduced by $2260 ([$20,000 − $15,480] / 2 = $2260). Therefore, people who are under full retirement age and who are still working full time should think hard before starting their retirement benefits.

However, in the actual calendar year that you turn full retirement age, the earnings limit is higher (e.g., $41,400 for those reaching full retirement age in 2014) and the reduction is lower (i.e., $1 for every

$3 over the limit). For example, if you reached full retirement age in 2014, for every $3 you earned over $41,400, your benefits would be reduced by $1. If you were born in August, then seven months of benefits (January through July) would be adjusted. Complicated? Absolutely. Just remember that you can earn more money in the year you turn full retirement age without the earnings limit cutting into your benefits.

Keep in mind that the earnings limit applies to earned income only. Earned income includes earnings from work or self-employment. It does not include dividends, interest, capital gains, retirement plan distributions (e.g., IRA distributions), or rents. You can earn unlimited amounts of investment income without worrying about the earnings limit.

Spousal Benefits

Spouses can receive retirement benefits. To add simplicity in explaining spousal benefits, let's assume in these examples that the benefits are to be paid to a wife. They can, however, be paid to either spouse – the husband as well as a wife.

The general rule is that a wife can receive half of the husband's benefits based on his record. While this is a good rule of thumb, this is not exactly true. The rule actually states that the wife receives half of the husband's full retirement benefits reduced for each month she starts her benefit before her full retirement age.

Let's give an example. Suppose Gordon starts receiving his benefit at age 66. His wife, Judy, age 62, starts her spousal benefit at the same time. Since Judy is below her full retirement age, her benefit will be reduced to less than half of his full benefit.

Of course, if Judy has earned income on which she paid Social Security taxes, she can receive benefits on her own earnings record instead. Social Security will pay Judy the higher benefit amount she is due – whether it is Gordon's spousal benefit or benefits due on her own record. If Judy is due $750 per month on Gordon's earnings record or $500 on her own earnings record, she will receive the higher amount of $750.

While Judy is allowed to start benefits from her own earnings record whenever she qualifies, she cannot start her spousal benefits until Gordon starts receiving his retirement benefits. To continue the illustration, let's say that Gordon has not started his own retirement benefits. In this case, Judy can receive only $500 per month based on her own record. Once Gordon starts his benefits, she can then increase her benefit to $750 per month based on his earnings record.

Single Divorcees

Spousal benefits can also be paid to single divorcees. To get benefits from the earnings record of a divorced spouse, a divorcee must have been married to that spouse for at least 10 years, be at least 62 years old, be unmarried, and not be eligible for a higher benefit on her own (or someone else's) record. I've found that spousal benefits are an often overlooked but important resource for divorced spouses. If you're single (and don't have a big earnings record), you need to be sure to check if you are due benefits on a previous spouse.

Widow's Benefits

Another type of spousal benefit is available to widows (or widowers) or divorcees whose ex-spouse is deceased. These are known as *widow's benefits*. Widow's benefits are a form of spousal benefits in which payments are calculated from a deceased spouse's record. Unlike straight spousal benefits, these payments can be taken as early as age 60 (or even 50 for those who are disabled). Calculating these benefits is more involved, so I won't explain that here. But be aware that if you're single, at least 60 years old, and a widow, you could be due some benefits.

On many occasions, I've used an often-overlooked twist in widow's benefits to help women retire early. Widow's benefits not only cover widows, but also single divorcees whose ex-husbands have died. If the divorcee qualifies for spousal benefits (on her ex-husband's record), she would also qualify for widow's benefits. For example, Ms. Jones had been married to Mr. Jones for 12 years when they divorced. She then married Mr. Robinson whom she divorced two years later. Later in her life, at age 60, she learned that Mr. Jones had died. Since she is currently single and had been married to Mr. Jones for over 10 years, she could receive widow's benefits on his earnings record.

Taxation of Benefits

Nothing irritates retirees more than paying income tax on their Social Security retirement benefits. Amazingly, many of these folks are unaware that they may be able to reduce or eliminate this tax. How? The IRS uses a somewhat complicated calculation to determine how much of your benefits are subject to tax. I haven't the space to go into that here, but be aware that the amount of your Social Security benefits subject to tax depends on your adjusted gross income (on your 1040), tax-exempt interest, and the amount of Social Security benefits you receive each year.

Sometimes you can lower the tax on your benefits by simply repositioning some of your investment assets into tax-deferred annuities. Like IRAs, the interest, dividends, and capital gains paid inside tax-deferred annuities are not included in your Social Security taxation calculation. An easy way to find out if this strategy would work for you is to simply "rerun" your tax return. Delete the interest, dividends, and capital gains from your return and recalculate your tax. If the taxation on your Social Security drops, you may want to examine an annuity strategy. If you don't know how to juggle the numbers on your tax return, just ask your tax professional for help. Using annuities to reduce the taxation on Social Security is a powerful, yet often-overlooked, tax strategy.

Your Social Security Office Is Very Helpful

In my experience, there is no agency in the U.S. government more helpful or more thorough than the Social Security Administration (SSA). All of us have had unpleasant experiences with one government agency or another. Against this governmental gloom, Social Security stands out like a shining light. My experiences with the SSA have been sterling. I continually hear wonderful stories of their efficiency and courteousness. They are extremely helpful and provide personable service.

If you would like to get more information about your benefits, the SSA provides a wonderful assortment of information and publications. Just call 800-772-1213, or log onto their Internet site at http://www.ssa.gov.

Conclusion

Without Social Security retirement benefits, fewer people would be willing to retire. For millions of people, it has become a cornerstone of their financial security at retirement. Since Social Security plays such a large part of your security, it is important that you understand your benefits. By learning more about Social Security, you can make intelligent and informed decisions. ◆

Chapter 14

Pension Rollovers

Some of the most irrevocable choices made at the time of retirement concern pensions. In addition to choosing a distribution method, you also have survivorship choices to make. Once elections are made, your choices are irrevocable. They cannot be changed. Because these once-in-a-lifetime decisions have enormous implications for your security, you need to give them your full attention and careful consideration.

Lump Sum vs. Lifetime Income

There are two basic ways pensions are paid out – in a lump sum or through a lifetime income. However, pensions differ significantly in their flexibility. Some allow for few or no choices. Other pension plans are extremely flexible and allow extensive choices on how the benefits are paid and what the beneficiaries will receive upon the death of the pensioner.

In addition to lifetime payments, many pensions offer a large, one-time payment choice known as a *lump sum*. In essence, a lump sum choice allows you to gain control of the pension's principal. Most of the time, you can simply roll (transfer without tax implications) the money into a self-directed IRA. Within the IRA, you can invest the money any way you wish and distribute cash as you need it.

There can be advantages to taking a lifetime income vs. taking a lump sum payment. Without question, a lifetime income provides dependable income for paying bills. Moreover, a lifetime income generally is free from investment worries. The retiree doesn't need to sweat over stock market troubles or low interest rates.

However, when a lump sum choice is offered, retirees need to seriously evaluate whether this might be a better decision. In many cases, the lump sum choice gives you much more flexibility, diversity, and ability to create a rising income. Even if you decide to have a fixed lifetime income, many times you can purchase a string of higher payments by making investments in the open market. Let's discuss the implications of each choice and the questions you should ask.

Flexibility

One of the biggest advantages to a lump sum is flexibility. You control the cash flow. If you need more money, it's there for you. If you need less money, you can simply leave it invested. Likewise, choosing a lump sum allows you to control your taxes.

For example, after paying off his mortgage, Phil found himself needing less cash for living expenses. To save taxes, he simply lowered the distributions from his lump sum rollover (his rollover IRA). By simply reducing his distributions, he reduced his tax bill, as well. Unlike lifetime pension payments that are irreversibly fixed, a lump sum rollover gives you the power to control your distributions and subsequently your taxes.

Rising Income

Taking a lump sum also gives you the opportunity to create a rising income stream. Most monthly pension amounts (on corporate pensions) are fixed. They pay the same amount every month for life. In the face of ever-increasing prices, these payments can quickly lose their ability to meet your needs. A good pension today may not meet your bills 10, 20, and 30 years from now. Suppose Franklin retired in 1970 with a $1500 per month pension. Life was sweet for him back then. He had plenty of income to meet his needs. However, by the late 1990s, Franklin and his wife were barely getting along. Inflation eroded away 80 percent of his pension's buying power. Had he taken a lump sum instead, he could have used the money to create an ever-increasing income stream. A good investment strategy could have increased Franklin's monthly income to keep pace with inflation.

Exceptions to the Rule

Even though taking a lump sum is usually better, sometimes taking life payments is the right choice. A good example of this is the Teacher Retirement System (TRS) of Texas. In that system, teachers are usually better off taking the life income payments. The lump sum choice is usually so low that it would be very difficult to invest it in order to generate a comparable income. Before you take your lump sum, carefully evaluate whether it is enough to generate a solid income stream. I recommend you enlist the help of a Certified Financial Planner™ Certificant to help you make this evaluation.

Pension Alternative Strategy –
Use a Life Annuity

Many people like the idea of a lifetime income and often take one of the life annuity choices instead of the lump sum. However, if the retiree is clever, a lump sum payment often can create lifetime payments that are much higher than the choices offered by a pension.

A frequently used strategy to increase lifetime income is to take the lump sum and invest the money in a life annuity. A life annuity works just like the employer pension, and if you shop around, a life annuity can often offer a higher monthly payment. If you are facing a pension choice and would like to see if you can increase your monthly amount, simply to go to:

http://annuity.MichaelDallas.com/lifeannuity.html

After you enter your age, state, gender, and investment amount, the page will display your payment choices. The annuities listed on this page are a great way for retirees to put more money in their pockets. If you want to compare other types of annuity choices such as joint life annuities, just call my toll-free number for a quick quote.

Heir Protection

Another aspect of pension decisions is heir protection. When making pension decisions, you need to ask what might happen to those you love if you died unexpectedly. If you choose a lump sum option, obviously, the survivorship considerations take care of themselves. Your heirs simply inherit the money. On the other hand, if you receive a life income benefit, your heirs (such as your spouse) may be at risk. A loss of pension income could cause hardship.

To protect surviving spouses, many pensions offer survivorship choices. In essence, you can choose to take a smaller pension income now in exchange for your spouse's right to continue receiving all or part of the pension income after your death. If losing your pension would cause hardship to your surviving spouse, you should seriously consider taking a lump sum or an income choice with benefits for your surviving spouse.

Many times, pensions don't offer lump sum or survivorship choices. In this case, you may want to seriously consider getting life insurance. For example, many government pensions don't contain lump sum or spousal survivorship benefits. Should the pensioner die, his spouse may be left with little income. Purchasing a life policy on the life of the pensioner can protect the spouse against the pensioner's death. Of course, whether this strategy will work depends upon the age and health of the pensioner. The younger and healthier the pensioner, the cheaper the life insurance. When taking a pension without provisions for a surviving spouse, consider whether life insurance might be useful.

Hire a Professional

I believe the best way to make a pension choice is to hire a Certified Financial Planner® Certificant to run an analysis of your choices for you. In essence, you need to compare how much income can be generated from each choice and what risks are involved. Factors such as inflation, interest rates, life expectancy, and spousal protection need to be considered. Making a pension choice is a one-time, irrevocable decision. Seeking professional help can be well worth the investment.

Conclusion

Because decisions made about pensions are often irrevocable, it is critical that you consider all the choices available to you at the time of your retirement. Your decisions may include the distribution method, as well as survivorship selections. I highly recommend that you get professional help to make this once-in-a-lifetime choice. ◆

Chapter 15

Health Insurance and Medicare

Of all your decisions made at retirement, none is more important than making sure you have good medical insurance in place. One serious, uninsured illness can wipe out a lifetime of savings and prudent investing. I caution every soon-to-be retiree not even to think about retiring without suitable health insurance in place.

Medicare

Without a doubt, the Medicare program has been a tremendous liberator for American retirees. Medicare coverage has made it possible for millions of people to retire. If not for Medicare, I believe many retirees would have had to continue working just to qualify and pay for medical coverage. Since Medicare forms the bedrock of your health care during retirement, you should understand how this important program works and the steps you should take to maximize your benefits.

Medicare Basics

Before we begin, there are several simple facts you need to know about Medicare. First, you need to understand that unlike Social Security retirement benefits that can begin "early" at age 62, Medicare only starts at age 65. Until then, you will need to secure other health coverage – even if you are retired. Similar to Social Security spousal retirement benefits, stay-at-home spouses can qualify for Medicare on their working spouses' records. If you are 65 and older but don't qualify for Medicare under your or your spouse's work record, you can still buy it. You will just have to pay more for it.

Next, you need to understand that Medicare comes in a variety of "parts" titled *Part A, Part B, Part C*, and *Part D*. Except for Part A, you have decisions to make about every part.

For decades, Part A and Part B made up the benefits we know as *traditional Medicare.* However, in the past few years, two additional parts to Medicare have appeared – Part C and Part D. Understanding all the parts and how they work together will help you make better decisions about your Medicare benefits.

Medicare Part A

Medicare Part A pays for hospital bills. It covers in-patient hospital services, skilled nursing care after a hospital stay, home health care, and hospice care. We pay for Part A throughout our working career with our payroll deductions. For those who have worked and paid into Medicare for 10 years or more (i.e., 40 quarters), there's no monthly charge for it when you retire. If you don't have 40 quarters of Medicare taxed earnings, you can still get it. You just have to pay for it; in 2014, Medicare Part A cost $426 per month.

Medicare Part B

Part B covers 80 percent of medical expenses (such as physicians' services and supplies), clinical laboratory services, and outpatient hospital treatment. Unlike Part A, Part B has a direct cost and is optional.

Most everyone knows that Part A Medicare is extremely valuable to retirees. However, many people may not realize that Part B Medicare is a fantastic bargain, as well. Since Part B has a cost, it is considered optional; however, it is only optional in the sense that you can turn it down. It is not optional in the sense that you don't need it. You need it! In fact, if you turn down Part B Medicare, you are probably making the biggest financial mistake of your life. You'll not only be neglecting the best deal on medical coverage you'll ever find, you'll also be exposing yourself to horrendous financial risk.

Part B provides fantastic coverage at a great price. Over the past few years, the way Part B is priced has changed. It is now charged on a sliding scale based upon income. In 2014, those who made less than $85,000 in Modified Adjusted Gross Income paid $104.90 per month for Part B. These people are getting a 75 percent discount on high quality health insurance. The federal government picks up the other 75 percent. Furthermore, if it weren't for Part B Medicare, many, if not most, people over 65 probably could not buy this coverage at any price. Because seniors can easily run up significant medical bills, few companies would want to offer them coverage.

A few years ago, everyone 65 and older received the same 75 percent discount on the cost of Part B. Today, the discount phases-out (i.e., it is reduced) for those with incomes over $85,000. The phase-out is on a sliding scale. Those at the top end of the scale who make $224,000 or more per year will pay the full cost of Medicare Part B – $335.70 per month in 2014. I have included the phase-out schedule in Chart 1 on the next page.

Don't make the mistake of thinking you don't need Part B Medicare because your supplemental insurance will pay those costs. It won't. Medicare supplemental insurance will not pick up the costs that would have been paid by Part B. If you don't take Part B Medicare, you will be picking up those expenses yourself. One serious illness could easily mean financial ruin from excessive medical bills.

Part B premiums by income

If your yearly income in 2012 (for what you pay in 2014) was			You pay (in 2014)
File individual tax return	File joint tax return	File married & separate tax return	
$85,000 or less	$170,000 or less	$85,000 or less	$104.90
above $85,000 up to $107,000	above $170,000 up to $214,000	Not applicable	$146.90
above $107,000 up to $160,000	above $214,000 up to $320,000	Not applicable	$209.80
above $160,000 up to $214,000	above $320,000 up to $428,000	above $85,000 and up to $129,000	$272.70
above $214,000	above $428,000	above $129,000	$335.70

Chart1

If you don't remember anything else in this book, remember this one thing: Don't turn down Medicare Part B. You need it. If illness or an accident strikes, the lack of Part B coverage could turn out to be the worst financial mistake of your life. The uninsured expenses could easily wipe you out.

Medicare Part C

Known as *Medicare Advantage*, Part C is an alternative to the coverage provided by traditional Medicare (i.e., Parts A and B). The Part C program attempts to incorporate the cost-saving measures of *managed care* into the Medicare program by allowing beneficiaries to participate in coordinated care programs such as HMOs, PPOs, and Medical Savings Accounts. To date, more than one-fourth of Medicare beneficiaries have opted out of traditional Medicare in favor of Part C.

The main reason many people choose Part C is the potential for out-of-pocket cost savings. Where the traditional Medicare Part B has a monthly charge, many HMOs advertise that they will offer Part C coverage for very low or even no monthly fees to the beneficiaries. Moreover, many HMOs and PPOs will pay costs not covered by Part A or B.

Many people mistakenly believe that if they take Part C, they are stuck with it for life. In fact, you can make changes to your Medicare coverage once per year. If you decide you don't like Part C, you can always switch back to traditional Medicare Parts A and B the next year.

Special Note: If you are considering using an HMO under Part C, I recommend that you also consider maintaining a Medigap policy until you're completely comfortable with the HMO's service. Should you find the HMO isn't meeting your needs, you can simply convert back to traditional Medicare with your Medigap policy intact. (See "Medigap Insurance" below for more information.)

You are eligible to switch to Part C at any time if you are entitled to Medicare Part A and enrolled in Part B (provided you reside in the plan's service area).

Medicare Part D

People frequently refer to *Part D* as the *Medicare Prescription Drug Coverage*. Part D was added to Medicare to help beneficiaries pay for prescription drug costs. While many people have been critical of Part D, I believe it provides tremendous relief against spiraling pharmaceutical bills. According to Medicare, the typical beneficiary sees his or her total drug expenditures cut in half by using the benefit.

Like Medicare Part B, Medicare Part D is optional and has a monthly cost to beneficiaries. There are several costs associated with Medicare Part D: premiums, deductibles, copayments, and the "donut hole," which I'll explain in a moment. (People with low incomes may apply for a subsidy from the Social Security Administration to reduce these costs.)

In 2014, Part D premiums range from $12 to $69 per month (depending on availability and the particular plan you choose). The deductible for most plans in 2014 was $325. After you meet the deductible, Medicare will pay about 75 percent of your prescription costs. After your total drug costs reach a certain amount (in 2014 the amount was $2850), you hit the *donut hole*. Your plan stops paying and you must pay the full cost of your prescriptions. (However, you will receive a discount on the cost of your medications while you are in the donut hole coverage gap.) The plan begins to pay again (about 95 percent of all further costs) when your pharmaceutical expenditures reach a *catastrophic level* (in 2014 that level was $4550). If you initially decline the coverage, you may have to pay a late enrollment penalty to start the coverage later.

Medicare Part D has a wide variety of plans from which to choose. The variety of policy choices has caused a lot of confusion and anxiety among beneficiaries. However, making good decisions about Part D coverage is not hard. Let's look at some of the strategies you might use.

First, lets look at who may not need a Medicare Part D policy:

1. If you have *credible drug coverage* (according to Medicare) and you like it, you may not need Medicare Part D. There are also no premium penalties for getting Part D in the future should you want or need it. If you like your coverage, there may not be a reason to change. A good strategy is to call your insurance carrier. Ask whether your coverage is considered "credible" by Medicare and discuss how it compares with Part D.

2. If you don't take prescription drugs and are a veteran or retired military personnel, you may not need Medicare Part D. A special provision has been made for veterans and retired military personnel. They can start Medicare Part D at any time with no premium penalties. Since there is no penalty for starting coverage later, people under this provision may want to consider coverage only after they begin taking prescription drugs.

Next, let's look at the people who benefit from Part D the most — those who take prescription drugs but have no coverage. For these people, the biggest concern is finding the best coverage. Fortunately, Medicare has done the work for you. Simply write down names of the prescriptions you take, the dosages, and how much you pay for them. With that information in hand, you can shop for coverage in two ways – through Medicare's Internet site or by getting personal help.

On the Internet, Medicare has provided a feature it calls the Medicare Prescription Drug Plan Finder - (https://www.medicare. gov/find-a-plan/questions/home.aspx). By entering information about your prescriptions, this handy web page will present the five best plans available to you and will estimate how much money you will save.

If you are not Internet savvy, don't worry. There is plenty of help. Simply call Medicare at 1-800-Medicare. They will give you the names and phone numbers of local counselors who can help you find the best drug plan coverage.

Let's now look at those lucky people who currently don't take prescription medications. Should they get Medicare Part D or not? If you are one of these fortunate souls, you may consider two options. First you may decide to skip the coverage for now and simply pay a higher premium later if you need it. For example, in 2014, the premium increase for those who didn't take Part D coverage was $.3242 per month, so if you waited 1 year (12 months) and then started the coverage, your premium would be $3.89 per month higher than if you had not waited (.3242 x 12).

A second strategy is to start an inexpensive policy now and change it later if necessary. In 2014, Part D policies could be found as cheap as $14 per month. By getting a low cost policy now, you can avoid the late enrollment penalties. Should you start taking prescription drugs in the future and need better coverage, you can simply change your coverage (once per year) without any late enrollment penalties.

Covering the Gaps in Medicare

Even though Medicare provides wonderful coverage for Americans over age 65, it doesn't pay all the costs. This shortfall or *gap* in the Medicare program can be either met out of your pocket or by various insurance plans. The most popular method of meeting this shortfall is by purchasing supplemental insurance. However, employee group coverage or HMO arrangements can be extremely useful, as well.

If you determine that you need a supplemental policy, you need to be an educated shopper. Even though supplemental policies have been standardized, you need to understand the benefits of each and the tips and tricks that will make the most of your retirement, health-care coverage dollar.

Medigap Insurance

The most popular way of meeting the shortfalls in Medicare coverage is to buy a supplemental policy from an insurance company. These Medicare supplemental policies are often referred to as *Medigap* policies since they help you cover part of the gap in your Medicare benefits. Buying this type of supplemental insurance can be an excellent means of protecting against medical costs not covered by Medicare. For example, Medicare does not cover the following costs; you must either pay them out-of-pocket or cover them through Medigap insurance:

- Custodial care, such as help in walking, getting in and out of bed, dressing, eating, and taking medicine
- More than 100 days of skilled nursing-home following a hospital stay
- Private duty nursing care
- Homemaker services
- Most dental care and dentures
- Most health care received while traveling outside the United States
- Cosmetic surgery and routine foot care

- Eye examinations, eyeglasses (except after cataract surgery), and hearing aids

Note: Long-term-care costs are not covered by Medicare supplemental insurance. To learn more about strategies for dealing with long-term-care issues, please refer to Chapter 15, "Long-Term Care."

Even though Medigap is private insurance, insurance companies that offer Medigap policies must sell you a policy during the first six months after you enroll in Medicare Part B, despite any existing health problems you may have. This period is called *open enrollment*. However, after that period, insurance companies can (and probably will) require you to qualify for a Medigap policy. You may have to answer a battery of questions and take a physical exam. Should your health be less than sterling, your premiums could be high. For this reason, it is important that you get your Medigap policy as soon as possible.

Nevertheless, not everyone needs a Medicare supplemental policy. If you are enrolled in certain other types of health plans, the gaps in Medicare coverage may already be covered. For example, you may not need Medigap insurance if:

- You receive Medicaid.
- You are a qualified Medicare beneficiary (QMB is explained below).
- You are covered by an employer-sponsored group health insurance that covers the gaps in Medicare.
- You belong to a Medicare health maintenance organization (HMO).

Employee Group Plans

If you don't retire at 65, you may be able to continue group health insurance at your place of employment. If so, as long as you are working, you will not need Medicare Part B or Medigap insurance. Likewise, if your spouse is over 65 and remains employed, you may be included on your spouse's policy and will not need a Medigap policy. Nor would you need Medigap coverage if you have health-care coverage through a union or fraternal organization.

Some people are fortunate to have health plans at work that follow an employee into retirement and provide Medigap-type coverage. Because each health plan works differently, be sure to consult with your employer's benefits coordinator before making a decision about Medigap insurance.

Medicare Health Maintenance Organizations (HMOs)

Generally, if you have Medicare Part C and are in a Medicare health maintenance organization (HMO), you won't need a Medigap policy. However, you may want to own a Medigap policy until you're sure you are happy with the HMO. To understand this strategy, you need to know how Medicare HMOs work and why maintaining a Medigap policy might be advisable.

Medicare HMOs work differently than straight Medicare. Instead of paying for each claim separately, Medicare pays a monthly premium to the HMO. In return for these regular payments, the HMO provides health care services. In addition to Medicare's payments, the HMO may charge an additional premium and a copayment when the services are used.

If your Medicare HMO terminates its contract in your service area, many states guarantee participants the right to purchase available Medigap plans. For example, Texas allows participants an open enrollment time of 63 days after they lose coverage to apply for any available A, B, C, or F Medigap policy (see "Standardized Policies" below). During that period, companies operating in Texas may not place restrictions on these policies such as preexisting conditions or exclusions.

On the other hand, if you voluntarily leave the HMO before it terminates, this option is not guaranteed. Therefore, it is good to have a Medigap policy in place before joining an HMO and keep it intact until you are completely satisfied with its services. Leaving an HMO without a Medigap policy (even if you leave in disgust) could leave you without coverage.

If you are considering using an HMO, I recommend that you maintain a Medigap policy until you're completely comfortable with the HMO's service. Should you find the HMO isn't meeting your needs, you can simply convert back to regular Medicare with your Medigap policy intact.

Medicaid

Medicaid is not the same as Medicare, although the two are often confused. Medicaid is a state-administered health insurance program for low-income people. You do not need a Medigap policy if you receive Medicaid. It pays eligible expenses in full.

Qualified Medicare Beneficiaries (QMB)

The federal Qualified Medicare Beneficiaries program pays the Medicare Part B premium and covers all Medicare deductibles and copayments. This program is for people with incomes below a certain level. Those persons in the QMB program will not need Medicare supplemental insurance.

Standardized Policies

Standardization of Medigap policies has made shopping for Medigap insurance much easier. Since 1992, federal law has required insurers to provide standardized Medigap plans labeled A through N. Forty-seven of the states offer these plans. (Massachusetts, Minnesota, and Wisconsin do not offer the standard Medicare Supplement plans. Instead, each state has its own unique Medicare Supplement plan offerings.) Each lettered plan offers a different level of benefits. While all companies that sell Medigap insurance must offer plan A, they do not have to offer the other nine plans. This standardization makes it easy to shop around and compare prices.

Note: If you bought a Medigap policy before the 10 standardized plans were first required (1992), you may choose to keep your existing policy. It is not mandatory that you switch to one of the 10 standardized plans.

Medicare Select

Medicare Select is a specific type of Medigap policy offered in some states. In return for using only hospitals in an insurance company's network providers list, you may get a lower price. Should you leave a Medicare Select plan for any reason, the company must make available to you any comparable non-Medicare Select policy it has on the market.

Open Enrollment

If a person is at least 65 and applies for coverage within six months after enrolling in Medicare Part B, insurance companies are required by federal law to offer a Medigap policy regardless of any preexisting health conditions. This period is called an *open enrollment period*. During open enrollment, an insurance company must allow free choice among all the Medicare supplement policies it offers. These open-enrollment rights can be used more than once during this six-month period. For example, you may change your mind about a policy, cancel it, and still have the right to buy any other Medigap policy. As long as the sale takes place during the six months after you enroll in Medicare Part B, you can buy any policy (or policies) you want.

Note: Even though a company must sell a policy during the open enrollment period, it may require a waiting period of up to six months before covering preexisting conditions.

The right to open enrollment is absolute. For example, if because of continued employment you wait for several years after age 65 to enroll in Medicare Part B, you still have an open enrollment period at that time.

30-Day Free Look

If you are dissatisfied with your Medicare supplement policy, you can return it within 30 days after receiving it and get your money back. Be sure to keep a record of when the policy is received, and read it as soon as possible. If you return the policy, use certified mail with a return receipt.

Renewability

All Medicare supplement policies are guaranteed renewable. A company cannot cancel your policy or refuse to renew it. However, the amount of the premium is not guaranteed and may change once per year.

Buying Tips

Family members and friends are good sources of information about a company's service. Ask around for their experiences with different Medigap companies.

Although it is illegal for insurers to sell you more than one Medigap policy, federal law does allow them to offer other policies with benefits that may overlap Medigap coverage. These include cancer insurance and other policies, such as specified disease, and hospital indemnity. Any duplication of benefits must be disclosed in writing. In general, duplicate coverage wastes money. Before buying, carefully consider your budget and your health-care needs.

Group insurance through an employer or former employer often is cheaper and more comprehensive than individual policies. Be sure to find out if you can keep your employee health insurance or convert it to suitable Medicare supplement coverage after you turn 65.

Before buying any new policy, read your existing policy and closely compare it with the new policy. Never switch policies just to get a lower price. Benefits may be different and premiums can increase.

If you want to switch coverage to another company after the free enrollment period has expired, keep your old policy in force until you receive the new policy. Letting the old policy lapse without securing the new policy could leave you without coverage.

Always discuss your doctor's charges before getting service. This could help avoid incurring charges that Medicare or Medigap insurance will not pay.

Retiring With Healthcare Coverage Before 65

I've met many people who would like to retire before age 65 except for one thing – they would be without health insurance. While many employers allow their employees to continue their health coverage into retirement, many do not. Since retirees don't qualify for Medicare until they turn 65, many people continue working just to stay on their employer's health plan. If this is you, you should be aware that you might not have to wait until age 65 to retire. Two federal laws may help. First, if you have an employer plan, you may be able to continue your employer's plan for 18 months after you leave employment under a plan known as *COBRA*. Second, the *Affordable Care Act* (*ACA*) provides benefits even for people who don't have an employer plan.

COBRA

In 1985, Congress passed a federal law known as *COBRA* (the Consolidated Omnibus Budget Reconciliation Act of 1985). This legislation provides health plan coverage for workers, their spouses, and their dependent children when their health insurance might otherwise be dropped. Because of its benefit to workers and their families, COBRA has been applauded as a wonderful safety net for workers in the middle of a crisis or a change, such as unemployment, divorce, death, or retirement.

If you resign from a job or are terminated for any reason (other than gross misconduct), COBRA guarantees you the right to continue your former employer's group plan as individual or family health-care coverage for up to 18 months at your own expense. Sometimes, your spouse and dependent children are also eligible for COBRA for up to three years.

It is important to understand that COBRA only applies to employer group plans. Individual plans – plans you buy on your own – are not subject to COBRA.

You also need to understand that even though you can continue your employer's group coverage, you will be responsible for covering the cost of the premiums. Since you must pay the full premium, it can be a significant monthly cost.

Affordable Care Act

One of the biggest game changers for many would-be early retirees is the Affordable Care Act (ACA). For many, the law removes two large hurdles to getting affordable health care before age 65 – accessibility and price. However, because the ultimate cost of health insurance depends on taxable income, the law adds another layer of complexity to maximizing an early retiree's overall financial solution. Let's look at the law and strategies early retirees should consider.

Before we get too far into the topic, you must know that I wrote this section in early 2014 – just as the Affordable Care Act's insurance elements were coming online. I am certain that as a new program, many changes and tweaks will be made in the near future. After reading this chapter, I would encourage you to visit my website where I will keep you updated on the program. Just log on at:

http://www.MichaelDallas.com/ACA

New Opportunities

For many people, the biggest obstacle to early retirement was getting affordable health care coverage before age 65 (when they qualified for Medicare). Often policies were unaffordable or worse, impossible to get at any price. With the *Affordable Care Act* (*ACA*), coverage is available to everyone no matter their health history. Moreover, for many people, the government subsidies make the premiums much more affordable.

If you are thinking about early retirement and need health insurance, your first stop should be to the ACA site:

http://www.healthcare.gov

Let's take a look at the potential benefits of the ACA for early retirees. According to the calculators, the annual full cost of a *silver policy* (used as the benchmark for most comparisons) for a 62-year-old couple in Fort Worth, Texas, would run between $14,256 (2 x $7128 per policy) and $18,264 (2 x $9138) per year. If they had a taxable income (i.e., MAGI) of $40,000, they would receive a subsidy of $11,376 which would bring their total cost as low as $2880 per year.

In this example, I have used a specific scenario for illustration. Just remember that each situation is different. The cost of insurance, the amount of the subsidy, and the net cost of the insurance depend on several things – the size of the family, the age of the family members, the total household income, and the cost of the insurance.

Conclusion

Unlike Social Security retirement benefits, Medicare is only available once you turn 65, not before. For this reason, it is very important that those who retire before 65 secure their medical coverage before leaving a job. Needless to say, retiring without health care coverage can be a disastrous decision. For many people, federal COBRA provisions allow them to carry their employer's insurance for 18 months after retiring. For others, the Affordable Care Act provides opportunities for access and affordability. Even after qualifying for Medicare, you have many decisions to make.

Even though putting a good health care plan in place can take time and effort, nothing can make retirement more wonderful than being healthy. By planning ahead, you can take comfort that you have a sound safety net to help you stay financially and physically fit. ◆

Chapter 16

Long-Term Care

When the subject of long-term care comes up, most people think mainly of nursing home care. While long-term care does include nursing home care, it is, in fact, much broader than that. Long-term care refers to the type of medical or personal care services needed if you become unable to care for yourself because of chronic illness, disability, loss of functional capacity, or cognitive impairment.

Unlike traditional medical care, which attempts to permanently cure or control illness, long-term-care services help people maintain their ability to function, perform normal daily activities, or maintain a normal lifestyle. Long-term care comes into play when a person becomes physically or mentally unable to perform normal daily activities, such as eating, bathing, dressing, and walking. The care is not only provided in nursing homes but may also be furnished in the home, in an adult daycare center, an adult family home, or an assisted-living facility. Long-term care is the daily help needed to make life more livable and comfortable.

The Cost

Costs of long-term care vary widely depending on your location and the services that you need. Choices include services provided through the framework of nursing homes, assisted-living arrangements, and in-home services. The most expensive long-term-care services are generally provided during a nursing home stay and can cost from $30,000 to well over $100,000 per year, depending on the location, facility, and the services provided.

Even though nursing homes are an important provider of long-term-care services, most long-term care is received through assisted-living and in-home care. These services are often more comfortable and help the individual maintain independence for a longer period of time. Assisted-living and in-home services are often less expensive than a nursing home. Because available services and costs vary, it will require a little investigative work by calling local nursing care facilities, assisted-living facilities, and home-care service organizations to compare services and prices.

Who Pays

Long-term-care expenses are met through three sources: Medicaid, long-term-care insurance, and your pocketbook. Don't confuse Medicaid with Medicare. Medicaid is a state-administered health insurance program for low-income people with a small amount of assets. The federal government provides a portion of the funding for Medicaid and sets guidelines for the program. States also have choices in how they design their program, so Medicaid varies state by state and may have a different name in your state.

Medicare is federally backed medical insurance for those 65 and older. Ironically, Medicaid covers a substantial amount of long-term-care expense, while Medicare pays very little for these services. If you don't qualify for Medicaid, almost all your expenses must be met either by long-term-care insurance or out of your own pocket.

To receive Medicaid, state and federal guidelines for income and assets must be met. The more income and assets you have, the less likely it is that you will qualify for Medicaid. Oftentimes, the drain of paying nursing home expenses shrinks people's assets enough for them to become eligible for Medicaid. This is called *spending down*. It is a nice term for becoming impoverished by nursing home expenses and then qualifying for welfare assistance (Medicaid).

On the other hand, Medicare is a federal program that pays a substantial portion of health care for people over age 65 and for some people with disabilities. Many people wrongly believe that Medicare will pay for their long-term-care needs. It will not. While Medicare will pay for a limited amount of skilled nursing home care after a hospital stay, it won't pay for the ongoing need for daily assistance.

Long-Term-Care Insurance

Insurance that covers long-term care works best for people in a specific wealth bracket. People who have very little in the way of assets don't need it because they qualify for Medicaid. People who have substantial assets don't need the insurance either; they have plenty of assets to pay the costs out of their own pocket. It is the people between the very rich and very poor – the comfortably affluent – who should examine long-term-care insurance. They have enough assets to meet retirement needs but not enough money for the additional costs of a long-term nursing home stay. Long-term-care insurance best meets the needs of people who are in this affluent middle class.

The first thing to consider when looking at long-term-care insurance is whether you can afford it. If you're stretching your income just to pay for utilities, food, or medicine, it is not a good idea to buy a long-term-care policy. The cost to your current lifestyle might outweigh the potential benefits of the insurance protection. A good long-term-care insurance strategy not only needs to provide you with long-term-care protection, it must also fit into your budget.

Long-Term-Care Risk Factors

Research indicates that several factors determine the need for long-term care at some time in your life. The likelihood of needing long-term care might be affected by these factors:

- Life expectancy: The longer you live, the more likely it is that you will need long-term care. Does your family have a tendency for long life?
- Gender: Women are at a much higher risk of needing long-term care. They have longer life expectancies and often outlive their husbands.
- Marriage and children: If you have a spouse or adult children, you may be more likely to receive informal care at home from family members. You need to ask, "Can my family take care of me?" as well as "Do I want my family to take care of me?"
- Health factors: If chronic or debilitating health conditions run in your family, you could face a greater risk of needing long-term care.

Long-Term-Care Policies

Long-term care insurance policies are not standardized like Medicare supplement insurance (Medigap insurance). Each policy is different, with many combinations of benefits and coverage. To buy effective and affordable long-term-care coverage, you must decide what combination of benefits, services, and costs best fit your personal needs. A good strategy is to find a trustworthy long-term-care agent who works with many different insurance companies. A good agent will be able to evaluate your specific needs and budget and help you find the best coverage. Since the large variety of policies and benefits makes it difficult to shop and compare long-term-care policies, a good long-term-care professional can be invaluable.

Tax-Qualified vs. Nonqualified Plans

A few years ago, Congress acted to help people pay for their long-term-care insurance premiums. Through an act called the *Health Insurance Portability and Accountability Act* (HIPAA), our legislators gave favorable tax treatment to certain long-term-care policies. The policies that meet the requirements of this act are known as *qualified plans* because they qualify for the special tax treatment provided by the law. Policies that don't meet the requirement are known as *nonqualified plans* since they don't qualify for any special tax treatment.

There is debate on whether it is better to buy a qualified or nonqualified plan. The two main differences between them are when benefits will be payable and the tax treatment of premiums and benefits. Those who argue for buying a qualified plan point out that you may be able to deduct part of the premium from your taxes as a medical expense. Furthermore, the benefits paid out by a qualified policy will not be taxable as income. On the other hand, many people argue that nonqualified long-term-care plans may provide an easier standard for which to receive benefits. When designing the act allowing qualified plans, Congress required the language in the plans to be more restrictive on when benefits should be paid; therefore, it may be easier to collect benefits from a nonqualified policy than from a qualified policy. When selecting a policy, carefully examine the differences between qualified and nonqualified policies and determine which type is right for you.

Tax-Qualified Plans

So how does one determine the difference between qualified and nonqualified policies? In the law, Congress proclaimed that all policies sold before January 1, 1997, are automatically qualified. If you bought a long-term-care policy before this date, that policy is grandfathered to receive all the tax benefits of a qualified plan. Any policies sold after that date must be identified as either tax qualified or nontax qualified. Look for a statement on your policy similar to this:

"This policy is intended to be a qualified long-term-care insurance contract as defined by the Internal Revenue Code of 1986, Section 7702B(b)."

Because policies explicitly state whether they're qualified or nonqualified, it is not hard to determine which type you own.

Tax Deduction

To claim a personal tax deduction for long-term-care premium payments, your out-of-pocket medical expenses, including the long-term-care premiums, must be more than 10 percent of your adjusted gross income (or 7.5 percent of your income for taxpayers 65 or older). The expenses over this amount can be deducted. Once that hurdle has been cleared, the maximum amount of long-term-care premium you can deduct depends on your age at the end of each tax year. The chart below lists the deduction limits for the year 2014.

2014 maximum deductible (amounts change annually):

40 or less - $370

More than 40 but not more than 50 - $700

More than 50 but not more than 60 - $1400

More than 60 but not more than 70 - $3720

More than 70 - $4600

On the other hand, if you control a C-corporation, partnership, S-corporation, or sole proprietorship, it is much easier to deduct premiums. Premiums paid by a C-corporation are 100 percent deductible when paid. Premiums paid by a partnership, S-corporation, or sole proprietorship are partially deductible based on age. By providing long-term-care insurance through a business entity, you may be able to create tax advantages on policy premiums.

Tax-Free Benefits

In addition to providing partial deductibility of premiums, the Act also bestows tax-free status on the benefits paid. Should you collect benefits from a qualified long-term-care policy, they will not be included in your taxable income.

Non-Tax-Qualified, Long-Term-Care Plans

As I discussed before, the two main differences between qualified and nonqualified policies are (1) when benefits should be paid and (2) the tax treatment of premium payments and benefits. Nonqualified plans may have less strict language on when benefits are due than qualified plans. On the other hand, the tax treatment of nonqualified plans may make them much less attractive. Compare the potential benefits and disadvantages of qualified and nonqualified plans before deciding which is best for you.

Services Covered

When choosing a policy, it is important to know the type of facility, services, and care that is covered. While nursing home care is generally recognized as the main benefit in long-term-care policies, other types of care could be as important, or even more important, than an institutional stay. Many policies may also pay for a variety of coverage including assisted-living care, care in the home, daytime care in an adult daycare facility, hospice care, respite care, and care coordination. Check any policy you are considering against the following services to make sure it offers the benefits you think are important.

- Nursing home services: Most policies pay for care in a licensed nursing facility.
- Assisted-living care: This type of care is becoming extremely popular. Assisted living allows retirees to have their own space while getting the help needed. Typically, the facilities provide a

private apartment and on-site services such as housekeeping, meal preparation (such as a cafeteria), and emergency help. Assisted living allows independence while offering needed services.

- Home health-care services: Care or personal assistance in the home is called *home health care*. Many policies cover these part-time services, which include skilled nursing care, physical therapy, homemaker services, and assistance with activities of daily living.

- Adult daycare program services: Many policies cover care received in licensed adult daycare facilities. These services can be valuable for individuals who do not need to live in a nursing home but need daytime help, such as nursing or therapeutic care, social and educational activities, or personal supervision because of cognitive impairment, such as Alzheimer's or a similar disease.

- Other services: Some policies may include or optionally offer other benefits such as respite care, home assistance services, and training for family members. Respite care benefits provide a part-time service to caregiver family members. This service allows them to have some time off from continual care of their loved one. Home assistance provides ongoing help with chores like cleaning and shopping. Training for family members can give family members insight and help with how to best meet the care needs of a loved one.

Benefit Eligibility Triggers

Payment of long-term-care insurance benefits is triggered when you are unable to perform activities of daily living (ADLs) or if help is needed because of cognitive impairment.

Activities of Daily Living (ADLs)

Under most policies, if you are unable to perform at least two of the six activities considered essential to a normal lifestyle – bathing, dressing, toileting, transferring (mobility), eating, and continence – you will be eligible for covered services provided by the policy.

Cognitive Impairment

If a licensed health practitioner certifies that a loss in intellectual capacity requires you to have substantial supervision to protect your safety or the safety of others, benefits are payable on your plan. Impairment can be the result of Alzheimer's disease, senility, an accident, or other causes.

Items Not Covered

Many policies exclude coverage for certain conditions. Some conditions may be excluded for a limited period of time, while others may be permanently disallowed. The following are typical exclusions:

- Primary exclusions: Many plans exclude coverage for conditions resulting from alcoholism, drug addiction, illness caused by an act of war, care already paid for by Medicare or by any government program (except Medicaid), attempted suicide, intentional self-inflicted injuries, service in the armed forces, aviation activities (if not a fare-paying passenger), and participation in a riot, felony, or insurrection.

- Preexisting conditions: A preexisting condition is an illness or disability for which you have already received medical advice or treatment. When shopping for a policy, make sure you know if it excludes preexisting conditions. Some policies exclude preexisting conditions from coverage for up to six months. Most good policies have no preexisting condition exclusions.

For example, if your doctor had previously treated you for arthritis, your policy might not cover that condition for six months. Should the arthritis require you to need long-term care during the first half year of your policy, the insurance company may refuse to pay benefits. However, after the six months have passed, any care resulting from your arthritis would be covered.

- Mental and nervous disorders: Long-term-care policies may exclude coverage for some mental and nervous disorders. Even so, the policies do cover age-related disorders such as Alzheimer's disease and senile dementia.

- Payment to family members: While most policies will not pay your family members to take care of you, other policies will. The policies that do offer family care compensation refer to this benefit as total home care. As you might guess, including this benefit increases the cost of your policy.

Premiums

There are six primary variables that affect the premiums on the policy. They are as follows:

- Age
- Health status
- Daily benefit amount
- Elimination period (the time before benefits begin)
- Benefit period
- Type of inflation protection

While you can do nothing about your age or current health status, the other four factors are within your control. Carefully consider each before buying a long-term-care policy. Any such policy should meet your individual needs without busting your budget.

Daily Benefits

When choosing a daily benefit amount, first consider where you live and the rising cost of long-term care. Nursing home costs vary widely across the nation. In general, highly populated urban facilities tend to be more expensive than their suburban and rural counterparts. According to CareGiverList.com, the average cost of a nursing home stay in Texas is $167 per day. Costs in California average $260 per day. A stay in New York State will set you back on average $322 per day.

It is important to know the costs of nursing facilities in your area before selecting a benefit amount. Contact and visit several local nursing facilities, assisted-living centers, home health-care agencies, and adult daycare facilities to discover the current price range. Don't be afraid to visit the facilities. You will find that nursing homes vary widely in prices and in the quality of care provided. It may be that you'll need to choose a higher benefit amount to get the quality of care you want.

You also need to understand how policies determine benefits – they either pay benefits using an *expense-incurred* method or an *indemnity* basis. An expense-incurred policy pays the actual charges as eligible services are received. An indemnity policy pays a flat amount no matter what the charges. For example, suppose you have a policy with a daily benefit of $100 and are staying at an assisted-living facility that charges $65 per day. An expense-incurred policy will pay $65 per day since the actual charge is less than the daily benefit. An indemnity policy would pay $100 per day even though the actual charges are less.

Elimination Period

Most policies contain a deductible, often referred to as the elimination period. This is the length of time that must pass before benefits begin and usually ranges from 0 to 100 days. Most policies have elimination period choices of 0, 20, 30, 60, 90, 100, 180, or 360 days. For example, if you choose a 30-day elimination period, the policy begins paying benefits on day 31. Premiums can be lowered if you choose a longer elimination period. Most good policies have only one elimination period. Other plans start a new elimination period for each new period of care. Be sure you understand how the elimination period works and choose a time frame that is within your means.

Benefit Period

Maximum benefits are measured in two ways: they can either be stated as a period of time or a total dollar amount. Policies that set a maximum time period often provide benefits stretching from one year to a lifetime. The most common benefit periods are one year, two years, three years, five years, six years, or a lifetime. As you might guess, the longer the benefit period, the higher the premiums.

Instead of stating a maximum period of time, some policies state a maximum dollar amount. For example, if you bought a policy with a lifetime benefit of $50,000, the policy would pay all the charges for care until the maximum dollar amount had been reached. In this case, if the current charge was $100 per day, the benefit would last for 500 days (over one year, four months). Make sure you understand how benefits are determined – either by a maximum period or by a maximum dollar amount – and carefully consider which is right for you.

Inflation Protection

In planning for future health needs, keep in mind that it will probably be many years before you actually need long-term-care services. Over that time, costs for long-term care will probably increase substantially. A benefit that would adequately cover expenses today may cover only a portion of the costs 10 or 20 years from now. According to some experts, a nursing home stay that now costs $100 a day could cost more than $200 a day in 10 years. Because care costs continue to rise, protection against inflation can be very important.

As you might guess, adding inflation protection will increase premiums. The amount of additional premium mainly depends on your age when you purchase the policy. The younger you are, the more inflation protection costs. On the other hand, since it could be many years until you receive any benefits, having inflation protection can be extremely important.

Inflation protection can be offered in one of three ways:
- Simple fixed-percentage increase
- Compounded fixed-percentage increase
- Optional fixed-percentage increase

Simple Fixed-Percentage Increase

A fixed-percentage policy automatically increases your benefits each year by a stated percentage of the original benefit. For example, suppose you had a policy with an original benefit amount of $100 per day. If it had a 5 percent per year simple inflation increase, in the second year, it would have a benefit of $105. The third year would provide a benefit of $110. By the twentieth year, it would provide a benefit of $200 a day.

Compound Fixed-Percentage Increase

Fixed-percentage policies can also come with a compounded percentage. Rather than simply adding a fixed dollar amount each year to the benefit, these policies add an ever-increasing amount. For example, suppose that you had a policy with a $100-per-day benefit and a 5 percent compounded inflation increase. Like the fixed-percentage policy, in the second year you would have a benefit of $105. However, in the third year your benefit would be $110.25. While the difference seems small, by the twentieth year, the policy would provide a benefit of $265 per day – $65 more than the simple fixed-percentage method. Given the same percentage increase, compound fixed-percentage policies will always have a higher future benefit amount than simple fixed-percentage policies.

Optional Fixed-Percentage Increase

Instead of being automatic, some policies give you a choice of whether you want your benefits increased every two or every three years. Since these policies tend to recalculate new rates on the holder's attained age, this inflationary strategy tends to be expensive. Even though the benefits increase, the premiums will increase as well. The older you get, the more substantial your premium increases will become.

Inflation Strategy

There is a simple rule of thumb to use in defending your long-term-care policy against inflation.

- Generally, those who are less than 65 years old should consider policies that have a compounded inflationary increase, because it could be decades before the policy is used. Compounded protection gives the most protection against inflation.

- Those who are 65 to 75 years old may want to consider a fixed-percentage policy. Since inflation has less effect in the short term, there is less risk of inflation diminishing the benefit amounts.

- Those over 75 may want to consider simply buying a higher benefit amount, since those in that age group will probably need the benefits sooner. A higher benefit amount may take care of any increases in care costs without the need of paying for an inflation benefit.

Nonforfeiture Benefits

Many companies offer the option of purchasing a guarantee that the policyholder will receive some long-term-care benefits even if their present coverage is cancelled or lost. This guarantee is called *nonforfeiture benefits*. In my opinion, this benefit has little value.

A typical nonforfeiture benefit usually will provide long-term-care payments up to the amount of all the premiums paid. For example, suppose you paid $3000 in premiums on a long-term-care policy for 10 years. For one reason or another, you quit making premium payments and let the policy drop. In the twelfth year, you started using long-term care. If the plan contained a nonforfeiture benefit, the policy would pay up to $3000 of your long-term-care costs. You and I both know that

$3000 would make very little difference in anyone's financial situation. With nonforfeiture benefits, higher premiums are charged for a benefit that offers very little assistance.

Other Benefits

Waiver Of Premium

All good policies include a waiver of premium provision. This feature allows you to stop paying premiums once your policy has begun paying benefits for institutional care (a nursing home or assisted living) or home health care. Some companies waive the premium as soon as they make the first benefit payment. Others wait 60 to 90 days.

Bed Reservation Benefit

If you are hospitalized during a nursing home or assisted-living stay, all good policies will pay to reserve your nursing home bed or assisted-living room for a specified number of days or until you return.

Refund Of Premium Benefits

Under this feature, some or all of the premiums, minus any claims paid under the policy, will be returned to the insured's beneficiaries after he or she dies.

Restoration Of Benefits

Some policies offer to restore benefits to the original maximum amounts if you remain treatment-free for a specified period (often 180 days). For example, suppose your policy has a maximum benefit of three years and you have already used one year. If you don't require long-term-care services for six months, a restoration of benefits provision could automatically restore the benefits to the original three years.

As might be expected, adding either of these last two benefits generally increases the premium cost.

Life Long-Term-Care Insurance Policy

A different type of long-term-care policy is a *life long-term-care insurance policy*. This type of policy can be an excellent choice for people who dislike receiving nothing back from their insurance coverage. This type of plan is simply a life insurance policy with long-term-care benefits. It can provide three choices of benefits:

- Death benefits for the heirs
- Long-term-care benefits for the policyholder
- Completely liquid funds should the premiums be needed

For example, suppose you purchased a policy with a $100,000 death benefit and a $200,000 long-term-care benefit for a single premium payment of $50,000. Like standard life insurance, if you died, your heirs would receive $100,000. On the other hand, if you needed long-term care, the policy will cover costs up to $200,000 – twice the death benefit. If, instead, you needed the cash from the policy, your original $50,000 is always available. The policy can be liquidated at any time for a full refund. This type of policy overcomes the drawback of having insurance that may never be used. One way or another, the policyholder gets something back.

Qualifying for a Long-Term-Care Policy

To provide coverage and still make a profit, companies want to be sure they understand your health and chances of needing long-term care in the future. They will look at an applicant's health history to determine whether or not they will issue a policy and, if they do, to determine the cost. Most good companies ask detailed questions regarding health status and will examine an applicant's medical records. Applicants 70 and over are often required to have a face-to-face interview. During such an interview, all health questions should be answered as truthfully and thoroughly as possible. If a company later learns that the truth was not fully disclosed, they may refuse to pay a claim or even cancel the policy.

Premium Increases

Once you own a long-term-care policy, the insurance company cannot change your rate because of age or health status. Nevertheless, all companies reserve the right to do a class premium increase (a bulk increase of policy premiums) for the state in which you reside.

Policy Cancellation or Modification

The only way a policy may be terminated is if you deliberately falsify information on the application, fail to pay premiums, or exhaust your benefits. In addition, companies cannot make any other changes to your policy unless you request such changes. It is important to note that generally after a policy has been in force for two years, a company cannot cancel it or refuse to pay claims because of misstatements in the application unless those statements were made with the intent of committing fraud.

Third-Party Notification and Reinstatement

Insurance companies provide two modes of protection to keep policyholders from losing a policy in case of being incapacitated. These are known as *third-party notification* and *reinstatement*. At the time of purchase, you are asked to designate another person who also will receive notice that the long-term-care policy is about to lapse (be canceled) because of an unpaid premium. This courtesy is called *third-party notification*. The third person can be a relative, friend, or a professional such as your lawyer or accountant.

Likewise, if a policy is canceled for nonpayment of premiums, the insurer will reinstate the policy if proof is received by five months of the cancellation date that the failure to pay was a result of mental or physical impairment. Third-party notification and reinstatement protect policyholders if they are physically or mentally unable to pay the premiums.

Free Look

In most states, insurance companies must give you at least 30 days to look over your long-term-care policy after you receive it. This is called a *free look period*. This is the time in which you may look over the policy closely to see if it is exactly what you wanted to purchase. If you decide to return the policy within the 30 days, you will receive a full refund of any premiums paid. Should you opt for the refund, use certified mail so you will have proof of when the policy was returned. For your records, you need to keep a copy of everything you return.

Replacing a Policy

Before replacing a long-term-care policy, several things should be considered. You need to determine how the current policy differs from the new one. There could be big advantages and disadvantages to replacing a policy. For example, the current policy might contain undesirable benefit limitations that are no longer allowed, or it might not contain benefits that must be offered in new policies. On the other hand, a new policy may be much more expensive than an older policy and provide no more benefits.

Older policies could include the following limitations:

- They may require a hospital stay before nursing home benefits are available.
- They may provide no or minimal home health care or adult daycare benefits.
- They may provide no inflation protection or benefit increases.
- They may provide no protection against cancellation because of a loss of mental or physical capacity.

- They may not provide nonforfeiture benefits.
- The benefit amounts may be too low to cover today's long-term-care expenses.

Likewise, an older policy may have advantages over a new policy. The old policy may be less expensive and provide tax advantages. Without a doubt, you've aged since buying the old policy. If you combine the additional age with any health problems experienced since the policy was purchased, you may find that the better benefits on a new policy cost substantially more than you are currently paying. Also, if the current policy was purchased before January 1, 1997, you may be able to deduct the premiums on your income tax return and enjoy tax-free status on any benefits received. This tax treatment will come into effect only if the new policy is qualified.

Before replacing any current long-term-care policies, carefully consider all the factors. If the current policy is replaced, the new company is usually required to give credit for any probationary periods (including waiting periods for coverage of preexisting health conditions) that have already been served under the current policy. Under no circumstances should you cancel a current policy until the new one is issued, or you may find yourself without any coverage at all.

Shopping Tips

- Retirees who qualify for Medicaid generally do not need long-term-care insurance.
- You may want to check on long-term-care coverage through your employer's group insurance plan before retiring. Keep in mind that your employer's plan may not be necessarily the best value. Many times a more competitive plan may be found by shopping around.
- The older you are when you buy a long-term-care policy, the higher the premium will be. Buying a policy long before you expect to need benefits will save money.

- Take the time to compare the policies, costs, and services of several different companies. Call the insurance department in your state to request a written company profile showing the company's history, complaint record, and financial rating. Again, take your time, and never be pressured into buying a policy. If an agent pressures you, walk away and get another agent.

- Never buy a policy or sign something you do not understand. Ask questions and discuss the policy with a trusted friend, relative, or advisor before making any purchases.

- Never sign a blank insurance application. Instead, answer all questions carefully and truthfully. An insurer can deny a claim or cancel a policy if an answer is not truthful.

- Examine all premium payment methods. Many policies will take premiums on a monthly, quarterly, semiannual, or annual basis. You may be able to get a discount on the premiums by paying for longer terms.

- Decide whether or not you want a paid-up plan. This type of plan allows you to make premium payments for a specified period and then keep the policy with no further contributions. For example, if someone in his forties wanted to own a paid-up plan for his retirement, he might choose a 10-year pay plan. Once the 10 years were up, the plan would be completely paid for and no further payments ever need to be made.

- Avoid purchasing multiple policies. It is not necessary to purchase several policies to get enough coverage. One good policy should be all you ever need.

Questions to Ask Yourself

The following are questions to ask yourself. By answering each one to the best of your knowledge, you will be able to decide if a long-term-care policy is right for you.

- How would I pay for long-term care if I ever needed it?
- If I needed long-term care, how long would my money last?
- What is my current annual income?
- Do I expect my income to change over the next 10 to 20 years? Will it stay about the same, increase, or decrease?
- Will I change from regular employment to a fixed or retirement income during that period? How will my ability to pay premiums or expenses be affected?
- How much per month and per year is the premium for the policy I am considering?
- Can I afford to pay long-term-care expenses during the elimination period for this policy?
- Will I pay each year's premium from my income, savings, or investments?
- Will my family pay premiums?
- Are my assets and income large enough that I need to protect them with a long-term-care insurance policy?
- Could my family members provide care for me?
- Would I want my family to provide long-term care for me?
- Based on my answers to all these questions, do I believe a long-term-care insurance policy is my best alternative?

Conclusion

Preparing for the risk of long-term care can be challenging and time-consuming. The factors affecting such a decision include every aspect of life from finances to family relationships. While there is no one right answer for every person, you can create a plan that is right for you. The peace of mind you get from knowing you and your loved ones are protected is worth the effort of planning. ◆

Chapter 17

Turning 70½: Required Minimum Distributions

There's an adage in the tax world that says, "The government giveth and the government taketh away." The idea being that when we get a tax break in one place, we usually get it taken away some place else. It is not surprising then that there are rules that "taketh away" some of the benefits of tax-qualified accounts such as IRAs and employer plans (such as 401k's). One such rule is commonly referred to as the *required minimum distribution* (*RMD*). Most investors enjoy the deferral power of IRAs. However, many people don't realize that when an investor turns 70½ years old (or when a nonspouse inherits an IRA), a new set of rules come into play. These rules require that money be withdrawn from the IRAs and employer plans each year.

In theory, the government designed the RMD rules to disgorge the deferred amounts on qualified accounts (IRAs and employer plans) so the taxes would eventually be paid. In reality, with a little forethought, retirees can stretch the distributions over many decades.

Beware of Mistakes

There are many missteps that can cause you (and your heirs) to pay higher taxes unnecessarily. For example, failure to distribute enough money during your lifetime can incur a stiff 50 percent penalty tax. Likewise, omitting beneficiary information on an IRA can cause your heirs to pay higher taxes. Your objective in learning about the RMD rules is to minimize your taxes now, minimize your heirs' taxes later, and avoid paying any penalties. In this chapter, I will go over some of the common mistakes and give you an easy-to-follow path.

Types of Plans under the RMD

The RMD rules generally apply to the following types of tax-qualified plans:

- Pension plans
- Employer plans such as profit sharing, 401k, and stock bonus plans
- Individual retirement accounts (IRAs)
- Simplified employee plans (SEPs)
- Tax-sheltered annuities, aka: 403(b)s (except for account balances existing on or before December 31, 1986, if not commingled with other funds.

Required Beginning Date (RBD)

It is generally understood that the RMD must be started when a person turns 70½ years old. This, to me, is rather strange. As a kid, I kept track of my half birthdays. They are very important when you long to be a year older. When someone asked how old I was, I would reply, "Eight and a half," or "Nine and a half." Evidently, the folks in Washington still think this way.

Here's an easy way to figure out which year you turn 70½. If your birthday is in January through June, you turn 70½ in the same year you turn 70. If your birthday is in July through December, you turn 70½ in the year you turn 71. Wasn't that easy?

As with all tax rules, the RMD guidelines have some tricks and exceptions. The first exception is that you don't actually have to take your first distribution in the year you turn 70½. Instead, you need to take your very first RMD distribution by April 1 of the year *after* you turn 70½. This date is known as your *required beginning date* (RBD). For most people, that date passes uneventfully and without a second thought. However, it is a focal point of many RMD rules.

The first choice to make in the year you turn 70½ is whether to take your first distribution in the year you turn 70½ or by April 1 of the next year (your RBD). If you decide to put off the distribution until the second year, you will be making two distributions in one year – the one for the year in which you turned 70½ and one for the year in which you turned 71½. If you think you might be in a lower tax bracket the second year, putting off the first RMD could save some money. On the other hand, putting off the distribution could force you into a higher tax bracket or disqualify some of your deductions (such as medical deductions). To answer the question of which year to distribute your first RMD, you will need to work closely with your tax professional.

Distribution Myths

I've found that many myths and misconceptions surround the RMD rules. The number one misconception is that you are required to distribute all of your retirement accounts at age 70½. This is absolutely false. In fact, the most any 70½-year-old must distribute for the first RMD is 3.79 percent of any qualified accounts.

Another question I hear is, "I took more money out of my IRA than I needed this year. Can I apply the overage to next year?" The answer is, no. The RMD is recalculated each year. Your distributions apply only to the year in which they are taken.

Keep in mind that the RMD rules only dictate the minimum amount to be disbursed from a retirement account. In no way do these rules impose a maximum amount that can be taken. If you need to take more money out of your retirement accounts than is dictated by the RMD rules, that isn't a problem.

Finally, retirees often ask if there is a way to completely avoid the taxation on RMD distributions. The answer is, no. If you inherit an IRA or turn 70½, there will be distribution requirements. The best way to fight the taxman on this issue is to lower your RMDs to their legal limit. After you've done everything in your power to minimize the distributions (e.g., making sure your IRAs list a beneficiary, using the recalculation method, setting up spousal takeover of the IRA after your death), you just pay the tax and go on. The distributions made from IRAs are simply added to your taxable income at tax time.

Distribution Calculation

Calculating the RMD is easy. Simply divide the total amount of your qualified accounts (e.g., IRAs) on December 31 of the previous year by a number found on an IRS table that corresponds to your age at the end of the year. The table used is called *IRS Table III* and is found in IRS *Publication 590*. For your convenience, I've included it as Illustration 8 on the next page.

Table III Exception: If your spouse is more than 10 years younger than you and is the sole beneficiary of your IRA, it is to your advantage to use Table II of IRS *Publication 590* instead of Table III. In this case, Table II provides for a lower RMD than Table III.

Two Calculation Methods

The IRS code provides you with two ways of using this table to calculate your RMDs. One is known as the *term certain method*. The other is known as the *recalculation method*. Understanding these two methods is not only important to your lifetime distributions but also for your heirs. While the distribution rules allow spouses to choose the recalculation method, nonspousal heirs must use the term certain method when they inherit qualified accounts.

Term Certain Method

The term certain method is easy to understand. After starting your initial distribution, the divisor goes down by 1 year for each distribution. For example, suppose Wilmer was age 70 at the end of the year in which he turned 70½ (i.e., his birthday is in the first half of the year). He would use the divisor of 27.4 from the table for his first RMD. In that year, he would need to distribute at least 1/27.4 (3.65 percent) of the account. The next year, he would use a 26.4-year divisor. In other words, at 71, he would need to distribute 1/26.4 (3.79 percent) of the account. At 72, he would distribute 1/25.4 (3.94 percent) and so on. The distribution percentage would continue to increase until finally, when he turned 97, he would distribute the balance (100 percent) of the account.

Table III (Uniform Lifetime)			
(For Use by: • Unmarried Owners, • Married Owners Whose Spouses Are Not More Than 10 Years Younger, and • Married Owners Whose Spouses Are Not the Sole Beneficiaries of Their IRAs)			
Age	Distribution Period	Age	Distribution Period
70	27.4	93	9.6
71	26.5	94	9.1
72	25.6	95	8.6
73	24.7	96	8.1
74	23.8	97	7.6
75	22.9	98	7.1
76	22.0	99	6.7
77	21.2	100	6.3
78	20.3	101	5.9
79	19.5	102	5.5
80	18.7	103	5.2
81	17.9	104	4.9
82	17.1	105	4.5
83	16.3	106	4.2
84	15.5	107	3.9
85	14.8	108	3.7
86	14.1	109	3.4
87	13.4	110	3.1
88	12.7	111	2.9
89	12.0	112	2.6
90	11.4	113	2.4
91	10.8	114	2.1
92	10.2	115 and over	1.9

Illustration 8 – Table III

While easy to calculate, this method may not be the best. By using a different method, the *recalculation method*, you can decrease your distribution percentage and resulting taxes.

Recalculation Method

The recalculation method allows you to stretch (and reduce) distributions by recalculating the divisor each year. As discussed earlier, Wilmer would have to distribute 1/27.4 of the account at age 70. This is the same for either RMD method. The difference in distributions occurs in following years.

With the recalculation method, instead of reducing the divisor by one, we go back to the *Publication 590* tables and get the next number. At age 71, he would use a divisor of 26.5 instead of 26.4. While this difference is small at first, the older you are, the bigger the difference between the methods. For example, when Wilmer reached 97, the term certain method would require him to distribute 100 percent of his qualified accounts, while the recalculation method would require him to distribute only 13.16 percent of the accounts in that year.

Distributions To Beneficiaries

Carefully complying with the rules will have the greatest impact on your beneficiaries. Making bad choices could mean beneficiaries have to distribute all the accounts within a year. Good choices can enable beneficiaries to enjoy tax-deferred status for many decades.

The Mythical "Stretch IRA"

People frequently ask me, "Which is better, a traditional IRA, a Roth IRA, or a stretch IRA?" I always have to explain that nothing in the tax code describes a *stretch IRA*. It simply doesn't exist. The term "stretch IRA" is a marketing moniker created by people selling financial products such as mutual funds. Brokers and other salespeople use the mythical creation to pack sales seminars with eager learners. The reality is that you can turn any traditional IRA into a so-called stretch IRA by simply naming your beneficiaries on your IRA.

Name a Beneficiary and a Contingent Beneficiary

One of the biggest mistakes made on IRAs and other qualified accounts is not naming beneficiaries. Since the accounts will go to their estate, anyway, many people don't consider naming beneficiaries such a big deal. However, when it comes to the distribution rules, naming or not naming beneficiaries is a very big deal. If you fail to name beneficiaries, the estate may have to completely distribute the accounts over a short period of time and pay the resulting income taxes. By simply naming your beneficiaries, your heirs can stretch the distributions out over time. If done well, the distributions can be made over decades instead of months.

Nonspousal Beneficiaries (e.g., Children, etc.)

Nonspousal beneficiaries have few distribution choices about their RMDs. In general, when you inherit an IRA from someone other than a spouse, required distributions are based on your single life expectancy as listed in Table I of IRS *Publication 590*. (For your convenience, I have included the table for beneficiaries 56 and older – Table I – as Illustration 9 on the next page.) Remember that nonspousal beneficiaries cannot use the recalculation method. They must use the term certain method.

For example, a 56-year-old woman who inherited an IRA from her mother would have to distribute the inherited IRA over 28 years or less. (The first RMD would be 1/28.7 or 3.48 percent.) As a nonspousal beneficiary, she would be able to use only the term certain method for the distributions.

There is an important exception to this general method: if someone inherits an IRA from a widowed spouse who never "took over" the IRA. (I'll discuss "spousal takeovers" next.) In that case,

Table I (Single Life Expectancy) (For Use by Beneficiaries)			
Age	Life Expectancy	Age	Life Expectancy
0	82.4	28	55.3
1	81.6	29	54.3
2	80.6	30	53.3
3	79.7	31	52.4
4	78.7	32	51.4
5	77.7	33	50.4
6	76.7	34	49.4
7	75.8	35	48.5
8	74.8	36	47.5
9	73.8	37	46.5
10	72.8	38	45.6
11	71.8	39	44.6
12	70.8	40	43.6
13	69.9	41	42.7
14	68.9	42	41.7
15	67.9	43	40.7
16	66.9	44	39.8
17	66.0	45	38.8
18	65.0	46	37.9
19	64.0	47	37.0
20	63.0	48	36.0
21	62.1	49	35.1
22	61.1	50	34.2
23	60.1	51	33.3
24	59.1	52	32.3
25	58.2	53	31.4
26	57.2	54	30.5
27	56.2	55	29.6

Illustration 9 – Table I

the IRA must be distributed over the assumed life expectancy of the widowed spouse at the time of his or her spouse's death. Since the widowed spouse will probably have a much lower life expectancy than her beneficiaries (often her children), it could mean that the IRA must be distributed much quicker. This exception can have serious implications for the unwary.

Spousal Takeover

When a spouse dies, the widow has a choice to make. The spouse can either continue the IRA under the deceased spouse's name or *take over* the IRA. A spousal takeover is just that. The IRA account is renamed into the name of the surviving spouse. Generally, at a death, a spousal takeover is advised. Often, this move will give the surviving spouse and the surviving spouse's heirs lower distribution requirements and added flexibility. (Takeovers are only available to surviving spouses – nonspousal heirs, like children, cannot take over an IRA.

For example, let's look at the Jensons. In January 2008, Herbert Jenson turned 70½ and started taking his RMDs from his $200,000 IRA. A year later, he died and left the IRA to his wife, Marie. Unaware of the tax consequences to her only daughter, Marie continued Herbert's IRA unchanged. She reasoned that since she needed the cash for living expenses, there was no reason to change the IRA or its distributions. In 2012, Marie died at the age of 70, leaving the IRA to her 40-year-old daughter, Laura. Because no thought had been given to the IRA, Laura faced a much higher annual tax bill than if her mother simply had taken over the IRA by putting it in her name and naming Laura as her beneficiary.

Had Marie taken over Herbert's IRA, Laura would have been able to distribute the IRA over her life expectancy (43.6 years according to IRS *Publication 590*). Unfortunately, since Marie left the IRA alone, Laura will have to distribute the IRA over her mother's published life expectancy of 17 years (again IRS *Publication 590*). In other words, by the time Laura is 57, she will have to distribute and pay tax on the entire IRA balance. Had her mother simply taken over the IRA, Laura could have enjoyed the tax-deferred status of the account until she was in her 80s.

Because it is such an easy mistake to make, a widow's failure to take over the retirement accounts is probably one of the most common RMD mistakes. Once the remaining spouse dies, there is no way to go back and undo the damage. The heirs have to do the best they can.

As I mentioned before, when taking over the retirement accounts, the widow needs to be sure he or she doesn't forget to name a beneficiary – a potentially even more costly mistake for the heirs since the IRAs might then have to be distributed far more quickly – as short as one to five years after death. The RMD rules are complicated and tedious. Rather than my boring you with the details, just remember that naming a beneficiary on your retirement accounts and IRAs is very important.

Where to Take Distributions

If you have several qualified accounts (e.g., several IRAs), you don't have to take distributions from each. After calculating the amount of total distributions (total RMD), you can take them from any account.

Suppose a retiree named Darlene has two IRAs, each worth $50,000. If her total RMD is $2000, she can distribute from one account or both accounts. She can take the entire $2000 from one account, or she may decide to take $500 from one account and $1500 from the other. As long as Darlene distributes $2000, it doesn't matter which account it comes from.

Also, if you are taking income from your IRAs during the year, these distributions count toward your RMDs, as well. Any money that is distributed from IRAs during the year, counts toward required minimum distributions.

Note: As with most tax laws, there is one exception to this general rule. Required minimum distributions from tax-sheltered annuities (403(b)s) must be made from 403(b)s only. Likewise, RMDs from other qualified accounts cannot be made from 403(b)s. For example, Sarah has several IRAs worth a total of $50,000 and a 403(b) worth $60,000. She must take the RMDs on her IRAs from her IRAs and her RMD on her 403(b) from her 403(b) plan.

In-Kind Distributions

Another distribution strategy is to take distributions *in-kind* rather than in cash. When taking an in-kind distribution, you take the actual investments out of the qualified accounts rather than cash. While this type of distribution is still taxable, investments need not be liquidated.

Suppose Kenneth has 1,000 shares of ABC Growth Fund (selling at $10/share) in his IRA. His required minimum distribution is $1000, but he doesn't need or want the cash. Instead of liquidating $1000 from his fund and distributing the cash, Kenneth could move $1000 worth of shares (100 shares at $10/share) to a nonqualified (regular) account. Just like a cash distribution, the transaction would be a taxable event. But since Kenneth doesn't need the cash, the transaction lets him satisfy the distribution requirement while keeping his investment portfolio intact.

New Variable Annuity Rules

In 2006, the IRS began enforcing special RMD rules for variable annuities in retirement accounts. Instead of simply using the account value of the variable annuity to calculate the RMD (as was done in the past), investors must now include part of the value of the "other benefits" (e.g., living benefit, death benefit), as well. While the change probably will not increase most investors' RMD much, it will substantially increase the difficulty in calculating it. Investors with (retirement account) variable annuities will now have to get their *RMD values* each year from each insurance company before they can calculate their RMDs correctly.

You Must Do It

Many people make the mistake of thinking that their RMDs will come automatically. They won't. You must initiate the process. If you don't, your distributions won't be made.

To simplify the RMD process, many mutual fund and annuity companies offer an automation service. When you give them instructions, many companies will automatically send your RMDs out each year. The money can be taken either monthly, quarterly, or annually. It is up to you. If you don't need the money, I usually recommend taking the distribution in late December. This strategy allows the money to grow tax-deferred until you absolutely have to make a distribution.

IRS *Publication 590*

The cornerstone guide to IRAs and required minimum distributions is IRS *Publication 590*. It describes the general rules for RMDs. You can order the publication by calling 800-829-3676 or logging on at http://www.irs.gov. However, since many of the rules in the publication have exceptions that are not listed or explained, I recommend getting sound professional advice before starting a distribution strategy.

Roth IRAs

With Roth IRAs, I frequently get two questions. The first question is, "Do I have to make required minimum distributions from a Roth IRA?" The answer is, no. Roth IRAs do not require any distributions during the owner's life. However, once the owner dies, the distribution rules that apply to traditional IRAs apply to Roth IRAs, as well.

The second question is a little slyer. People often ask me, "Can I roll my required minimum distributions into a Roth IRA?" Or asked another way, "If I convert some of my traditional IRAs to Roth IRAs, will those taxable amounts apply to my required minimum distributions?" This shows that people are always thinking. Unfortunately, the IRS is way ahead of us on this one. The IRS has answered this question with an emphatic, no. Roth conversion amounts don't count toward RMDs, and RMDs cannot be rolled into a Roth IRA.

Typical Strategy

It is easy for us in the planning community to get bogged down in the rules and exceptions when we try to explain RMDs. In this chapter, I've listed a few of the high points. However, to clarify your understanding, I'm going to give you a final example of how planning for a RMD can stretch out the distributions.

Example of Good Planning

Roger retired from a large corporation. He rolled over his pension and 401(k) into a self-directed IRA. Getting good advice from his advisor, he named his wife, Theresa, as beneficiary. Years later, when he started taking his required minimum distributions, he used the recalculation method. This strategy allowed him to take the smallest distributions possible.

Several years later, Roger died. After consulting with her financial advisor, Theresa used the IRS's special spousal provision and took over the IRA as her own. Since Theresa was 68, she did not need to make any additional distributions until she turned 70 ½. She quickly named their only daughter, Beth, as her beneficiary. Several years later, Theresa died. By being proactive and taking over the IRA, Theresa had given Beth the ability to spread her required minimum distributions into her 80s.

While taking RMDs is simpler and much easier than in the past, there are still pitfalls to avoid. In the above example, there are many mistakes that easily could have been made. Roger might have failed to take his RMDs. He might have neglected to name a beneficiary before his death. Theresa might have neglected to take over the IRA. She might have failed to start her RMDs. She might have failed to name her daughter as beneficiary. Any one of these errors would have caused the distributions (and resulting taxes and penalties) to be much higher.

Conclusion

We all enjoy the power that tax-deferred investing, such as IRAs and employer plans, provide. These plans have given millions of people the opportunity to enjoy the financial freedom we call retirement. However, you need to be aware that what the government gives with one hand, it often takes away with the other. The required minimum distribution rules are an excellent example of this. Nevertheless, by putting a sound distribution strategy in place, you can significantly reduce your distributions and extend your IRA benefits over many decades. While the strategies are not difficult, they do require vigilance and planning ahead. ◆

Chapter 18

You Desperately Need An Estate Plan

In the decades I have served as a financial planner and advisor, I have found that the most neglected area in people's financial picture is estate planning. When I raise the subject of estate planning, people often tell me, "I don't need an estate plan because my estate is not worth enough. I don't have an estate tax problem."

Herein lies the biggest myth about estate planning – thinking that estate planning is only about avoiding taxes. For some, it is true that avoiding an estate tax gouge can be very important, especially if the estate value is very high. However, avoiding tax is just a small part of an estate plan. The real purpose of an estate plan is to protect yourself and your loved ones in a crisis. Without an estate plan, you have a huge hole in your Retirement Solutions. You need to act now to protect yourself and your loved ones during your life and at the time of death.

Estate plans should address two areas:

• Who will you depend on?

• Who gets what?

In this chapter, I will discuss both areas and the tools that are used to meet your goals.

Who Will You Depend On?

While elbow deep in writing this chapter, I began discussing it with my friend Nancy. Like many people, Nancy said she didn't need an estate plan because she didn't have very many assets. "My retirement plans and IRAs will transfer without a will," she assured me, "and my other assets would make a poor garage sale."

I let Nancy talk about how little she had to her name, but then I asked her a very important question. If she became disabled, who would make the decisions about her care? Who would pay her bills and make her money decisions? Likewise, who would be in charge of "pulling the plug," if such a thing ever became necessary?

Nancy thought about my question for a minute, her eyes growing wide. "Oh my gosh!" was all she could say. The next day, she contacted an estate attorney.

An important aspect of estate planning is to give the people upon whom you depend the legal right to help you in a crisis. An unanticipated injury or illness could put you at the mercy of others. Without your input and the appropriate documents, the decision-maker you trust may not be able to help if you became incapacitated. The time to specify the person you want making your decisions is now.

It is common for retirees and soon-to-be retirees to look to their children for decisions during an illness or long-term disability. Often, several siblings are involved. While on the surface this may seem like a good plan, it may be a recipe for trouble. For example, many families have a "responsible child" and a "less-than-responsible child." Unless the responsible child is specifically authorized to make the decisions, she may not have the power to help. I have frequently witnessed intense sibling fights over "what's best for Mom." It is not pleasant. The best thing you can do for yourself and your children is to specify who will make your decisions when you cannot.

The areas that require assistance fall into two broad categories: money and health care. Sometimes, people divide the responsibilities. One sibling can make the money decisions while another makes the health-care decisions.

Money decisions include paying bills, managing investments, and selling real estate and other property. Choose someone who not only is trustworthy but also has a good head for business. The financial aspects of a crisis situation can become complicated whenever a person is incapacitated.

For example, if you were unconscious, you wouldn't be able to answer questions such as what bills have not been paid or who your financial professional is. Furthermore, these situations usually incur a mountain of bills that must either be paid or handled by insurance. The person who jumps into this type of situation has a very difficult job.

The health-care decisions can be just as trying. For example, the person designated to "pull the plug" must carry the burden of that decision for the remainder of his or her lifetime. Likewise, making the decision to admit someone into a long-term care facility can be emotionally trying. Even if everyone involved agrees that it is the right thing to do, these are never happy decisions. Be sure you discuss your wishes with your decision-makers now, before the decisions have to be made; you will get the decisions you want and your decision-makers will feel better about making them.

It goes without saying that it is best to ask your decision-makers if they want the job before naming them in the legal documents. Most people consider it one of life's honors to be trusted enough to be asked to help in time of trouble. Nevertheless, anyone who has ever served in this capacity will readily admit that the responsibility is grueling and often thankless. Asking permission before naming them is the least you can do for the people on whom you will ultimately depend.

Planning For Death . . .
"Yuck, Do I Have To Do This?"

It is kind of depressing to execute documents that we know will be read after we are dead. They not only serve as a reminder that we're going to die, they also create tangible monuments to that fact. Nevertheless, this is the one part of our estate plan that absolutely will be used. It is critical that we prepare for death.

Who Gets What

One of the biggest issues upon death is "who gets what." Even if you only have a vague interest in where your stuff goes, you probably have some preferences. Surely you would prefer that your assets go to sound charities than to strangers, attorneys, and the government. Some of the issues that tend to complicate who gets what are marriage, divorce, disputes, and taxes.

Marriage

Without question, marriage passes more estates to strangers than any other cause. Even honest, well-meaning people can produce the wrong results if definite plans are not in place.

Let's look at the story of Juanita, whose estate ultimately went to people she didn't know. A few years ago, Juanita died at age 80. Her only daughter, Lisa, inherited her mother's home and her rather substantial portfolio. Lisa had three grown children and more than a dozen grandchildren. Before she died, Juanita told Lisa that she was entrusting her to use the money for her numerous great-grandchildren. She wanted Lisa to use her estate to pay the expenses of those who attended college. Lisa was doing a good job until the unexpected happened. Lisa died.

Lisa's husband, Karl, was a great guy. He had met Lisa five years before Juanita died. After a whirlwind romance, they married. Karl was a good man who had children of his own. He knew Lisa had been helping her grandchildren and was supportive of her efforts. After her death, Karl honored Lisa's (and her mother's) wishes: He continued to support Lisa's grandchildren. This would have been perfect except for one thing. Karl died, too. Because of a lack of an estate plan by both Lisa and Karl, all of Lisa's estate went to Karl's children. Lisa's heirs got nothing. Because no legal provisions were made, Juanita's great-grandchildren have to look elsewhere for their college funds.

Divorce

Another area that causes more problems in an estate than death is divorce. Inheritances are routinely split with ex-spouses. However, in most states, this need not happen. With a little planning, heirs can keep their entire inheritances during divorce. Unfortunately, once the divorce is started, it is usually too late to start planning. When working with your estate planner, be sure to do two things. First, be sure you understand your state's marital laws and how your planning will affect your heirs during a divorce. Ask your estate planner to explain how spouses can protect themselves and their heirs. Discuss what tools should be used. Understand in what name(s) accounts should be held. Finally, learn how to avoid commingling your money with your marital property.

Be sure to communicate with your spouse about the provisions you've made. No one should be afraid of offending his or her spouse in this area. Loving spouses want their mates to be protected. Objections usually come when there's already trouble in the marriage. All retirees or soon-to-be retirees need to protect themselves against the consequences of divorce.

Disputes

I find that people can be unpredictable. When an inheritance is up for grabs, I've seen nice people become mean and grabby. Brothers and sisters often fight bitterly when Mother or Father dies. All too frequently, fights spill over from the living room to the courtroom. In the courtroom, attorney fees and court costs burn up much of a parent's life savings. Entire estates are often transferred to attorneys and the court system because of disputes.

The best way to resolve disputes is to avoid them. Identify potential trouble while you're still alive and take actions now to preserve the peace. Each family is different. Some have cooperative siblings: everyone gets along and the estate transfer goes smoothly. Other families are more contentious. Without proper provisions in place, dividing an estate can amount to the civil equivalent of World War III.

To further complicate matters, in-laws often stir up what otherwise would have been a peaceful situation. When thinking about who gets what, examine the personalities involved and the events that are likely to occur. Then instruct your estate attorney to craft your estate documents to minimize possible disputes.

As everyone knows, women usually outlive men. It goes without saying that a husband should be especially sensitive to how his wife might fare in the event she became a widow. I've seen situations where a manipulative child needled Mother to change the estate plan after Dad died – particularly as Mom became more dependent.

If you're a husband, ask yourself what would happen if you died and your wife became disabled or less mentally aware. Just like death, your spouse's disability can cause disputes. Take steps now to be sure that any individual who may take advantage of the surviving spouse is prevented from doing so. By deciding who will be the decision-makers and taking steps to ensure your wishes aren't thwarted later, you can protect your spouse and promote family harmony.

Transfer Taxes – Estate and Gift Taxes
History Of The Estate and Gift Tax

Before 1986, there were two separate transfer taxes, the *estate tax* (aka, *death tax*) and the *gift tax*. Each had a separate set of rules. Later,

Congress combined or unified these two taxes into a single tax code covering transfers of assets. Together, these taxes are now called the *unified transfer tax*. Even though the tax code on transfers has been unified they are still considered two taxes but with the amounts combined in the calculations and the tax computed from a single table.

Originally, estate and gift taxes were designed to fleece only the very rich. Over several decades, inflation eroded the dollar to the point that a vast number of Americans were subject to transfer taxes. After dilly-dallying for years, Congress finally instituted changes. Now, only estates worth over $5,250,000 (or $10,500,000 for couples) are subject to the taxes. If your estate is worth less than these amounts, you probably won't be subject to transfer taxes.

Applicable Exemption Amount

Two numbers are thrown around when talking about transfer taxes: $5,250,000 and $14,000. The $5,250,000 number (which goes up from time to time with inflation) represents the amount of assets an individual can ultimately transfer without paying any transfer tax. The IRS calls this number the *applicable exemption amount* (formerly the *unified exemption amount*).

Annual Exclusion

The $14,000 number (which also goes up from time to time with inflation) represents the amount you can gift to individuals each year without filing a gift tax return, also called the *annual exclusion*. It is often mentioned as a *tax-free annual gift exclusion*. It is simply the amount of assets that may be given to an individual each year without digging into the giver's applicable exemption amount.

For example, let's suppose that in 2013, Estelle gave each of her five grandchildren, the three neighbors across the street, and her mailman $14,000. Since each gift was $14,000 or less, they were exempt from gift tax and did not affect her applicable exemption amount. Since the amounts were all under the annual exclusion amount, she did not have to file a gift tax return either.

In 2014, Estelle is feeling even more generous. She gifts $20,000 to each of her five grandchildren, $15,000 to each of the three neighbors across the street, and $14,500 to her mailman. This time, each of her gifts exceeds $14,000. She must reduce her applicable exemption amount by $33,500 ($5,250,000 − $33,500 = $5,216,500).

This is easily calculated by taking the amount of each gift which exceeds $14,000 (5 x $6000 + 3 x $1000 + $500 = $33,500 reduction). Since she had never used any of her applicable exemption amount before, her remaining exemption amount in 2014 then becomes $5,216,000.

Notice that even though all her gifts in 2014 were over the $14,000 annual exclusion amount, no tax is due when she makes these gifts. She just uses up part of her applicable exemption amount. The only time she will pay tax is when she makes lifetime taxable gifts beyond $5,250,000 or her lifetime gifts plus bequests that fall beyond the applicable exemption amount. It is also worth noting that the exemption amount will go up over time with inflation.

As far as reporting to the IRS goes, since Estelle made gifts over the annual exclusion amount, she will need to file a gift tax return for 2014 even though she doesn't owe any tax.

Exemption Amounts For Married People

When Congress increased the exemption amount, it also simplified another aspect of the law. Just a few years ago, when a spouse died, any unused exemption amount was lost. This created a potential tax nightmare for the surviving spouse if he or she inherited the estate. To solve this problem, many couples used a sophisticated system of trusts to capture the exemption. Today, the exemption of the late spouse is automatically preserved. This means that without using a trust, a couple can pass $10,500,000 to their heirs without estate or gift taxes.

Trusts – Your Artificial Best Friend

Trusts are used in estate planning for a variety of reasons. But before we get to why you would use a trust, let's discover just what a trust is. I like to visualize a trust as an artificial person. This person's only purpose in life is to follow your written instructions. When you give or entrust your assets to this person, those wishes are handled exactly to your specifications.

Since a trust will follow any instructions you give, it can help you accomplish many goals. Perhaps you have an heir who cannot handle receiving a large sum of money at one time. You're afraid that this person would blow through an inheritance within a few months. You can protect the heir by putting your bequest in a trust. Through your instructions, you control how this person receives the money. For example, you could instruct the trust to pay the person a monthly income, pay for medical needs, pay for education, or whatever you decide but without giving this person access to the assets.

Trusts can also make sure that your money actually goes to your heirs. As an example, let's look at how a trust can help avoid problems in a blended family situation. Last Christmas, Alex married Rebecca. Both Alex and Rebecca had children from previous marriages. The couple discussed what would happen to Alex's assets should he die first. Alex wanted his assets to support Rebecca during her life with the remainder going to his son, Brandon. To make this happen, Alex and Rebecca drew up their wills with instructions on where the money would go, but they didn't use a trust.

As often happens, Alex died first. A few years after his death, Rebecca's daughter, Kristy, convinced her mother to change her will and cut out Brandon. A year later, Rebecca died. All her assets, including Alex's, went to Kristy. In spite of their agreement and original wills, Brandon received nothing.

In this case, Alex could have left his money to a trust instead of his wife. He could have instructed the trust to support Rebecca for the rest of her life. At her death, the remainder of his assets would have been distributed to his son, as he wanted. By using a trust, Alex's transfer to Brandon would have been secure.

Types of Trusts

You will hear all types of names given to trusts: A/B Trusts, Living Trusts, Charitable Remainder Trusts, Charitable Income Trusts, and Loving Trusts. The list goes on and on. Generally, attorneys assign fancy names to trusts for identification and marketing purposes. Don't worry about the name, just focus on what the trust accomplishes.

Hire an Attorney

Under no circumstances should you craft a do-it-yourself trust. To do so is to invite disaster. There are many complicated laws governing the use and taxation of trusts. When creating a trust, hire an attorney who specializes in estate planning. Avoiding the pitfalls that could spell disaster for your estate plan will more than offset the attorney's fee.

Living (in vivos) vs. Dead (testamentary) Trusts

The birth of a trust can occur at either of two times – when you're alive or when you're dead. Trusts created when you're alive are commonly called *living trusts*. Usually, people will transfer their assets to a living trust to avoid having their assets go through probate. Since the trust is immortal, it will be around after you die to distribute your assets without court intervention.

Nevertheless, some people feel uncomfortable with putting their assets in a trust while they're alive. No problem. Simply put instructions in your will to have the trusts created after you die. These *testamentary trusts* pop into existence at the time of death. The main problem with testamentary trusts is with their funding, or getting the assets into the trust. If the assets are probate assets (transferred by will or state law), then they have to go through a probate court to get into the trust. This brings up an important subject – how assets pass at death.

How Assets Pass At Death

While we are alive, the law provides each of us with the right to own property. However, dead people don't have property rights. At death, our property transfers to other people. But who has the authority to decide who is entitled to our property and to transfer it? Let's look at how transfers at death work.

There are two general ways assets pass at death – in court and out of court. Some assets, by their very nature, are out-of-court assets. For example, when someone is designated as the beneficiary of a life policy, that beneficiary collects the money upon the death of the policyholder without going to court. The insurance company simply pays whoever is designated as beneficiary on the policy.

Likewise, you can change an in-court transfer to an out-of-court transfer by how an asset is held. A good example of this is when you take title to real estate as joint tenants with rights of survivorship. At the death of the first tenant (owner), the surviving tenant receives the entire real estate interest – without going to court. As we all know, going to court is rarely a joyous occasion. With careful planning, many estates pass to the heirs entirely without the cost and hassle of court intervention.

In-Court Assets

In-court assets are known as *probate assets*. Very simply, probate is the court process of deciding who gets what. If you die with a will (*testate*), that document generally guides the probate process. If you die without a will (*intestate*), the court uses the law and its best judgment to decide who gets what. Either way, these in-court assets have to pass through the court system and under the nose of a judge. In general, if an asset isn't an out-of-court asset, it must pass through the probate process.

Out-of-Court Assets

Out-of-court assets or *nonprobate assets* are just as they sound. They are assets that pass outside the court system. Some of the out-of-court transfers occur by contract. Examples of these include life insurance, IRAs, retirement plans, annuities, and assets held with rights of survivorship. Those persons listed as your beneficiaries will receive these out-of-court assets. For example, suppose Harry listed his son, Matt, as his beneficiary on his IRA. But in his recently completed will, Harry listed his daughter, Jamie, as the recipient of these assets. At Harry's death, who do you think gets the IRA? The answer is Matt. On contract assets, whoever is listed as beneficiary, will receive the assets.

The second type of out-of-court assets are those held by irrevocable trusts. These assets do not go through probate, because, technically, you don't own them – the trust does. When you die, only the assets you own are included in your probate estate. Since assets in a trust don't belong to you, they are not included in the probate action. After your death, the trust merely follows your instructions about who gets what and when. By putting your assets in a trust before you die, you can turn in-court assets (those that would have passed through the court system) into out-of-court assets (those that pass without the oversight of a judge).

Be Careful Naming Beneficiaries

Keep in mind that the reverse is also true; out-of-court assets can also be converted into in-court assets – often by accident. Several years ago, one of my dearest clients died. He left a variable annuity to his daughter. Since he named her as the beneficiary, the annuity passed to her very quickly and easily. No probate hearing was necessary.

After the account was transferred, I called the daughter to discuss her financial future and the annuity. Unfortunately, she had no interest in financial planning or discussing the investment. Over the next two years, she continued the variable annuity without any changes whatsoever. Then she died.

Her husband called me wanting to get the annuity changed into his name. I had to be the one to tell him that there was bad news and there was worse news. The bad news was that since no beneficiary had been named, he was headed for probate court. The worst news was that since she had not named him as her beneficiary, he could not use the spousal continuation rule. In other words, the annuity had to be completely disbursed. All the gains – in this case about 75 percent of a very large investment – would become subject to income taxes.

It was a shame, too. He described to me the extensive estate planning they had done. They had even created a living trust so that they could avoid probate. Unfortunately, since the annuity had no named beneficiary, it needed to go through probate court. The time and money spent on a living trust had been wasted. Had his wife simply named him or the trust as the beneficiary, the assets would have passed easily and quickly – and without triggering income-tax consequences.

This story illustrates how easy it is to mess up an estate plan by making beneficiary mistakes. To avoid unnecessary expenses and taxes, be sure you understand how each of your assets will pass – either in-court or out-of-court. Also, be sure that your beneficiary designations coordinate with your entire estate plan. Costly mistakes are extremely easy to make when filling out the forms for IRAs, annuities, and life insurance policies.

When You Need Help

A large part of your estate plan is naming those who will help you in time of need. The two issues that you should address are who will make your money decisions and who will make your medical decisions. It is not uncommon for families to erupt in fighting when Mother or Father needs help. Disagreements about a parent's care and how that parent's money should be invested have split many families apart. Designating who should have control not only will ensure that the surviving parent is well cared for, it also keeps family harmony and makes it easier for the chosen decision-makers to do their jobs.

Durable Power Of Attorney

A *durable power of attorney* gives the person you designate (your *attorney-in-fact*) the power to execute your financial affairs. This person (or agent) has the right to act on your behalf as your legal authority to handle your business. Their powers would include the ability to execute agreements, write checks, pay bills, trade securities, and so on. It is as if you were taking these actions yourself.

Notice the word "durable." Unlike a general power of attorney that becomes powerless when the issuer becomes incompetent, a durable power of attorney stays in effect; that's what the durable means. Your disability or incompetence doesn't invalidate the power. It is the *durability* during your time of need that makes the instrument work.

Since the durable power of attorney legally binds you to your decision-maker's actions, choose someone you trust – someone who is competent in financial affairs and who is familiar with your financial situation. Remember that this is the person who will be making your decisions when you cannot. Under no circumstances should you name a person as your agent if you have the slightest doubt about that person's trustworthiness or competence.

It is a good idea to discuss your affairs with that selected person before you become disabled and to organize your business so that this person can take over smoothly. Make sure he or she knows where your financial records, checkbook, and legal documents are kept. The more organized your books, the better your designated durable power of attorney will be able to help you.

Problems With Durable Powers Of Attorney

While durable powers of attorney are excellent estate-planning instruments, they do have drawbacks. First, a durable power of attorney terminates at the time of death. This is an extremely important point. If you die with incomplete business, your agent could face serious difficulties in completing unfinished business. Second, your agent may have difficulty using his or her power to follow through with your wishes. Banks and financial institutions are not obligated to honor a power of attorney. They could require your agent to get a court order.

Terminates At Death

Even though a durable power of attorney is active during disability, the power terminates at the time of death. At the moment of your death, your attorney in fact can no longer conduct your business. Your estate administrator (i.e., the person authorized by the probate court to administer your estate) takes over. This is an extremely important point. Durable powers of attorney work for the living only; therefore, it is important that your agent be advised of this. Any business your durable power of attorney conducts for you following your death is invalid and could possibly be construed as fraudulent.

May Not Be Honored

Lately, I've had several people tell me that banks and financial institutions have refused to honor their durable powers of attorney. To transact business, they had to get a court order enforcing their authority. When an institution refuses to honor the power, it pretty much ruins the reason for executing one. Avoiding court is exactly what a durable power of attorney is trying to accomplish.

We cannot blame the institutions though. It is a sign of our times. Banks are extremely fearful of fraud. They bear the risk should the power be phony or inappropriately used. For example, suppose Melva took off on a vacation to Europe for a month. A criminal could approach the bank with a durable power of attorney claiming that Melva was in the hospital and then proceed to access her funds. When Melva returned home, the bank would have to replenish her account at its own expense.

Directive To Physician

The *Directive to Physician* is also known as a *living will*. This document simply states the kind of medical treatment you want or don't want should you become unable to make your own decisions and are unlikely to recover. For example, you may state that should you become vegetative, you don't want heroic actions to be taken such as breathing assistance, intravenous feeding, or kidney dialysis.

The most useful aspect of a directive is to make your wishes known at a time when you are thoroughly cognizant. The problem is, no matter how thorough the document, it cannot cover every situation. Because of that, you will need to appoint someone to make the tough decisions for you. The document that designates that person is known as a *health-care power of attorney* or *medical power of attorney*.

Medical Power of Attorney

Like a durable power of attorney, a *medical power of attorney* appoints someone to help you in your time of need. As you can tell from the title, the power covers your medical decisions. The advantage of using a medical power of attorney over a living will is the flexibility. The appointed person is free to exercise his or her judgment. The designee can consult with doctors, understand the ramifications of all possible decisions, and apply this knowledge to what he or she believes you would want. There is no way a living will can deal with every contingency.

Appointing someone you trust with your health-care decisions helps you get the necessary help in time of crisis.

Small Businesses

Frequently neglected areas of estate planning concern small businesses. If you have a small business or are in a business partnership, you need to be sure that you, your heirs, and your partners are all protected. Consider what would happen if you died. Would your heirs be protected? Would they be able to take your place? Could they access the business's assets? Would your customers or partners want to be in business with your heirs? If the business had to be sold, would your heirs know what to do or whom to call?

If you're in a partnership, consider what would happen if one of your partners died. Would you be in business with his or her heirs? How would the business be valued? How would you fund paying the heirs their equity?

There are many issues surrounding small businesses and partnerships. I could write a separate book on that subject alone. Be aware that if you own a business or are a partner in a business, you need heavy-duty estate planning. You need to talk with an attorney (and your partners) now. After the death of a small-business owner, the problems pile up quickly.

Review Your Life Insurance

In general, retirees need very little life insurance. The two most common reasons life insurance is needed are estate tax planning and pension planning.

Funding Estate Taxes With Life Insurance

As discussed earlier, there are many strategies that can be used to minimize estate taxes. Another strategy is simply to fund the payment of estate taxes with a life insurance policy. For example, suppose that Donald died today and his estate owes $1,000,000 in estate taxes.

If Donald is in good health, he could simply buy a $1,000,000 life insurance policy before his death to pay the taxes. Compared to the taxes owed, the policy would be very inexpensive. In other words, life insurance is a very cheap way to pay estate taxes.

The biggest mistake people make when using this strategy is not giving the policy away while they are still alive. Using the above example, if Donald owned the $1,000,000 life policy, the death benefit would be piled onto his estate. While his heirs would owe no income tax on the proceeds, they would owe estate taxes. Since estate taxes start at 40 percent, the tax could be substantial.

To avoid this tax, Donald can simply get the policy out of his estate by gifting it to his heirs or to a trust. Since he is not the owner when he dies, the policy is not included in his estate. If he wants to make the premium payments, he simply gifts cash to the heirs or to the trust each year. They can then use the cash to make the premium payments. If Donald decided to use a trust, he would need to form an *irrevocable life insurance trust* or *ILIT*. After his death, the trust will distribute the proceeds as he proscribes.

Protecting a Pension with Life Insurance

The second most common life insurance need for retirees is to protect a pension. While most pensions offer survivorship choices, many do not. For example, some government pensions cease when the pensioner dies. The spouse is left with nothing. To protect the surviving spouse against this risk, life insurance is often used.

To protect a spouse, a pensioner simply purchases a life insurance policy that will provide enough money to replace the lost pension income. At the pensioner's death, the money is invested to provide a new income stream. Keep in mind that the policy's death benefit needs to be large enough to replace the pension income for life. In the case of a government pension, the amount needs to be enough to provide inflationary increases, as well.

Final Arrangements

Of all the estate-planning decisions, making the final arrangements is probably the most dreaded. But this is the one area in which you can save your loved ones emotionally wrenching decisions and a good chunk of money, as well.

Issues to think about:

- Do you want your remains to be buried, cremated, or donated to science?
- If buried, what kind of casket do you want?
- Where will the service be conducted?
- Who will conduct the service?
- What music will be played?
- Do you want donations to a favorite charity in lieu of flowers?

Burial

It is no secret that families often overspend when burying loved ones. By arranging your own funeral – picking out your own casket and avoiding the add-ons that the funeral directors often try to sell – you can save your family a lot of money.

Be careful when purchasing a prepaid funeral plan. Many people purchase these plans and never use them. In addition to situations such as getting remarried and buried with a subsequent spouse, prepaid expenses are often not honored. It is not uncommon for prepaid plans to be refused when a funeral home goes bankrupt, is bought out, or becomes financially unsound.

I met one young man who decided to have fun with making his own funeral plan. In addition to purchasing his plot ahead of time, he also purchased his casket, and stored it in his garage. He was always popular at Halloween when he loaned his coffin out to the neighborhood haunted house. He figured that since he was buying the casket, anyway, he might as well enjoy using it. He also discovered another use for the container. When daily problems started to get him down, he would meander out to the garage and take a good look at that casket. He said it always put his troubles in perspective.

Cremation

Without a doubt, cremation is much less expensive than burial. But even here, a little shopping around can save a lot of money. For example, I recently spoke to a man who was making this type of arrangement. He said that by contacting a service outside his metropolitan area, he was able to save 80 percent of the cost. The crematorium would even pick up the body and deliver the ashes.

Donation to Medical Science

For many people, the best bargain in final funeral plans is a donation to medical science. Medical science desperately needs people to make donations for training and research. By donating your body, you will have the satisfaction of knowing you are helping others while sparing your family the expense and worry of final disposition of your remains.

Donation to Medical Schools

As we all know, medical schools have an ongoing need of bodies for teaching and research. Since there is usually little or no expense for the family with this plan, body donation may be an economical, as well as generous, choice. Most medical schools pay for nearby transportation as well as embalming and final disposition. The school may have a contract with a particular firm for transporting bodies, so it is important to inquire about the specific arrangements to be used at the time of death in order to avoid added costs. After medical study, the body is usually cremated. If requested, the remains can be returned to the family for burial within a year or two. Contact your local medical school to learn their policies.

If you don't have a local medical school, you can contact the National Anatomical Service in New York at 800-727-0700. The NAS has been in the business of procuring and transporting cadavers for various medical schools since 1975 and is aware of the schools with the greatest need.

Organ Donation

With the advances in medical science over the last decade, organ transplants have become fairly common. Organ donation at the time of death could mean the gift of sight or even a second chance at life to the recipient. When wishing to make your organs available, you need to make sure your next-of-kin and physicians know your preference. Your intent should be noted on any medical or hospital records. It is important to note, though, that a body from which organs have been removed usually will not be accepted for medical study.

Conclusion

Obviously none of us likes to contemplate our disability or death. But as someone who has created an estate plan for himself, I know the satisfaction of being prepared for the unexpected. In addition to protecting those that you care about, you can be assured that those whom you trust will be making decisions for you in your time of need. Estate planning is simply preparing a plan to protect you and your loved ones against the unexpected. Each person desperately needs an estate plan. ◆

Retirement

Chapter 19

Forecasting Depressions

I n a bookcase in my home, I have an entire shelf dedicated to what I call "disaster books." When these books were published, they all predicted that a severe economic and financial disaster was just around the corner. Copyrights in my collection date as early as the 1960s and as late as this year. The authors in each decade focused on the issues of the day. For example, the books from the 1960s predicted a disaster through the international devaluation of the dollar. Writers from the 1970s focused on runaway inflation. In the 1980s, the authors predicted that runaway deficit spending and crushing debt would end the western world. In the 1990s, the tomes predicted a horrendous stock market crash would cause economic ruin. Disaster in the new millennium received an early start when countless books predicted that a catastrophic computer bug named *Y2K* would finish us off. Besides being wrong, all of these alarmist books have one thing in common: They predicted an economic depression was near at hand.

Only these "Chicken Little" authors themselves know whether they published their books to simply earn money or if they actually did believe that the "sky was falling." One thing is certain: They scare a lot of people into making bad financial choices. I've seen people wait years to invest or make critical financial decisions because an author predicting disaster convinced them of impending doom. Worse, I've seen people squander their money on questionable assets based on their belief that civilization was near the end. In my opinion, unrealistic fear is the number one hazard that deters otherwise logically thinking adults from taking positive, productive action for financial success.

History Haunts Us

These disaster-book fear mongers get much of their alarmist power from an event that occurred decades ago – the Great Depression. The Great Depression of the 1930s made such an impact on our American psyche that the reverberations are still felt today. Early in my career, I found that many older seniors would not invest in anything but government-guaranteed certificates of deposit. But who could blame them? The Depression was an extremely difficult time in their lives. Huge parts of the economy were completely shut down. Businesses failed. Factories closed. One-third of the workforce was unemployed. Farming was no better. Food prices were so low, farmers couldn't make a profit. Many went out of business and lost their land. Millions of people crisscrossed the country looking for work. Disaster writers tap into our deep cultural fear that this might happen again.

Ignorance and Misinformation

Unfortunately, most people don't understand what happened. In fact, most of the information and popular theories about the Great Depression are just plain wrong. The most popular theory frequently taught in our schools states that overspeculation in the financial markets (stock market) was to blame. This is wrong.

The theory states that by the end of the 1920s, participation in the stock market by the general public had reached an all-time high. This popularity created a bubble of investment. Money poured through the financial markets into industry. Factories were built at a frenzied pace and grew so fast that our industrial capacity to produce outstripped our capacity to consume. In other words, supply exceeded demand.

As a result, unsold goods remained on the shelves. Factories suffered terrible losses and were soon closed for lack of profits. When the factories closed, people lost their jobs and the stocks of those businesses became worthless. Unemployment surged. The stock market crashed. As stock prices crashed, people who had borrowed money from banks to buy stock went broke. As these people became destitute, banks couldn't collect their loans and they folded, as well.

Problems with the Conclusions

There are serious problems with this idea. The fatal flaw is under-estimating our power to consume. The idea that Americans could ever produce more than they could consume is ridiculous. Think about it for a second. Do you think that if the American public were given the opportunity to have twice as much as they do now, that they would pass on it? No way! We Americans love to consume. The more we have, the better we like it. We can always use a newer car, bigger house, better food, and more entertainment. The idea that Americans in the 1930s produced so much that they could consume no more is laughable.

Furthermore, we can plainly see that Americans during the depression had tremendous shortages of every product imaginable. If overproduction were the problem, why was everyone living in lack? In fact, everyone was ready, able, and willing to produce (they needed jobs) and ready, able, and willing to consume (they were hungry). The idea that overspeculation in the stock market and overproduction in the industrial sector caused the Great Depression doesn't hold up to examination. Clearly, something else was wrong.

In this chapter, I'll discuss what caused the Great Depression. Keep in mind that if you ask 10 economists why the Great Depression occurred, you will get 10 different answers. Nevertheless, my goal is to distill my best thinking on the subject into an entertaining chapter of information you can use. I'll discuss why depressions occur and how you can predict them in advance.

Hurricane Watch

Don't misinterpret this chapter. It is not intended to help you forecast the most common varieties of financial changes. In normal times, we experience all types of financial and economic weather – the stock market goes up and down; interest rates go up and down; inflation goes up and down; recessions come and go. This chapter is not designed to help you in forecasting any of these. Instead, the information given here is designed to help you understand and identify the most vicious storm of the economic world – a depression. If a recession is a thunderstorm, a depression is a Category 5 hurricane. It leaves an unimaginable wake of financial destruction in its path. While we generally can predict the daily weather with mild accuracy, no one can miss a massive hurricane approaching the shore. In the same way, you can identify the monster storm of an economic depression before it reaches your financial beach.

Mother Of All Indicators

The good news about a depression is that you can predict when it is going to occur by using what I call the *Mother of All Indicators*. This indicator, unlike any other, will tell you when a depression is approaching. In fact, I have been able to use this indicator to predict with astonishing accuracy which countries would emerge from the financial crisis of 2008 and which ones would be mired in ongoing depressions.

The media have familiarized us with a variety of financial and economic indicators. We all have heard about the unemployment rate, the inflation rate, leading indicators, and gross domestic product. At best, these indicators only give a foggy idea of the future and for a very simple reason. These indicators show only what happened in the past. As you know, the past is not always a good indicator of the future. Using indicators to predict the future is like steering a forward-moving car by looking in the rearview mirror. Most of the time, the road ahead is a continuation of the road behind. However, you only have to miss one turn to know that driving by looking behind doesn't always work.

On the other hand, the Mother of All Indicators strongly predicts the future, regardless of the past. The Mother of All Indicators sounds a clear warning when a depression is imminent. What is the Mother of All Indicators? Very simply, it is the health of the banking system. When the banking system gets sick, the economy and the financial markets catch pneumonia.

Three-Headed Monster

Like a three-headed monster, every depression contains three crises: a banking crisis, a financial crisis, and an economic crisis. A banking crisis is when the banks fail. A financial crisis is when the stock market plunges. An economic crisis is when factories close and people are put out of work. As I mentioned earlier, most theories state that the financial crisis (the stock market crashing) occurs first. In fact, a banking crisis will always come first. A massive banking crisis always signals a coming depression.

The three crises occur in the following sequence:

1. Banking crisis (massive failures throughout the banking system)
2. Financial crisis (the stock market crashes severely)
3. Economic crisis (factories close and unemployment runs high)

From Banks To Soup Kitchens

The best way to illustrate how a banking crisis sets off a depression is with an example. Let's pretend that you own a business. In your business you manufacture tables. Today, you're very excited; your best salesman has just brought in a fantastic order from your best customer. In fact, his sales ticket sets a record. It is the biggest order you've ever received. Unfortunately, the order is so big your plant is unable to fill it. There isn't enough machinery, factory space, or workers. How are we going to handle these problems? Expand!

As with most typical businesses, there's not enough cash on hand to fund the expansion; financing is needed. Several options are available for raising money. You could go to the public capital markets and raise the cash by selling part of the business through a stock offering, or you could borrow the money by selling bonds. Both of these alternatives are fairly expensive and time-consuming. Instead, you decide to use your main source of financing that you have used in the past – your banker.

Your banker has proven to be an invaluable source of capital. In fact, most of your capital needs have been met through bank loans. Compared to issuing stocks and bonds, bank loans are relatively inexpensive and quick to get.

When you arrive at the bank, you have no worries. You have good credit, solid equity in the business, and an order in hand. In the past, you've received loans on riskier projects with far less collateral. How could the banker possibly say no? After a few thoughtful grunts, the banker lays your proposal on his desk and removes his glasses.

"This looks like a great sale," he says. "In fact, I bet this is the biggest order that you've every received." Just as you are expecting him to pull out the checkbook, he drops the bombshell. "Unfortunately, I have some bad news and some worse news. The bad news is that I can't make the loan to you." You brace yourself as he continues. "The worst news is this: You know those loans you have outstanding? I need those repaid by the end of next month." Shocked and stunned, you ask why. He mumbles something unintelligible about your financial condition and capitalization ratios. What he doesn't tell you is the truth. The bank is in trouble.

Pale and shaken, you return to the factory. With your loans being called, you will have to scale back. Instead of hiring, you start passing out pink slips. As older machines break, they aren't replaced. With fewer people and machines, operations start slowing down. Think about what this slowdown means to the value of your business. Slowing operations mean shrinking profit. As you learned earlier, when businesses earn lower profits, their stocks go down in value. Notice how this banking crisis quickly triggers an economic crisis (people lose their jobs and factories go idle) and a financial crisis (stock values plunge). One or two small bank failures are not that serious. You can always find another bank. On the other hand, if the bank failures are system wide – when most all the banks fail – then this scenario will play out millions of times. The financial markets and the economy will nose-dive.

How Banks Work

To understand how banks get in trouble, you need to understand how banks work. Few people believe that when they deposit money at their bank, it is taken into the vault and left there for safekeeping. We all know that the money we deposit at the bank doesn't stay there for long. The bank uses our deposits to make loans. Making loans with their depositors' cash is a primary way banks earn money.

A bank doesn't loan all the cash though; it keeps some for daily transactions. For example, you and I will pay bills and occasionally cash a check at the bank. For those transactions, the bank keeps part of our deposits held back for our use. This unloaned money is known as the *bank's reserves*.

The system works fine as long as everyone behaves normally and leaves their deposits in the bank. But what if everyone decided to take their cash out of the bank at the same time? The bank would not have the cash on hand to pay it all. Does this lack of ready cash mean the bank is broke? Of course not. The bank has plenty of assets such as boat loans, car loans, and business loans. Unfortunately, when you go to the bank to withdraw $1000, you don't want to be paid with a $1000 boat loan from the guy down the street; you want U.S. currency.

Bank Runs

Suppose you went to your bank to cash a check. Instead of honoring your request, the bank tells you that it is out of cash right now. "But don't worry," the teller says, "the bank isn't broke – we have plenty of assets. We're just a little short on ready cash right now."

The teller asks you to come back in a few days. What would you do? You'd become very angry and demand to speak to the manager. When that didn't help, you would go home and call all your friends to tell them that the bank is out of money. What would they do? They would call all their friends and an angry mob would descend on the bank. As you probably already know, this chain reaction is known as a *bank run* or, simply, *a run*.

Before 1913, banks protected themselves against runs by forming alliances with other banks. When there was a run on an individual bank, the neighboring banks loaned the troubled bank the cash it needed until the depositors settled down. The strategy worked fine unless all the banks were being run at the same time. In that case, the neighboring banks couldn't loan the needed cash; they had their own problems. Until the early 20th century, the United States suffered periodic national bank runs. Growing up in this environment, depositors were very sensitive to banking troubles. Everyone knew someone who had lost his life savings in a failed bank. With this widespread fear, a single bank failure often sparked national frenzies where depositors all over the country would make runs on the banks.

The Federal Reserve System

Of all the institutions in the United States, I believe none is more misunderstood than the *Federal Reserve Banking System* (aka *Federal Reserve Bank* or *The Fed*). Myths abound. People believe that the Federal Reserve is everything from a socialistic institution to a conspiracy of billionaires seeking world domination. I'm afraid that the truth about the Federal Reserve is not quite that melodramatic. The Federal Reserve was created simply to stabilize the banking system and end bank runs once and for all.

The Federal Reserve System is designed to be the lender of last resort – the bankers' bank so to speak. The role of the Federal Reserve is fairly simple to understand. Imagine depositors getting anxious about their banks. In a panic, the masses run to the banks to get their money out. As I discussed before, the banks' money is tied up in loans; they don't have enough cash on hand to give everyone their money on demand.

Before the Federal Reserve was established, these massive runs meant that the banks had to close their doors or face the wrath of their depositors. After 1913, however, the banks could simply use their assets (the loans they had made) as collateral to borrow the cash they needed from the Federal Reserve Bank. Because the Federal Reserve always stood ready to lend the banks cash, the banks could always meet their depositors' demand for cash – even if all the depositors took all their money out at the same time.

Where does the Federal Reserve get all this cash? You guessed it ... from thin air. Since the Federal Reserve has the legal right to create money, it is never short of cash to lend the banks. By establishing a bank with an endless supply of lending power, Congress put into place the tools needed to eliminate national bank runs and the resulting banking crises.

The Oil Pump Of Our Economy

In addition to ending bank runs, the Federal Reserve evolved into a sophisticated system that matches the amount of cash in the banking system with the amount of goods and services in the economy. I will explain this role in more detail in the next chapter. But for now, just visualize the Federal Reserve as the "oil pump" of our economy.

Every car engine has an oil pump inside it. The oil pump's only job is to make sure that oil continually flows throughout the engine so the parts don't stick together. An oil pump has no other role. A mechanic can fiddle around with a car's oil pump all day long making it pump more or less oil. But, no matter how hard he tries, he cannot add any power to the engine by adjusting the oil flow. In fact, if the pump adds too much oil, the engine will smoke terribly. On the other hand, if the pump provides too little oil, the engine will seize and die. The role of an oil pump is to pump only the right amount of oil – not too much and not too little.

Likewise, the Federal Reserve's job is to keep just enough cash (oil) in the economy to make sure transactions flow smoothly. Too much cash, and the economy starts smoking with inflation. Too little cash, and the economy will seize up in a recession or depression. Before the Federal Reserve was created, the economy regularly seized up in depressions when panicky depositors drained their cash from the banking system. Today, if the banking system needs cash, the Federal Reserve stands ready to "oil" it.

In my opinion, the establishment of the Federal Reserve was a landmark event. It helped create a business environment that allowed the United States to produce a standard of living unequalled by any civilization in history. By maintaining a stable banking system, the public and businesses were suddenly free from ever-present worry over bank failures. People and businesses could confidently deposit their money. Similarly, this stability allowed much freer use of credit. The public and businesses could borrow without fearing that their loans would suddenly be called because the banks were in trouble.

1929

I can hear some of you saying, "Okay, Mr. Smartypants," if the Federal Reserve was established in 1913, why did the United States suffer a horrible banking crisis in 1929?" This is an excellent question that deserves an excellent answer. The answer is, "Benjamin Strong died."

Over the years, confusion about what the Federal Reserve is supposed to do has not been limited to conspiracy theorists. Misunderstanding over the Fed's primary mission has extended into the Federal Reserve System itself. Even people running the Federal Reserve Bank have misunderstood the role of our national bank.

One of the men who fully understood and appreciated the role of the Federal Reserve was Benjamin (Ben) Strong – governor of the Federal Reserve Bank of New York until October of 1928. I believe that Ben Strong is probably one of the most underrated financial heroes of the 20th century. Ben's insight and leadership helped nurture one of the biggest economic booms in history – the Roaring '20s. When the banking system needed cash, he argued for cash infusions. When inflation rose, he reined in the printing presses. For years, Ben Strong was a powerful influence on the Federal Reserve's policies.

This golden era came to an end on October 16, 1928, when Ben Strong died. In my opinion, his death marked the beginning of the United States' treacherous journey into the Great Depression. Ben's successors failed miserably. They did not comprehend the Federal Reserve's critical role in maintaining the health of the banking system. When a light recession struck the economy in 1929, the new leaders of the Fed made a deadly decision. In 1929, the banking system desperately needed an infusion of cash from the Federal Reserve. Instead of putting money into the system, the Federal Reserve drained it out. Just like a car engine with the oil drained out, the economic engine of the United States seized up quickly.

The reduction of cash caused banks to fail on a massive scale. Within a few weeks, national bank runs were back. Even while runs were underway, the Federal Reserve failed to help the banks. The resulting banking crisis threw the United States and ultimately the entire world into the deepest depression in history. In essence, the Federal Reserve drained the economic oil pan dry. In a very short time, the powerful economic engine of the United States seized up solid. Banks failed, factories closed, and people lost their jobs. Ben's legacy of the Roaring 20s died shortly after he did.

The Federal Reserve's On-the-Job Training

It is been a long learning experience for the Federal Reserve. Causing the Great Depression wasn't its last mistake. In the 1960s, the Federal Reserve proposed a new role for itself. Like a mechanic trying to enhance an engine's performance by adjusting the oil pump, the Federal Reserve believed that it could increase economic growth by adding extra cash to the system. Over the next 15 years, its leaders learned that adding excessive cash only causes the economic engine to smoke with ever-increasing inflation.

By the late 1970s, the Fed had escalated inflation into the double digits. The nation's economic engine was choking on inflationary oil. Something had to be done. In 1979, the Federal Reserve, under the leadership of Federal Reserve Chairman Paul Volker, changed course. Instead of trying to rev up the economic engine by adding cash, it set price stability as its goal. By 1992, inflation had dropped below 3 percent, and the banking system and the economy had never been stronger.

The Prodigal-Reserve Returns Home

After its experiences with the Great Depression in the 1930s and the double-digit inflation of the 1970s, the Federal Reserve has returned to its original role – preserving the health of the banking system. You will seldom hear the Federal Reserve's leaders express this goal explicitly. Instead, you will hear ideas such as price stability, economic growth, and unemployment targets. Make no mistake – the Federal Reserve has come a long way toward understanding what it should do (maintain a healthy banking system) and what it cannot do (induce economic growth). It has traveled a long way and is finally returning to its original purpose. If Benjamin Strong were alive today, he would be happy to see that the Fed has finally realized its monetary duties of not too little and not too much.

The Perils of Megabanking

I wrote the first version of this chapter in 1998. At that time, I expressed my belief that one of the biggest threats to our banking system was the formation of *megabanks*. While merging and consolidation in some industries can be healthy and competitive, I believed that the ongoing merger mania in our banking system had serious implications. I had fully expected a full-scale banking crisis to occur at some time in the future. I just did not realize how quickly our banks would take us there. Ten years later, the system almost collapsed.

In the next chapter, I will explain how we narrowly missed a full-on depression in 2008. We will get a little deeper into how money and banking work and why I believe Europe will be in and out of recessions for the foreseeable future. ♦

Chapter 20

To The Edge
Of Disaster and Back

2008

A lot of people realize that in 2008 the United States came very close to experiencing an unprecedented economic depression. I have explained that banking crisis occurs first, followed by financial crisis, then followed by economic crisis. Then the question becomes, in a modern banking system, what can cause a massive banking crisis?

I want to make you aware of three things. First, in the past 100 years, both major banking crises (1929 and 2008) share the same root cause. Second, the stories of what caused these banking crises are much simpler than you imagine. Third, the extreme differences in the performance between the economies of Europe and the United States post-2008, clearly demonstrates how the Federal Reserve's policies saved the United States from a very deep economic depression.

What Has Caused Modern Banking Crises

When reporters, commentators, and other financial experts try to explain what happened in 2008, they get bogged down in all sorts of details such as mortgages, housing bubbles, greed, fraud, and so on. The truth about how we narrowly averted the worst depression in history is a far simpler story.

The story of the 2008 banking crisis begins with the banking crisis in 1929. Use your imagination for a moment. Imagine a street dividing two sides of our financial system. On the left-hand side of the street is Wall Street. On the right-hand side of the street is the banking system. It's important to realize that these two institutions have completely different functions. Wall Street is all about taking risk and making returns. Banks are about keeping our cash safe.

Let's think about banks for a second. If we did not have the banking system, where would we store our cash? We could give it to a friend for safe keeping, bury it in the ground, hide it in the freezer, put it in the mattress. Each of these strategies suffers from similar risks – rot, forgetfulness, theft, robbery, and murder.

Now think about large organizations with millions or billions of dollars in cash. Their storage problems are even larger. Without banks, corporations would have to build special buildings, buy armored vehicles, and hire guards just to secure their money. Without banks, keeping our money safe is extremely difficult. Banks solve our collective problem by giving us a secure system in which to store our dough.

Now let's go back to our imaginary example. (In this example, I call the investing world "Wall Street" even though the investing world is much larger than Wall Street itself.) Wall Street performs an entirely different function than a bank. When an investor puts money into Wall Street, he "pays his money and takes his chances." Depending on how much risk he takes, an investor may win big or may lose everything. Wall Street is about risk and return. Make no mistake. It's not the role of Wall Street to protect your cash. Wall Street's role is to provide opportunities with risk.

In the 1920s, investors could walk from one side of the street (Wall Street) to the other side of the street (banks) with no interference. Money flowed freely from the banking system into Wall Street. Ultimately, this flow of money caused a massive nationwide bank failure and the Great Depression.

So how did Wall Street spark the Great Depression? Imagine an investor named Kit who bought $1000 worth of AT&T stock. A week later, Kit notices that AT&T has increased 10 percent in value. His account is now worth $1100. Kit is a very happy investor until his friend George shares something that changes his life. George put $1000 of his own money into AT&T as well, but he earned a 100 percent return or $1000 on his investment. Kit could not believe his ears and asked George to explain.

George tells Kit that he went to the Wall Street side of the street and bought $1000 worth of AT&T stock just as Kit had done. Later that day George went to the bank side of the street. While in the bank, George's banker asked him if he wanted to take out a loan. George said he could definitely use a loan because he just spent his money on AT&T stock. His banker said that was great! George could use the stock as collateral for the loan. The banker said George could borrow 90 percent or $900 on the stock. George was happy enough with this deal, but then he had a brilliant idea. After getting the loan, George went back across the street (to Wall Street) and bought more AT&T stock with his fresh new $900.

George felt pretty smug. Then while walking away with his fresh new stock shares, he had another brilliant idea. George walked back across the street to the banking side and took out another 90 percent loan or $810 on his newly purchased shares. George kept walking back and forth between the bank and Wall Street. At the end of the day, George had bought $10,000 worth of AT&T stock and owed $9000 to the bank. When the AT&T stock went up 10 percent, George had

$1000 gain on his $1000 investment. By using bank money, George increased his returns tenfold!

George and Kit continued this strategy for several years. In fact, they told all of their friends, who told all of their friends, who told all of their friends about the strategy, as well. Each time they had gains, they would go to the banking side of the street and get more loans to buy more stock. They all made a lot of money. But one day the unthinkable happened. The stock market declined. Since they owed 90 percent of their value, a relatively small decline in the market wiped them out completely. In an instant, George, Kit, and all their friends went from wealthy to broke. In fact, they owed millions and millions of dollars to the banks.

For Kit, George, and their friends, going broke was bad. For the banks, it was a disaster. The investors had no way to pay their loans. The banks were left holding the bag. Even though the banks collected the shares, once they were sold, the losses were staggering. In essence, depositor money from the bank flowed into risky Wall Street investments. Instead of protecting depositor money, banks were risking it on Wall Street.

In this example, I have simplified the mechanism of the transfer somewhat for clarity. But the essential truth remains: depositors' money had been exposed to the risks of Wall Street with disastrous consequences to the banking system.

As the Great Depression deepened, laws were passed, most notably the Glass-Steagall act, which specifically prohibited banking activities and investments that exposed depositors' money to Wall Street. Banks were strictly limited in the investments they could make. The few allowable investments had high levels of safety. These included high-grade corporate bonds, government bonds, and short-term collateralized loans to depositors (e.g., car loans, boat loans, business equipment loans). For 80 years, the Glass-Steagall Act acted as a brick wall down the middle of the financial street. Depositors' money could not flow into Wall Street. For eight decades Glass-Steagall protected our banking system.

Starting in the late 1980s, our leaders decided that the "archaic banking laws" of the 1930s needed to be disassembled. The mantra of our leaders was that the banking laws were hindering innovation in our financial system. According to them, our system had become so sophisticated that we did not need restrictive banking laws anymore. Our leaders took a wrecking ball to the Glass-Steagall wall.

Wall Street watched ecstatically at the financial demolition. After a half century of staring over the wall at an ocean of depositors' money, it was now ready to gush their way. At first, banks began investing in Wall Street investments tepidly. With so much money waiting, though, Wall Street worked night and day creating investments and presenting them to the banks. In the end, the investments that opened the floodgates were the mortgage vehicles and all the derivatives that nearly brought down the system. A flood of depositor cash flowed into Wall Street and mountains of money were made in commissions. When the mortgage bubble burst in 2008, the world banking system narrowly avoided catastrophic collapse.

In its simplest form, the global banking crisis of 2008 and the ensuing global economic crises are not a story about mortgages, derivatives, or other mind-bending concepts. It's simply about banks putting depositor money at risk in Wall Street. The end. If it had not been mortgage vehicles that opened up the floodgates to depositor money, I believe Wall Street would have found something else.

A Tale of Two Economies

Since 2008, a remarkable experiment in banking has been taking place. This experiment is clearly showing which one of two opposite economic theories is better – the one followed by the United States or the one followed by the European Union. To understand the experiment and what is happening in Europe and the United States, we need to learn how money is created and destroyed. We also need to learn about the Federal Reserve's most remarkable tool.

Where Does Money Come From?

In workshops, I frequently ask people where money comes from. In other words, where are United States dollars created? People usually say the Federal Reserve or the United States Treasury. These answers are slightly correct but mostly wrong. The Federal Reserve does create some money from thin air, and the Treasury does print the physical currency in our pockets, but most United States dollars are created by your local bank. Does your local bank have a printing press? Well, yes – sort of.

In the last chapter, we talked about how our local banks lend out depositors' money. For example, if you were to deposit $1000 in cash in your local bank, you would get a checkbook that notes your $1000 deposit. Later, your bank loans out a portion of that money to someone getting a loan. Let's say that your bank loans out $900 to John to buy a used boat. The person John buys the boat from then takes the $900 to his bank and gets a checkbook that shows his $900 deposit. Let's think about this for a moment. When the bank loaned out $900 of your deposit, did your checking account go down by $900? Of course not. You still have your thousand dollars in your checking account.

So let's do the accounting. In the beginning, you had $1000 in cash. After you deposited the $1000 and the bank made a loan, your $1000 stayed in your checking account and also became $900 in someone else's checking account. In essence, your bank created $900 of United States currency. Let's say the next thing that happens is that the bank with the $900 loans out a portion of that money, say $810. That $810 gets deposited in yet another bank. At that point, your $1000 in cash has become $2710 in United States currency – $1000 in your account,

$900 in the boat seller's account, and $810 in the final account. This cycle continues over and over until your $1000 in cash eventually turns into $10,000 of United States currency through bank lending.

The math is simple. Every time a bank makes a loan, it creates United States currency. If a bank loans out $100 million in depositor money, it creates $100 million of US currency.

Balancing Money With Stuff

The reason that banks are allowed to create currency is simple. For thousands of years this strategy has worked well at balancing the amount of money in circulation with the amount of stuff there is to buy.

Let's do another thought experiment. Imagine an ambitious politician gets a brilliant idea. To get elected he promises that he will make everyone in the country a millionaire. The day after his election, he delivers a fresh stack of currency to every man, woman, and child in the United States. Everyone has $1 million courtesy of a fancy new printing press. What would the world look like by the end of that day?

I think we all know intuitively that every new-car lot would be empty, all houses would have been sold, and grocery store and retailer shelves would be empty. The price of everything would be shooting through the roof as the ocean of money chased after a finite amount of goods. A loaf of bread might be 50 bucks. A gallon of gasoline might be $200. This thought experiment illustrates what happens when the amount of currency in the economy is not balanced with the amount of stuff for sale.

In this case, when the politician added cash to the economy, the amount of economic activity (i.e., buying stuff) increased enormously. If we did the thought experiment again and instead took away half of everyone's money, the opposite would happen. Economic activity would drop to a crawl. Car lots would be full of unsold cars. Grocery stores and retailers would have goods gathering dust.

While not perfect, allowing banks to create money by loaning out deposits has worked well at balancing the amount of money in the economy with the amount of stuff available for sale.

Attack Of The Zombie Banks

In the last chapter, I described how the Federal Reserve System was designed to be the lender of last resort – the bankers' bank. In that original role, the Federal Reserve stood ready to lend to any bank that asked. Banks usually ask for cash when they have a bank run. In this situation, the banks have assets (i.e., loans outstanding) but not a lot of cash on hand.

However, this lending tool only works against bank runs. What happens when the problem is not bank runs but instead a system-wide shortage of reserves?

Remember, fresh loans stimulate economic activity. Every time someone gets a bank loan, they buy something, but loans can only be made if a bank has adequate deposits.

This means that if the banking system as a whole does not have enough reserves to lend (from money deposited), lending will stop and the economy will come to a crawl.

When the banks lost money in the 1929 and 2008 banking crises, they lost their reserves. With no reserves, they quit lending. The question then became how do we get reserves into the banks. This process of putting reserves into banks is often called *recapitalization*. It just means that banks need to be fixed so they can operate in their role of lending and creating money.

In a massive banking crisis, most banks don't fail outright. They have enough deposits to stay afloat – but just. In this situation, banks just hunker down and quit lending. They are alive but just barely. These half-alive banks are often referred to as *zombie banks*. Since they quit making loans and participating in the financial system, zombie banks become a drag on the economy. If the banking system at large becomes zombie-like, economic growth will grind to a halt. Economic depression will set in and joblessness will skyrocket. In 2008, zombie banks threatened the world economy. To fight the attack of the zombie banks, the United States took two unprecedented actions – TARP and QE(1 and 2).

Throw A TARP On It

By 2008, banks around the world were so full of worthless Wall Street investments, that the banking system was essentially bankrupt. The first strategy employed by the federal government to fix the banking system was to simply buy these bad assets for cash. The banks would exchange worthless paper for hard currency. This program was known as the *Toxic Asset Relief Program* or *TARP*. Over $418 billion in Wall Street investments were purchased under this program by the federal government.

The Fed's Most Powerful Tool

Even after the TARP program, banks were still not lending. The economy was in trouble. Remember that bank lending expands the amount of money flowing through the economy. When banks stop lending, the opposite happens: Loans get paid off and the amount of money in the economy begins to shrink. A shrinking money supply is a very serious threat to economic growth. Millions of jobs are at stake. To address this problem, the Federal Reserve began in earnest using a tool it discovered in the 1920s.

One of the most powerful economic tools used by the Federal Reserve was discovered by accident. In the 1920s, the Federal Reserve found itself in a budget crisis. You need to understand that the Federal Reserve is not supported by taxpayer money. It operates on interest that it earns on outstanding loans. In the 1920s, the source of this income dropped to the point that the Federal Reserve could not support itself. To solve this problem, the leaders of the Federal Reserve decided to purchase some government bonds. The Reserve would then run on the interest.

When these bonds were purchased, something surprising happened. The Federal Reserve noticed that the overall amount of reserves (deposits) in the banking system increased. In essence, when the Federal Reserve purchased these bonds, the previous owners of these bonds simply deposited the cash into their banks. This infusion of fresh cash created new deposits from which banks could lend. The Federal Reserve discovered how to directly increase the amount of deposits in the banking system. All it had to do was to purchase something with freshly printed cash.

The Fed found the tool enormously powerful in keeping the banking system healthy and full of reserves. The part of the Federal Reserve that purchases things is known as the *Federal Open Market Committee* or *FOMC*. While the FOMC has always been active in the banking system, its role catapulted to a whole new level after the 2008 banking crisis. To restore the health of the banking system, the Federal Reserve embarked on a series of multi-trillion dollar purchases to keep the money supply from shrinking. These purchases were known as *Quantitative Easing* or *QE*. In 2008, the Federal Reserve took the unprecedented steps of not only purchasing government bonds but also purchasing a wide variety of other assets. These assets included mortgages and other financial instruments. The overall objective was to fill the banking system with cash and to get banks lending again. In my opinion, the program has been incredibly successful.

In Illustration 10, I have included a chart from the December 12, 2013, Wall Street Journal showing the increase in bank reserves after the 2008 banking crisis.

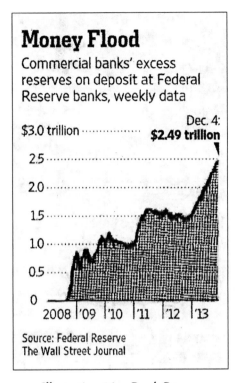

Illustration 10 – Bank Reserves

A Tale of Two Continents

In the world of scientific research, scientists create experiments to test their ideas about how the world works. Each experiment has two parts – a control and a test. The only difference between the parts is the variable being tested. For example, if a drug is being tested, one group gets the drug, the other a placebo. The groups are then compared to see if the drug was effective.

Unlike drug researchers, economists rarely get to run experiments with two parts. But since 2008, an extraordinary two-part economic experiment has been underway. One part of the experiment is the path of the United States. The other part of the experiment is the path of the European Union. The results are speaking volumes on what banking policies are most effective.

Many people have been critical of the Federal Reserve's expansive strategy after 2008. However, if we contrast its actions to the path that Europe took, we can clearly see just how successful the Federal Reserve's strategy has been. Unlike the Federal Reserve, the European Central Bank embarked on an opposite strategy. Instead of providing liquidity to the banking system, the European Union required its banks to tighten their belts. This program, in combination with the requirements for the European countries to balance their budgets, is widely referred to as the *Austerity Plan.*

As a result of these constrictive policies, the European Union found itself in the worst financial crisis since the Great Depression. While the United States experienced unemployment reaching 9 percent, the unemployment rate in many European member states (e.g., Italy, Spain, France, Greece) reached over 25 percent. While the United States economy recovered, the European Union slid deeper and deeper into a severe economic depression.

It's important to realize that the United States has followed the European model before, with disastrous consequences. Prior to the 1930s, the United States used a gold standard to back its currency. The gold standard made the job of balancing economic activity (i.e., the amount of stuff to buy) with the amount of money in the banking system difficult if not impossible. Until the United States abolished the gold standard, economic depressions occurred regularly. Each economic expansion would be crushed by the lack of money in the banking system. For the first hundred years of our nation, a depression followed each expansion.

Currently, the European Union operates under a banking system that is rigid like a gold standard. Even though the currency is not actually linked to the price of gold, the European Central Bank does not have the powers necessary to expand the currency (i.e., buy bonds and create reserves) when needed. For this reason, I think the European

Union will be in and out of severe recessions for the foreseeable future. Fundamental changes need to be made to its banking system. Moreover, if not for the bold actions of the United States government and the Federal Reserve in providing dollars to European banks, the European depression would have been much deeper than it was.

Illustrations 11, 12, and 13 clearly show the differences. In Illustration 11 (a chart from the November 8, 2013, Wall Street Journal), you can see that while the Federal Reserve bought bonds to increase the reserves in the United States banking system, the European Central Bank did just the opposite. It decreased the reserves of the European banking system from 2012 through 2013.

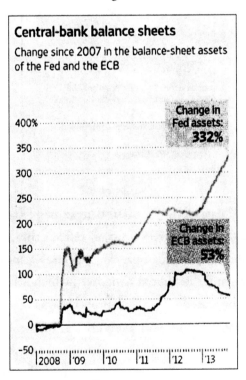

Illustration 11

Not surprisingly, the European economy experienced trouble from this. Illustrations 12 (a chart from the October 24, 2013, Wall Street

Journal) shows the United States economy growing while the European Union's economy shrank.

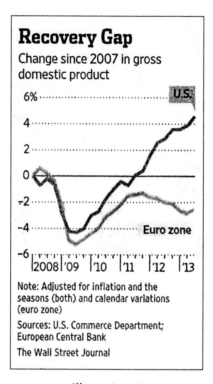

Illustration 12

Likewise, Illustration 13 on the next page (a chart from the November 1, 2013, Wall Street Journal) reflects this fact in the unemployment numbers. While unemployment decreased in the United States (as well as Japan and the United Kingdom, which followed the United States' lead), it increased in the European Union.

In my opinion, those who were critical of the Federal Reserve's actions since 2008 need to look at the numbers. At the writing of this book, the European Union continues to follow a restrictive and backward banking policy. My prediction is that the European Union will continue to experience economic problems until it reforms its banking system.

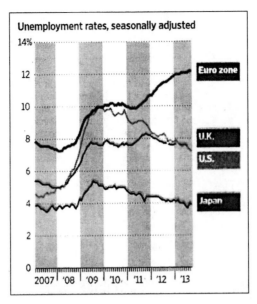

Illustration 13

Conclusion

When it comes to our investments, we should not underestimate the enormous implications of the banking system. The decisions our leaders make regarding our banking system have profound implications to our wealth. It's important that we understand how the system works and watch it very carefully. ◆

Chapter 21

Your Retirement Solutions

M illions of Americans look forward to the dream we call retirement – a time in life where you can enjoy the freedom to live where you want to live and do what you want to do. For many, however, retirement becomes a troubling nightmare instead of a peaceful dream.

Many retirees are surprised to find that when they achieve their financial freedom, their lives become complicated in ways they never imagined. They are confronted with a mountain of financial issues and decisions they never knew existed. They face decisions about pensions, rollovers, investments, Social Security, Medicare, medical supplements, long-term care, and estate planning. The sad thing is, one bad decision in any one of these areas can have huge and even catastrophic consequences. And what's worse, most bad decisions are made simply by omission – being blindsided by unknown issues. There's no doubt about it. Retiring in the 21st century is complicated and fraught with hidden dangers.

No matter how much a person is worth in dollars, a worried retiree is an unsuccessful retiree. Often, the difference between a stressful retirement and a stress-free retirement is getting hold of and acting on good information and wise advice. I derive a great deal of joy and satisfaction when I see retirees enjoying their golden years. I've found that retirees who have obtained good counsel, made wise choices, retain realistic expectations, and put appropriate Retirement Solutions into place are the happiest of all.

I wish you well in your retirement.

Michael Dallas, CFP® ◆

Michael Dallas, CFP®

Michael Dallas, CFP® provides investment advice and help to retirees and soon-to-retirees during their best years.

You may telephone Mr. Dallas any time the New York Stock Exchange (NYSE) is open for business at:
(800) 747-7384
(817) 763-8191

Mr. Dallas's business address is:
Michael Dallas, CFP®
6138 Camp Bowie Blvd.
Fort Worth TX 76116

Mr. Dallas offers securities and advisory services through:
Prospera Financial Services, Inc.
Member FINRA / SIPC
5429 LBJ Freeway, Suite 400
Dallas TX 75240
(800) 444-4428

MICHAEL DALLAS
RETIREMENT SOLUTIONS

"Trusted by Retirees"

Stay Connected With Us

 www.MichaelDallas.com/Facebook

 www.MichaelDallas.com/YouTube

 www.MichaelDallas.com/GPlus

 www.MichaelDallas.com/Twitter

 www.MichaelDallas.com/Linkedin

Visit Our Web Page For More Great Resources
www.MichaelDallas.com

 Retirement Solutions News Journal. Stay up to date with news that affect retirees.

 Free Online Retirement Seminar. Quick and easy lessons on the five most important retirement issues.

Install Our App: *Retirement Solutions*

Keep up to date and get all of your resources
with our smart phone app.

www.MichaelDallas.com/Play   www.MichaelDallas.com/iTunes